The Peanuts Papers

The
Peanuts
Papers

Writers and Cartoonists
on Charlie Brown,
Snoopy & the Gang,
and the Meaning of Life

Andrew Blauner, editor

A SPECIAL PUBLICATION OF
THE LIBRARY OF AMERICA

The Peanuts Papers

Published in the United States by Library of America.
www.loa.org

Interior design by Wah-Ming Chang.

Distributed to the trade in the United States by Penguin Random
House Inc. and in Canada by Penguin Random House Canada Ltd.

Library of Congress Control Number: 2019938570

ISBN 978–1–59853–616–4

1 3 5 7 9 10 8 6 4 2

Printed in the United States of America

For Sam

Contents

II. CHARACTERS

III. TWO POEMS

IV. OFF THE PAGE

V. TRUE STORIES

Preface

Nearly twenty years after the death of Charles M. Schulz, in the midst and perhaps the throes of the twenty-first century, there still seems so much to say about *Peanuts*, the singular comic strip that occupied the artist for the greater part of his life and, through a miraculous ensemble of hand-drawn children and an independent-minded beagle, won over the world. The book in your hands proves just how eager people are to think and write about the strip: over two-thirds of its pieces have been newly composed for this volume, and only two of the previously published essays reprinted here were written before 2000. To a degree that his cartoonist colleagues would surely have envied, Schulz's creations, those "li'l folks" dreamed up in a time and place now fairly distant from us, speak as powerfully as ever to so many people, including, as this book shows, some of the finest writers and cartoonists working today.

When it comes to *Peanuts*, the phrase "meaning of life" in this book's subtitle is well earned. The writers featured here reveal that to contemplate *Peanuts* is to move between two complementary spheres, one vast and existential, the other as small as the strip's diminutive characters. The overall mood and atmosphere of *Peanuts*—its braided threads of joy and melancholy, disappointment and wonder—suggest a philosophical orientation, a guide for the perplexed about how one might live in a world that is never easy and is often less than kind. But no one has ever read *Peanuts* as if it were a treatise, sermon, or self-help manual. Its individual frames and compacted scenes, unfolding over the four-panel vignettes that more than one writer in this book have likened to haiku, are what have stuck with us since our childhood encounters with Schulz's illustrated cosmos. Here on the tiniest of stages we find illuminated the ongoing human business of friendship and love, anger and frustration, fantasy and heartache—and pretty much everything else.

The Peanuts Papers, accordingly, adopts a dual perspective on Schulz's fifty-year magnum opus. Its writers think big but are attuned to particular moments, resonances, and their own highly personal associations. Especially in its opening section, "The Big Picture," they tackle the strip's larger significance in all its glorious entirety. Adam Gopnik invokes Chekhov, Beckett, and Thomas Merton while exploring "how instinctively, with how little effort, Schulz makes the big preoccupations of serious literature and spiritual crisis into an unforgettable set of daily comic parables"; Ivan Brunetti's trenchant thoughts about Schulz's achievement and influence include a comparison of the artist's seismic impact on the comics to Brando's on movie acting. Such brilliant high-altitude assessments are joined with nuanced examinations of individual strips, as with Peter D. Kramer's extended gloss on the running gag of Lucy and her psychiatry booth. The many recollections and memoirs included, particularly in the concluding section, "True Stories," provide powerful testimony of how *Peanuts* can be woven into the very fabric of a life, as it has been for so many.

This collection is varied, even kaleidoscopic, but it also offers the pleasure of detecting echoes and correspondences among writers who come to *Peanuts* from their own distinct perspectives. It's hard, for example, not to recall Sarah Boxer's remark about "uncomfortable truths" lurking beneath *Peanuts*'s "deceptive" ambience of "cozy suburban conviviality" when reading, a few pages later, this reminiscence of Jennifer Finney Boylan: "It was in reading *Peanuts*, lying on the floor beneath the piano in my parents' suburban home in Newtown Square, Pennsylvania, that I first saw evidence of the terrible truth: that my adorable parents resided in a cartoon universe. It was Charlie Brown and his friends—children who lived in a world defined by unrequited love—who resided in the real one." *The Peanuts Papers* celebrates Schulz's real-world cartoon universe by allowing this sort of dialogue among its contributors. Even matters they all can agree on, above all the view that *Peanuts* is of endless interest and remains deserving of the highest praise, can be expressed through a wealth of fruitful approaches. What you'll discover in the following pages is what many of the most passionate *Peanuts* fans already know: that like all the enduring monuments of American culture, Schulz's daily saga in miniature—of the Brown and Van Pelt children, their friends, and an indefatigable dog—is large and wise and contains multitudes.

Lights, please.

I

The Big Picture

Good Griefs

Adam Gopnik

Charles Schulz's great comic strip has hardly lacked for admirers or attention since it first appeared in 1950—in itself somewhat surprising, since the strip had a long ramp-up to sublimity—and so to join in the ranks of those who sing its praises might seem as redundant as Charlie Brown taking one more run at that football. But one point in particular is perhaps not made often enough, and so still worth making—that, for all of its charm and, and for all the television specials drawn from it that rightly occupy a place of affection in our revolving American holidays, Halloween to Christmas and back again, the actual comic spirit of the strip at its best, from the early 1960s to the mid-1970s, is astoundingly, "rewardingly," bleak and mordant. *Peanuts* is black humor before it is benign humor. Its inmates' predicament is closer to Chekhov than it is to *Gasoline Alley*, their stripped-down landscape of one-on-one exchanges of spiritual hopelessness more like Beckett than

Beetle Bailey. Each of the kids is perfectly mismated with his own ambitions—*Peanuts* is a mordant comedy of mismatched talents and desires, like life itself. It is not an accident that the peculiar cry of punctuation in the strip is "Good grief!" The simple cry of exasperation, which predates Schulz's use of it, becomes, in his characters' mouths, doubly loaded. They really do grieve their losses, which are real; the comedy with which their loss is articulated makes it "good."

The bleakness begins, perhaps, with the central condition of the strip: a world occupied by children alone, with the parents faint off-screen bugles, very rarely heard and never seen. This is a vision neither comforting nor "cute." The kids don't inhabit a more innocent world; they inhabit the recognizable grown-up world of thwarted ambition and delusional longing, only without even the capacity to take the kind of minimal actions that adults can take to bring their ambitions into at least an illusory compact with their circumstances. The kids can't make their own worlds, or furnish their own houses, or choose their own towns. They live permanently in that strange, empty, suburban landscape—one that recalls, perhaps inadvertently, the eerily vacant, if "safe," new "developments" of the period in which the strip reigned more than the small towns in which Schulz himself grew up. Only Snoopy has the capacity for homemaking, which is one with his capacity for self-making, becoming a World War I ace or a novelist simply by willing it so. The rest are as restlessly enslaved to their world of dusty sandlots and shallow lawns and rabbit-eared televisions and occasional sprouts of crabgrass as any mental patient in one of the period's hospitals.

Within this uniquely bleak world—one with none of the

decorative intensity of, say, Segar's *Popeye* strip, or the affectionate eye for bourgeois details of *The Family Circus*, much less the satiric specificity of the best of *The New Yorker* cartoonists of the time—each character is perfectly mismated to the role the character is asked to play, or else permanently crippled in some way from expressing his or her true heart. Only in *Peanuts* would the one character devoted to psychiatry be the most neurotic of all the characters we will meet. Lucy is the least fit person to offer psychiatric advice in the history of fiction—"crabby" and mean-spirited, thin-skinned and humorless, she is the least naturally empathetic or insightful inhabitant of this world. She's the last person in the world you would go to for heart-counsel—yet she is the only one arrogant enough to dispense it, and charge for it too. (Nearly bankrupting poor Snoopy at one point with a persistent bill for twenty cents.)

This dark joke is recognizably true. The rule of the mental mirror image rules here, as it does in life: we seek the thing we long to become, more often than become the thing we really are any good at being. Those among us who choose to be psychiatrists or therapists *are* as often as not thwarted or difficult people, who have chosen the healing professions because it opens a vista for them that feels intriguingly alien or, perhaps, appealingly authoritarian. I have known far more Lucys in my own adventures in being therapized than I have known, say, Linuses, though it would seem to be the Linuses whose gentle intelligence and wide erudition one would wish to share.

Linus, in turn, though represented as the most thoughtful and literate of the characters, is himself a "crippled" kind. First by the bullying of his big sister—to which he can respond only with stoic acceptance, a small boy with stars revolving over his head—and then by his dependence on his omnipresent security blanket. Linus, the one member of the family who might be a comfort in a storm, is himself so blazoned out as the victim of insecurity that he can hardly be relied on in a crunch. And then of course, his eccentric and completely isolated and un-rewarded religion of the Great Pumpkin—always represented not as a common faith in which many share, but a singular ob-sessive cult in which only he believes—sets him farther off from the mainstream of conversation in which his might otherwise be the most valuable voice. The sweetness of his talk and the reservoir of elaborate, punctilious goodwill are always touch-ing. There is his planned "sharing" time in school, when he will begin "with a few words of thanks and praise for our teacher, then perhaps an amusing anecdote followed by some pertinent statistics and an appeal to reason . . . How does that sound Char-lie Brown?" he asks. Charlie Brown's response is gently mock-ing more than insulting—"The remainder of the day will be an anti-climax"—but we know as he does that the only result of Linus's goodwill will be general and derisive laughter. The pure of heart, in Schulz's world, do not get worldly rewards for their purity.

In my own favorite of all the full-color Sunday strips, we see Linus's predicament, which is the predicament of every in-tellectual in Chekhov: to be imprisoned, rather than empow-ered, by the range of reference we bring to the world, trapped in a self-woven web of helpless allusiveness. You may recall that Charlie Brown and Lucy are, along with Linus, watching the clouds from one of the bare low hills that seem to fill their envi-ronment. (It is credible, by the way, that they are alone so often in this world, as kids so often were in the postwar period that

Schulz's strip immortalizes.) Asked what he sees, Linus tells us that "that cloud up there looks a little like the profile of Thomas Eakins, the famous painter and sculptor," while another "gives me the impression of the stoning of St. Stephen. I can see the apostle Paul standing there to one side." (In itself a fascinatingly obscure, not to say ornate, reference, since the only even moderately well-known representation of this scene is a relatively unknown painting by the Bolognese Baroque painter Annibale Carracci, in which the apostle Paul, recognizable by his turban, does indeed stand to one side, back turned but seemingly aghast.) (That last parenthesis, its author admits, is, to be sure, a truly Linus-like one.)

"Well, I was going to say I saw a ducky and a horse," an intimidated Charlie Brown announces, when asked by Lucy immediately after what *he* sees in the clouds. "But I changed my mind." Though the joke in one sense is on Charlie Brown's imaginative inadequacy, in a deeper sense the joke is about the futility of erudition. Linus knows an amazing amount, and he offers his learning with perfect sincerity. It is the key to his character that he is in no sense a show-off. But the effect of his learning is not illumination but isolation. In this great strip he is, in every sense, lost in the clouds. Nor does his learning immunize him against the daily and visible and, presumably, slightly shaming show of insecurity that his blanket bodes forth into the world, nor can it protect him from the desperate irrationality of the Great Pumpkin cult. Linus is a Pascalian intellectual—one whose learning has only increased his inner panic, and made him readier than not to make the gamble of irrational faith, on a blanket or a pumpkin-patch idol.

Throughout the strip, these serial mismatches persist.

Schroeder, Beethoven worshipper that he is, has only one truly faithful admirer, in Lucy. But he treats her not merely indifferently but disdainfully—her keen love for him does not offer him anything but annoyance. His compulsive musicality, like Linus's gentle erudition, does not help him communicate, but only further isolates him in his own obsession. He is happy playing, and annoyed when asked to talk—much less to flirt. *Everyone* loves the wrong person, as we all do in life. The irascible Sally Brown loves the phlegmatic Linus; the philistine Lucy the aesthetic Schroeder—even Marcie's devotion to the late-arriving Peppermint Patty feels one-sided in its infatuation. Though charming in their presentation, they are compulsive in their constant re-presentation. No one grows old in *Peanuts*, it's true. But no one grows up.

These spirals of unrequited love and renounced ambition lead us, inevitably, to the two central figures of the story, Charlie Brown and Snoopy. Charlie Brown has become a kind of universal type, in a way that perhaps only another Charlie, Chaplin, before him quite equaled, both because of the relentlessness of his suffering and the crushed complicity with it. More like Buster Keaton than Chaplin, though, Charlie Brown endures his fate stoically: not merely the badness of his baseball team, but their squabbling indifference to baseball; not only his failures in school, but his rueful recognition that they are deserved; not merely his infatuation with the Little Red-Haired Girl, but the relentlessly scrutinized public reality of his unrequited love. Everyone knows he loves her, everyone knows it's hopeless.

"I'm depressed, Linus," Charlie Brown begins many a strip, saying—and we don't stop to think sufficiently perhaps about how unusual, how rare, a strike into a story those words are in a comic strip that, if not meant for children, then is certainly likely to be read by them. Indeed, Charlie Brown's pet term, "depression," is one of the key terms of the period, the fifties and early sixties, in which *Peanuts* was molded, though it meant something different then than it does now. Today, we most often use it to describe the acute clinical condition that afflicts so many, the brutal darkness in light that Willian Styron wrote of. It is, though, also Holden Caulfield's favorite term—and Charlie Brown is in many ways a Holden Caulfield six or seven years before he runs away from school—and he uses it to mean not clinically incapacitated but . . . *depressed*, suddenly saddened by a turn of events that disclose the essentially resistant nature of all life. Holden is depressed when he thinks about tourists from Seattle getting up early to go to Radio City Music Hall, with the effort not worth the reward; he is depressed by seeing the words "fuck you" written on a museum wall—the small sordidness of life is what makes him depressed. It is the feeling that previous eras called not depression but "melancholia"— and that is what afflicts Charlie Brown as well. He is melancholy, and his melancholy is the tonic note of the strip. Camp is to be endured. The Little Red-Haired Girl will never be won, or even really wooed. Like any modern comic hero— Chekhov's Trigorin comes to mind again—he is trapped not just in his self but in his self-awareness. He cannot deflect responsibility. When Lucy, in another high-water mark, comes around blithely demanding that everyone sign a document that "resolves me from all blame and responsibility," Charlie Brown can only think, "That must be a nice document to have." He would never submit one of his own.

It is perfect, then, within the poetic-comic logic of the parables, that Charlie Brown will be the owner, though not in any sense the "master," of Snoopy. Snoopy is the only character within Schulz's world who is wholly free to exalt the life of the will and imagination, of extravagant choices made freely and artistic destiny pursued—he writes novels and lives ecstatically in his head and collects Van Gogh and Andrew Wyeth. The scale of Snoopy's imagination—and one must be of a certain vintage to recall the time when Snoopy was a figure of genuine mania, with pop songs sung about his obsession with the Red Baron—is so invigorating that we tend to forget his dilemma. He is locked in. Though his inner life is rich, it is a subtle point in the world of *Peanuts* that he remains ineluctably a dog, able to exercise his imagination but unable to articulate it—except as thought balloons to us, the readers, who can read, but not reach inside, the panels.

A world of bleak encounters and misfired loves, sporadically enlivened by acts of largely futile imagining. It does sound more like the world of Beckett or Ionesco than that of the comics. But in saying this one doesn't want to impose some other, exterior standard upon the strip. What makes *Peanuts* great is not that it imitates, consciously or not, some other "higher" form, but that Schulz arrived at his black comedy by much the same compass as the more literary humorists, if on a more demotic path. The crisis that lights twentieth-century black comedy, as many have noted, is the same crisis that his biographers tell us so affected Schulz: the crisis of faith in modern Christianity, the effort to reconcile a world that surely seems Godless in all its panels with the will to believe in Christ's message of hope. Schulz in his own life seems to have oscillated between the confident simple faith reflected in his Christmas story, with its forsaken tree and simple affirmations, and a series of doubts strong enough to make him, in the end, declare himself a "secular humanist" albeit one of a distinctly Protestant cast. This classic tangle of modern feeling—his contemporary John Updike illustrated in his books exactly the same push and pull of faith and doubt, belief and self-mockery for believing, all illuminating a similar prosperous if underfed American landscape—comes alive in the strip and in us because it was alive in Schulz. It was not a literary aspiration but a felt passion.

What we value most in *Peanuts*, perhaps, is how instinctively, with how little effort, Schulz makes the big preoccupations of serious literature and spiritual crisis into an unforgettable set of daily comic parables. And so much sly truth in them! "I don't know what to do," Charlie Brown at one point tells Lucy, in her psychiatric guise, with Charlie sounding like Thomas Merton in a funny sweater. "Sometimes I get so lonely I can hardly stand it . . . other times, I actually long to be completely alone." "Try to live in between," Lucy tells him, quickly adding, "Five cents, please." Live in between and pay your debts—if there's more wisdom in the modern world than that, no one has drawn it.

Yesterday Will
Get Better

Ivan Brunetti

Charles Schulz exposed me as a fraud. Nearly two decades ago, upon hearing of Mr. Schulz's impending retirement, I drew a clumsy comic-strip tribute to *Peanuts*; fancying myself a halfway decent mimic, I attempted to copy the strong, fluid lines of his mid-1950s work, which I long admired (idolized), but I quickly realized that I was going to fall far short, because I could only scratch the surface of his inimitable drawings—as natural as handwriting but even harder to forge—much less the emotional content he could pack into every molecule of ink. And anyway, the veneer is never the thing itself. You know how sometimes you might hear what sounds like a simple melodic line in, say, Mozart, and then you see the actual sheet music, which reveals an unfathomably complex, rich structure, an eternity condensed into tiny, elusive black marks flowing through, over, under, and beyond the staves, swimming like furtive cells viewed under a microscope, seemingly unfixed and unfathomable yet cohering into a unified and inextricable whole, all of this therefore outing you as an arrogant, deluded, oblivious fool? That was me.

While I hadn't been drawing comics for very long at that point, I should have known better. A teacher in high school once explained that drawing was simply observation; thirty-five years later, that still seems like a pretty thorough definition. For starters, I wasn't observing keenly or deeply enough. Even though in my pastiche/homage I was "drawing a drawing," I hadn't fully understood what I was looking at, because cartooning exists in a kind of liminal space somewhere between writing and drawing. Sure, one could imitate the telltale twirl of a brush winding its way through a stroke, or calculate the pressure applied to a nib traveling along a particular vector, but there was also something ineffable about comics, something more than the sum of its parts.

At the time, I had recently become good friends with Chris Ware, who articulated quite eloquently the difference between drawing and drawing comics. I had an inkling of what he meant, but it wasn't until I tried copying Schulz that I experienced comics as a special kind of calligraphy, formed and informed not only by an iconic mental map of the world but also by the intensity of life lived, the depth of feelings felt. Charlie Brown simultaneously is a beautifully proportioned, abstracted assemblage of marks, a conceptually pure and original character, a true expression of Schulz, and, through the act of reading *Peanuts*, a way also to understand myself. To communicate so much, to so many, with so little, as Schulz was able to do with *Peanuts*, takes a lifetime of practice, persistence, determination, focus, stamina, and dare I say: obsession. Dilettantes and imposters easily betray themselves.

The genius of *Peanuts* is that it seems simple, replicable. But simplicity and complexity are arbitrary categories; where is the *a priori* boundary that separates one from the other? The true undergirding of lasting works of art is the embrace of contradictions, and *Peanuts* is no exception: it is at once universal and idiosyncratic, miniature and vast, constrained and infinite, composed and improvised, claustrophobic and inviting, caustic and sentimental, funny and sad.

Moreover, what a wonderfully strange strip it is, this internal world play-acted by ciphers. A playwright famously noted that every character is the author, and *Peanuts* exemplifies this truth. Via the interactions of these captivating characters (themselves full of contradictions, with their own internal conflicts), we are inside Schulz's splintered psyche—unbeknownst to us, because it never feels that way as we read the strip; the content isn't self-conscious or pretentious or "meta." Despite the small, tight, even dense panels, Schulz wisely keeps at us at eye level with the characters, and thus we can easily enter a rectangle of *Peanuts* and imagine ourselves roaming along with the characters inside what paradoxically seems a boundless world; maybe this is what it feels like inside Snoopy's doghouse. We inhabit the drama (by which I mean comedy) as it unfolds, following these characters as if they were real people, despite their outsized heads, squiggly arms, and occasional graphic flourishes.

Peanuts has no discernible scale, because it exists simultaneously as small increments and a fifty-year totality, an epic poem made up entirely of haikus. Then again, maybe that's also what life is: short, packed moments of intense, concentrated awareness, minuscule epiphanies that accrete as we age, an accumulation of efforts, some meaningful and some meaningless, moments all too real that unsettlingly feel somehow also not real, jottings taking note of everything, within and without. One life, all life. An isolated four-panel comic strip of Charlie Brown and Linus debating a philosophical point can be appreciated just as it is, humorous, insightful, compact, and perfect; one strip a day documenting one man's thoughts for half a century has the weight of a full life. *Peanuts* endures, both from the closest micro-view and the farthest macro–vantage point.

Likewise, time also doesn't really exist in *Peanuts*. Maybe that's not the best way to put it. To be sure, the action always unfolds in a linear fashion, with dialogue often driving the action (dialogue perforce functions as a transcript of time). And there are surprisingly a greater number of topical references than might have stuck in one's memory of the strip. What I mean by time "not existing" is that Schulz is reliving his past, revising it into his characters' always-present. They aren't children who speak as adults, nor adults inhabiting child costumes. The characters and all that transpires in the strip are the sum total of one man's mind, memory, experience, history, speculations, and dreams, a self-contained universe revealing itself as if it were a slowly exploding singularity.

Take two: We are the same person from childhood to death, but we are always in flux, reacting to unpredictable stimuli, a little different after each experience, perhaps worse for the wear. We don't look the same from year to year, certainly not decade to decade, and our memory is imperfect (to put it kindly). We know there are ebbs and tides and biological upheavals as we age, but deep down we know we have always been one and the same person, the same one we are now and will continue to be. There is a continuity that seems odd to me.

Is there a latent self that exists in perpetuity, a Platonic version of each individual, that briefly flickers on Planet Earth? *Peanuts*, too, captures this odd sensation: Charlie Brown in 1950 looks quite different from Charlie Brown in 2000, but we always know it's the same Charlie Brown and weirdly: that there exists a Charlie Brown.

While the strip steadily evolved into a worldwide, near-ubiquitous phenomenon, it was by no means obvious that this strange, highly personal strip would ever achieve such success. Because it was designed to take up little space on a printed page, there wasn't much room for eye-grabbing visuals. But revolutions can sneak up on you. I often liken the effect *Peanuts* must have had on the comics page to the one Marlon Brando had on the movie screen. In Brando's first film (*The Men*, 1950), he is an incongruous presence: his messy but vivid style of acting is at odds with the overt theatricality of everyone else's, almost as if we are watching two different films simultaneously. Brando's performance is more naturalistic, and thus seems more modern, less stilted; in the same film, we can see the beginning of a new style of film acting, and the death of an older one. Similarly, before *Peanuts*, depression and neurosis were not topics commonly discussed in the funnies. With *Peanuts*, Schulz brought a gamut of new emotions and sensations to the comics: tenderness, melancholia, isolation, frustration, joy, spleen, fury.

Charles Schulz liberated the funny pages, all the while sustaining this self-examination under the microscope of public scrutiny, even through the debilitating pain that caused the lines to get shaky in the strip's latter years. What would have readily destroyed another artist was transformed by Schulz into the aesthetic of the strip. I can attest that giving up on drawing is the easiest thing in the world to do; Schulz must have been a rock made of 100 percent willpower. We cartoonists all owe him a debt of gratitude, even if we have absorbed *Peanuts* second- or thirdhand: every awkward pause, tragic punchline, stretched-out uncomfortable post-punchline moment, philosophical meandering, every strip with an inanimate object expressing its thoughts—all of these have their roots in *Peanuts*.

As for me, every decision I made in that one-page tribute strip, which at the time I considered an anomaly, a one-off project, unexpectedly but inescapably turned out to be the template for every drawing I have done since. This includes the nuts-and-bolts stuff, such as the ideal proportions of a cartoon body, the distances and angles of eye to nose to mouth, the shapes of noses and ears, and the size relation between a character and the panel perimeter; the touchy-feely stuff, such as rhythm, pacing, mood, flow, and overall tone; and the heady stuff, such as the blurring/merging of interior (monologue) and exterior (dialogue). That short strip was to dictate the next twenty years of my life. But *Peanuts* was already there, in the fabric of my being, its power and influence waiting to be acknowledged. Like many cartoonists, I found a way to examine myself by rediscovering and reconstituting the mechanics—and hopefully some of the feel—of *Peanuts*.

There is a Zen koan that asks, "What is your original face?" I can only answer that Charlie Brown is my original face.

Strip Mind

George Saunders

If you try to imagine, say, three kids sitting against the side of a suburban house on a summer afternoon, something interesting happens. What were originally three generic placeholder children will gradually, via the process of imagination and re-imagination, evolve into three distinct children. One child, who first leapt into your imagination as a seated amorphous blob with a sack of marbles, is soon seen to be somewhat overweight and fixated on those marbles, and on his face is a look of pleased ownership, and he is wearing an expensive blue shirt, and suddenly he has morphed into the very manifestation of Greedy Self-Satisfaction. Meanwhile, the child on his left, staring off into the distance, poor but clean, not the least bit interested in those marbles, is seen to represent Healthy Independent Renunciation. On the other side of Mr. Self-Satisfied Marble-Owner, a thin dirty kiss-up of a boy in high-water pants gazes hungrily at the marbles, the embodiment of Covetous Resentful Poverty.

If these characters are allowed to grow up and leave the suburban lawn and get jobs and fall in love, this is called a novel, and you, the creator, are called a novelist. If the imagined children are not allowed to grow up but are confined to the suburban lawn, where they continue for the next fifty years to be rich manifestations of their creator's psyche, and if this creator's imagination is supple and energetic enough never to tire of reimagining the children on the suburban lawn and never to make us tired of observing the children on the suburban lawn, this is called *Peanuts*, and the creator is called Charles Schulz, whose passing in 2000 left me with this gut-sinker of a thought: Charlie Brown will never again do something new.

Much has been written about Schulz: his happy, austere childhood in St. Paul, his loving barber of a father, whose frugal routine (days off were spent cleaning the shop) was brightened by a passion for comic strips (he bought four papers each Sunday). Young Schulz was nicknamed Sparky (after Barney Google's racehorse) and as a teenager enrolled in a correspondence art course, where he earned a C minus in the division called Drawing of Children. Just before he left for World War II, his beloved mother died of cancer, one of several reasons often cited for his lifelong feelings of loneliness, another being his early jilting by the young woman who would become the prototype for the Little Red-Haired Girl, although one comes to feel that his sadness was more biological than experiential, and that these hurtful events were more confirmatory than causative. He was by all accounts a wonderful man—a Christian in the very best sense of that word, a kind husband and father and a generous mentor to countless younger cartoonists, a man who fought off his depression with humor and common sense and devotion to craft.

Reading *Peanuts* back in the early 1960s, having just learned to read, sitting there in the dank basements and mod parlors of the time, poring over the compilation volumes my friends owned, I for the first time experienced the heady sensation of seeing the world I lived in represented in art. The strip was set in a new-lawned and new-treed and under-furnitured suburb much like the one where I lived. When I walked out into that suburb, certain vignettes—a single leaf falling down, a pearly-black late autumn sky, a picket fence, a concrete stoop—set off a delicious cross-firing in which the world seemed more beautiful because I had just seen it, stylized, in *Peanuts*. Likewise in its moral tone—I recognized, with a start, Charlie Brown as the tender loss-dreading part of me, Linus as the part that tried to address the loss-dreading part via intellect or religion or wit, Lucy as the part that addressed the loss-dreading part via aggression, Snoopy via joyful absurdist sagery.

Of course this recognition, at that time, was purely visceral. It manifested as a kind of *Peanuts* worship that permeated, in a low-grade way, my entire life. I spent childhood Halloweens mentally assessing my actual Halloween against the mythic Halloween depicted in *It's the Great Pumpkin, Charlie Brown*. At Christmastime I sometimes found myself unconsciously mimicking the Charlie Brown posture (face turned beatifically upward, hands jammed into the pockets of my car coat) while watching snowflakes fall past a streetlight. It was always a little startling to see a picture of Schulz himself—how could this man, who looked like one of my father's friends, know so much about the very private and alternately depressed and euphoric nine-year-old me?

What made *Peanuts* unique and even radical is the fact that it could evoke such complicated moral feelings under such tight constraints. These constraints were formal (typically four frames, except on Sunday), thematic (kids only, no adults), geographic (the kids will stay in the neighborhood), and visual (heads will be round; a furious scribble across half a face will represent Humiliation; three rings around a head, with a complement of fat stars, will indicate that the kid has just been knocked silly). If art is seen as a constant battle between freedom and constraint, then *Peanuts* was great not because it was joyfully unconstrained, but because it managed to be so joyful under constraint. *Peanuts* comprised a killer introduction to minimalism, to the idea that, to cover vast emotional territory, art need not be catalogic or vast. Years later, first encountering Beckett, I felt on familiar ground: two guys talking about loss and futility while standing in front of a tree was not so different from two round-headed kids talking about loss and futility while standing behind a brick wall.

"It is important for me, when I am discussing the comic strips," Schulz once wrote, "to make certain that everyone knows that I do not regard what I am doing as Great Art." In book form, the complete *Peanuts* (18,250 strips) would comprise some five thousand pages. Charles Schulz left us this fifty-year novel to remember him by. It is a beautiful thing, whimsical and bitter, neurotic and hopeful, proof that, despite his protestations to the contrary, he was a very great artist indeed.

It's Once Upon a Time, Charlie Brown!

Peanuts as Kidlit

Bruce Handy

Back in the 1970s and early 1980s, the *National Lampoon* ran a regular one-page comic strip called *Nuts*. It was written and drawn by Gahan Wilson, who is better known for the ghoulish yet whimsical single-panel cartoons he created for *The New Yorker* and *Playboy*—think Charles Addams but with more helium, less nightshade. *Nuts* was something quieter, lower-key, even drab. Its main character was an unnamed ten-or-so-year-old boy, a mid-century American everykid (and authorial stand-in). Not much happens to him, in a narrative sense. Wilson's real interest was granular explorations of childhood unease: the terror of unfamiliar food, the metastasizing guilt over a shoplifted candy bar, the unsettling smell of a hospital sickroom, the sweet dread of a first boy-girl party, the weirdness of knowing a dead person—and the occasional childhood joy, too, such as the satisfaction of setting out to do some dumb kid thing like building a fort and once in a while actually finishing it. The drawings emphasized a child's perspective: buffeted, confined, cut-off, low to the ground, with adult conversations literally going over the protagonist's head. It is about as authentic, vivid, and unsettling an evocation of childhood—only *slightly* exaggerated—as comics have produced. If you don't know *Nuts*, seek it out. But we are not here to praise authenticity.

As the title implies, *Nuts* was conceived as a response to *Peanuts*. Years ago, I had the opportunity to spend some time with Wilson and we talked about his strip vis-à-vis Charles Schulz's. *The kids in Peanuts aren't anything like real kids*, Wilson asserted, not with disdain but, let's say, annoyance. *Schulz's characters are just adults in kids' bodies*, he continued. *They don't act or talk like real kids in the least.* I was surprised by this: it had never occurred to me that Charlie Brown, Linus, Lucy, and the rest were meant to be thought of as "real," no more than I ever presumed Snoopy had anything to do with actual beagles. I love Wilson's work, but his is a silly objection, like complaining that George Herriman muffed cats and mice, or that Bill Watterson didn't know from stuffed tigers. I'm sure you agree, but just in case I offer two unrelated strips I came across not long ago on a single spread of one of my battered old *Peanuts* collections from the mid-1960s (*You Need Help, Charlie Brown*). On the first page, Linus is seen reading *The Brothers Karamazov* and then, opposite, he boasts about studying the letters of the apostle Paul; he is ostensibly five or six, maybe seven tops. (Age, like the presence of adults, is for the most part only implied in *Peanuts*—matters of faith, perhaps.) And then there is the business of Schroeder's playing Beethoven on his toy piano, and Lucy's moonlighting as a psychiatrist, and Sally's raging in one strip against "middle-class morality," and pretty much all the characters' impossibly articulate access to their every passing emotion. And I am only scratching the surface of *Peanuts*'s absurd precocity. Most college-educated adults I know would be thrilled to attain Linus's level of erudition.

Real? I was reminded of Wilson's criticism not long ago when my teenaged son and I watched *Double Indemnity* together. "People don't talk like that," he said, objecting to Billy Wilder's and Raymond Chandler's zingy dialog. "That's the whole point," I replied. No one wants Barbara Stanwyck to talk like a normal adulteress, and no one (Wilson excepted) wants Charlie Brown and Linus and Lucy to talk—or act—like normal children. By the way, that is not a *completely* strained comparison with *Double Indemnity*, given that the six deadly sins—pride, greed, envy, gluttony, wrath, and sloth (I am leaving aside the seventh, lust)—run as rampant in Schulz's oeuvre as they do in Wilder's. You might even argue that they are among Schulz's pet subjects. But it is kids, real or unreal, that he put front and center, and it is kids who have been among his most avid readers, my own younger self very much included; and it is that interplay, between real and unreal, youth and precocity, which I would like to explore—hopefully channeling Linus himself, of whom Charlie Brown marvels early on in Linus's life of the mind (ellipses Schulz's): "He's read 'Cinderella,' 'Pinocchio,' 'Snow White,' all of those books . . . And that isn't the *only* thing . . . He can also discuss them intelligently!"

A couple of ground rules for this essay. One, I am assuming Schulz's genius and also assuming that you and I agree on its worth; I am here only nibbling around the edges of a monumental body of work that at its best is as funny as anything humankind has produced and that also defies summation in a single essay and probably even a single book. Any cavils are proportionately petty. That said, every relationship between creator and muse has its rough patches, Schulz's not excepted. So, two, when I am writing about Peanuts I am primarily writing about the strip's decade-or-so-long golden age, which, in my humble opinion, ran roughly from 1956 to 1966, give or take a year or two on either end. Schulz's imagination was most free in those years, his wit at its sharpest, the strip's energy that of someone hitting his stride and reveling in it—or as much as Schulz's not exactly buoyant personality allowed him to. In this period, Charlie Brown, Lucy, and Linus form the nucleus, held together by strong forces of codependency, grandiosity, delusion, bad faith, and ill temper, with Snoopy to the side as a jester figure. But in the 1970s and beyond, as Snoopy and his eventual sidekick, Woodstock, and Peppermint Patty and her eventual sidekick, Marcie, along with later additions such as mopey Spike and innocuous Rerun began to preoccupy Schulz, the strip became, to my taste, cute and self-conscious, the humor flabby, even rote, with Schulz relying more heavily on stock punchlines ("Don't call me 'sir'!") and well-worn sight gags (Snoopy followed single file by his feathered Beagle Scouts). I should note that in real time, when Schulz was alive and drawing every day, these shifts in cast and sensibility coincided with, for me, the onset of adolescence—I was born in 1958—so I grant that my disaffection might have been as much about me as about the varying quality of Schulz's strip. Anyway, now you know where I stand as fan.

According to David Michaelis's Schulz and Peanuts: A Biography, the cartoonist found his way to children as a subject more through trial and error than a burning wish per se to create a comic strip about precocious school-age kids with big heads and remarkable tolerance for physical and psychic pain. Rather, as he honed his style and sensibility, comics about kids seemed to work for him—and, more to the point, they sold. But like a lot of creators whose work appeals to children, he didn't claim any particular affinity for them; Dr. Seuss and Margaret Wise Brown are another two who come to mind. Theodor Geisel (Seuss's real name) appreciated children more in the abstract than in the particular—he had his own childlike need to hog the spotlight and always claimed he wrote strictly to amuse himself—while Brown, the author of *Goodnight Moon* and *The Runaway Bunny*, once said, "To be a writer for the young, one has to love not children but what children love." As Schulz confessed to an interviewer in the 1970s, when *Peanuts* was a mammoth enough success that he could get away with saying things like this, "I have never been especially fond of children. I really haven't. I adore my own kids, but I'm not a children lover." And so you might have guessed, given the way he allowed—or directed—his cast to mock and torture one another. "Aren't all kids egotists? And brutal?" he asked rhetorically in a 1964 interview—blaming the victims, you might say. But he wasn't wrong. He would have appreciated the fact that my daughter laughed for the very first time at the age of ten months while sitting in her high chair eating peas and Cheerios and watching her mother slip and fall and land flat on her ass—my daughter thus revealing a Lucy-like inclination before she could even walk.

I suspect that school-age kids, who have to endure being shamed out of their natural inclination to laugh at others' misfortunes, enjoy *Peanuts*'s harshness as a vicarious, subversive thrill. I know I did. It helps that most of the jokes, references to Dostoyevsky and Beethoven notwithstanding, are accessible at a fairly early age, if not the deeper resonances of Schulz's wit (such as the implication that adults also like to laugh at other people's misery and pratfalls). It helps too that the strip's surface concerns are children's: friendships, pets, baseball, kite flying, thumb sucking, schoolyard crushes. Schulz met kids on their own terms, but then spoke up to them.

My own first encounter with *Peanuts* is lost to time—maybe I got a paperback collection as a birthday party favor?—but I know by third grade I was hooked, collecting reprint books and clipping the new strips that appeared every day in the *San Francisco Chronicle*, which defined it in my mind as the Bay Area's newspaper of record (that and its wonderfully lurid coverage of the Zodiac Killer case). A *Peanuts*-less rag such as the *San Francisco Examiner* was hopelessly Brand X, home to stale, depleted also-rans such as *Blondie* and *Bringing Up Father*, strips where people still had '30s haircuts and wore spats and stayed out late drinking at stag events. In those comics, adults—husbands, anyway—acted like children. Like most kids, I preferred children acting like adults, and doing so in a spats-less neighborhood that somewhat reflected my own (suburban and white, with one black family—exactly like Schulz's cast in that sense).

There is wisdom in *Peanuts*; the strip sometimes functions like a fable, the characters as archetypal, when viewed with a blurring squint, as the donkeys, lambs, wolves, and lions that populate Aesop. Just as wolves always eat lambs if given the chance, so Lucy will always yank the football just as Charlie Brown attempts to kick it—such is the nature of wolves and Lucys. I now think the strip also had a hold on me in a more primal way, somewhat analogous to the way traditional fairy tales enthrall children by helping assuage unconscious fears about growing up and finding a place in the world—real anxieties exaggerated and made grotesque. It's all the supercharged, often Oedipal stuff the child psychologist Bruno Bettelheim cited in *The Uses of Enchantment*: Snow White and Rapunzel punished by and ultimately defeating mother figures jealous of the heroines' fresher allure, or Jack growing his thick and towering bean stalk, slaying a powerful giant, and making off with the giant's golden-egg-laying goose. Not that there's much psychosexual tension in *Peanuts*, or even any; Charlie Brown's crush on the Little Red-Haired Girl and Lucy's on Schroeder and Sally's on Linus are all strictly aspirational, never in danger of consummation at even the cootie-exchange level.

A *Peanuts* narrative is the opposite of a fairy tale's. In the latter, good generally wins out, however messily: dragons get slain, witches are shoved in ovens, simpletons win fortunes, and so on. In Schulz, no one gets what they want and everyone is thwarted, not just in love but also on the baseball field or in the classroom or, where Snoopy is concerned, in the skies over World War I battlefields. *Happiness Is a Warm Puppy* notwithstanding—charming, but a cash-in and, I'd argue, maybe wishfully, not canon—the more quintessential *Peanuts* catchphrases are "Rats!," "Good grief!," "I can't believe it!," and "Aaugh!" Charlie Brown is, was, and always will be a blockhead. Lucy remains forever crabby, her pleasure in humiliating Charlie Brown eternally fleeting. Linus will never see the Great Pumpkin rise on Halloween. Pig-Pen cleans up nicely, but it will be a matter of only a panel or two before he's once again filthy.

Justice is almost as beside the point in Schulz as realism; rather, panel to panel, strip to strip, he just grinds his characters down, as if they were players in a children's theater adaptation of Camus or Sartre or Robert Johnson. One of my favorite strips, from 1954, depicts Charlie Brown sitting alone on a curb. In the first panel a few raindrops are falling. By the fourth panel, the rain is torrential, and Charlie Brown is still sitting in the same spot, mouthing the ostensible punchline to this otherwise purely visual cartoon: "It always rains on the unloved!" Is Schulz even trying to be funny? Not really, I don't think. "Winsomely depressing" might be the aspiration here. The drawings' wit is why I love this particular strip, Schulz's deceptively casual line capturing the subtle shifts in Charlie Brown's body language as he first sits up, noticing he's being rained on; then looks up, almost as if questioning the skies; then slumps in submission both to the deluge and to his miserable place in a disinterested universe.

What do kids take away from all this bleakness? On some level, Charlie Brown's relentless suffering comforted me, a lightning rod, I think, for my own anxieties about my place in the world—*Peanuts* as catharsis, as worst-case scenario, with the awaited thunderclap of laughter substituting for the reassurance of a fairy-tale happily-ever-after. I felt bad for Charlie Brown, but I confess I didn't feel *that* bad for him, no more than I did for less soulful, less worthy cartoon losers—Wile E. Coyote, Elmer Fudd, even that shill the Trix Rabbit. As a budding cynic and a kid congenitally impervious to religion, I may have found something confirming in Schulz's nihilism—I don't think that's too strong a word. I understand he took his Christian faith seriously, and I know people have argued that the suffering in *Peanuts* is somehow redemptive, but I'm not sure I buy it. What I took away from Schulz is that life is hard, people are difficult at best, unfathomable at worst, justice is a foreign tongue, happiness can vaporize in the thin gap between a third and fourth panel, and the best response to all that is to laugh and keep moving, always ready to duck.

I still hold to that philosophy, more or less. Maybe less: I'm older and softer-hearted now. Not incidentally, as I mentioned, I'm also a father, which in my case means I get a bit quivery when it comes to things such as children being bullied, humiliated, ridiculed, ostracized. Revisiting Schulz from this tender parental perspective can be eye-opening, just as rereading the Brothers Grimm can be—all that gore we shrugged at as kids! Or emotional gore, in Schulz's case. I now find myself dismayed at times by his sadism—and again, I don't think that's too harsh a word. Schulz likely would have agreed. As he himself once admitted, or boasted, "Maybe I have the cruelest strip going." He knew the blackness of his heart where playing God was concerned.

Flipping through my old *Peanuts* paperbacks, I am appalled by a Valentine's Day sequence from 1964. Charlie Brown is sitting on a schoolyard bench and, as per usual, eating his bag lunch alone. "There's that Little Red-Haired Girl. . . . She's handing out valentines," he says in the first panel. (Ellipses Schulz's throughout.) In the second panel, he leans forward, a look of embarrassed expectancy on his face: "She's handing them out to all her friends . . . She's handing them out one by one . . . She's handing them out . . . She's still handing them out . . ." Third panel. He's sitting back, his shoulders slumping and mouth drooping. "Now she's all done . . . That was the last one . . . Now she's walking away. . . ." Fourth panel. Charlie Brown turns away, his mouth now a quavering upside-down arc, his eyes wide, wobbly, and slightly askew. He looks as if he is trying desperately not to cry. His final word balloon is a simple, ironic "Happy Valentine's Day!" As in the rain sequence I mentioned above, Schulz's drawing is exquisite here. The devastating expressiveness he brings to Charlie Brown's face in that final panel: no one ever did more with only a few dots and squiggles. As well, it is quite a feat of draftsmanship to suggest slumping shoulders when, as a strict point of anatomy, Charlie Brown doesn't really have any.

The deluge strip was at least softened by a kind of "Rainy Days and Mondays" melancholy; this Valentine's Day strip is just . . . mean? Cruel? Of course Schulz wants us to empathize with Charlie Brown—he isn't heartless—but there's nothing the least bit droll or ironic here, not even the tiniest movement of the needle toward wit. I find it almost exhilarating the way the strip transcends anything we normally expect from the funny pages.

Cruel too is the climax of an August 1963 baseball story, running over several days, in which Charlie Brown is pitching for his perennially lousy team in a championship game. (The presumed miracle by which they arrived at a championship game is not explained.) This time, instead of giving up a homer or dropping an easy fly ball or striking out at the plate with the game on the line, Charlie Brown balks in the winning run. *No! Augh!!* His teammates cry out to the heavens with those wide, agonized mouths Schulz liked to draw, the ones that look like upside-down inked-in apples. The wordless fourth panel shows Charlie Brown still on the mound, being pelted by hats and gloves. That's it. No attempt at a punchline, no sad little observation. Just humiliation, like a Fassbinder finale. Did I laugh at this cartoon as a kid? If I did, I must have been a horrible child.

Returning to the Gahan Wilson objection, if Schulz's

characters were anything like "real" kids, his cruelty to them would be unendurable, rather than just curious and sometimes unpleasant. For this reason, I find the scene in *A Charlie Brown Christmas* where Lucy, Patty, Shermy, and the rest berate Charlie Brown for bringing back the homely little tree especially hard to take, since, on TV, the voices belong to actual children. They sound like kids one might know, or even be a parent to. I still love *A Charlie Brown Christmas*, and I still love *Peanuts* as a body of work, but I would be lying if I didn't admit that age—mine, not the strip's—has soured it for me, a little.

But here's a happier note to end on: my adult self has taken something positive from *Peanuts* that my younger self missed. When our daughter, Zoë, was born, my wife's aunt sent us a card in which she wrote that her wish for Zoë was that she have a passion. I didn't quite understand what that meant, at first, but as our children grew up, I began to see the difference between kids who cared deeply about something—soccer, books, flute, theater, social justice, whatever—and those who didn't. You could see that even as kids, in an embryonic way, they had found some kind of meaning in their lives—and what a gift that is.

I think Schulz felt this deeply. Look at his own passion for cartooning, his determination in getting his career off the ground, and look at how his strip evolved as he leaned into his imagination and let fly. Early on, the main characters were Charlie Brown, Shermy, Patty, and, soon, Violet. Aside from Charlie Brown's being something of a roughneck and practical joker, none of the characters had much personality; they were more or less interchangeable, plugged in as gags and visual variety demanded. But Schulz soon began fleshing out his cast with more eccentric, more specific, more driven characters: Schroeder, piano prodigy and Beethoven superfan; Lucy, vain fussbudget and perpetually aggrieved scold; Linus, thumb-sucking philosopher. Meanwhile, as Schulz turned the universe against Charlie Brown, as he became Schulz's alter ego, Charlie Brown's personality deepened and colored; he began life as "I Saw Her Standing There," a blast of fresh air, but within a decade he was the White Album: dark, troubled, raw here, refined there, embracing—magnificent. Colorless Shermy, meanwhile, never cast a shadow; even Schulz admitted he had "very little personality," barely serviceable even as a straight man. Schulz occasionally tried to spice him up by dressing him in a Hawaiian shirt or a snappy windbreaker, but it was useless. Patty and Violet survived as a kind of Greek chorus backing Lucy when it came to calling out Charlie Brown's blockheadedness, but Shermy grew more and more marginal, fading with the 1960s and finally disappearing in 1969—Shermy, who was given *Peanuts*'s very first line of dialogue. Shermy, who early on appeared to be Snoopy's owner. Shermy, *Peanuts*'s very own Pete Best.

So, if I were asked to pick the character most likely to find happiness if he or she ever grew up—the real kind, not just the glib, warm-puppy kind—I wouldn't hesitate to pick Charlie Brown. He feels his failures deeply, he suffers profoundly, and yet he remains ever willing to take another run at kicking the football or trying to get his kite aloft or pitching the next game or hoping this year finally to receive a valentine. Maybe he does find a form of redemption in his suffering. If he is a blockhead it is in part because he cares so much; diffidence doesn't merit the insult. Like his creator, he has passion *and* persistence. If he were real, I like to tell myself, Charlie Brown would be fine.

A Space for Thinking

Nicole Rudick

In his 1936 essay "The Storyteller," the German-Jewish philosopher Walter Benjamin describes what he sees as the beginning of the end of the oral tradition in Western storytelling.
The collective trauma of World War I and its aftereffects were
making the communication of shared experiences through the
telling of tales a thing of the past. He writes, "A generation
that had gone to school on a horse-drawn streetcar now stood
under the open sky in a countryside in which nothing remained
unchanged but the clouds, and beneath these clouds, in a field of
force of destructive torrents and explosions, was the tiny, fragile human body." At the heart of Benjamin's historical process
is a grim efflorescence of existential experience: the sense that
one is adrift in an unfamiliar landscape, a feeling that would
endure as a defining condition of the twentieth century, when
the world was expanding and becoming delimited at the same
time.[1] The writer Luc Sante's parents, recent immigrants in

the United States in the early sixties, couldn't speak English and, "tinged with a certain bitter realism," observed the foreign culture that surrounded them from an intimidating distance. "It wasn't surprising, then," Sante continues, "that my father, an intelligent, capable man who had been dealt a series of bad hands by life—poverty, war, a truncated education—should see himself reflected in Charlie Brown."[2] However he would come to be domesticated and beloved by Americans of all stripes, Charles Schulz's comic-strip boy also spoke to the émigré's sense of dislocation, tough luck, and calamity.

There may be no more tiny, fragile body than Charlie Brown's—the abbreviated torso, economized limbs, and naked, vulnerable pate. That head: with a modicum of lines, Schulz produced an untouched, capacious orb on which a world of expression could play. In the Sunday strip for October 15, 1961, the title panel shows Charlie Brown's head as a table globe, imprinted with a grid of latitudes and longitudes. The strip spins out the joke: to illustrate to Linus the distance between two locations (the absurd pairing of Texas and Singapore), Lucy plots the points over the top of Charlie Brown's bare, impassive head.

Surrounding this vulnerable human form is a wider world: hostile, exhausting, potent in its occasions for failure. Untethered from the historical moment, Benjamin's agents of change, those "torrents and explosions" (or Hamlet's enduring "whips and scorns of time," which extend even to include the intimate "pangs of despised love") are here as perennial humiliations played out in a fathomably unfathomable universe. *Peanuts*, Schulz once said, "deals in defeat."[3] At its core, the comic parses existential angst, strip by strip—not Cold War anxiety, a cloud under which *Peanuts* developed and flourished, but the

garden-variety anxieties found in everyday life. Charlie Brown
is *Peanuts*'s Everyman ("Of all the Charlie Browns in the world,
you're the Charlie Browniest," Linus complains in a 1965 TV
film), adept at losing one day and still rising the next to see
it through. And yet as grounded in real life as it seems to be,
Peanuts shows very little of the actual world. The comic is striking for its spare visual detail, its generic, repetitious settings,
and constrained action. With the exception of the early, busier
strips, it is formally minimal, there is little in the way of depth
perspective, and the action in each panel moves right and left,
as if on a stage.

I remember noticing, as a child, this circumscribed world
in which Charlie Brown and the gang air their problems, so
markedly different from that other deeply felt, philosophical
comic of my youth, *Calvin and Hobbes*, whose characters' domain
is visually and imaginatively bursting at the seams. In the *Peanuts* strip from Sunday, June 9, 1963, Charlie Brown and Sally
admire the night sky as he explains the future deaths of the stars
that make up the Big Dipper. All eight panels depict the same
scene: Charlie Brown and Sally atop a patch of earth, the dark
sky engulfing their bodies. Nothingness surrounds them—both
formally, on the page, and literally, in the black yawn of space
(Schulz uses this conceit frequently). Nothing much happens
here, yet in its openness and conversation, the strip is alive with
wonder, possibility, and humanity. Schulz does a lot with nothingness. In another Sunday strip, from November 19, 1961, the
title panel sets Charlie Brown's small round head astride the
great round face of a clock (his anxious expression and bird's
nest of hair make his features a topsy-turvy counterpoint to the
clock's regularity). We are invited to consider the solitude of

the school lunch hour, when Charlie Brown must sit alone with his thoughts—literally: each of the dozen panels below the title panel features the lone figure and a speech bubble giving voice to his interior monologue. The spareness of each frame rivals that of the stage set for Beckett's *Waiting for Godot*: only a bench and a paper-bag lunch. It's no accident that the evenly distributed, postage-stamp-size panels number twelve, like the hours on a clock. Each movement of Charlie Brown's head—he looks out and down, then up and right—is activated by the reader's eye moving in rhythm from panel to panel to panel, like the ticking of a second hand.

That rhythmic deliberateness—specifically its leisurely meter—is essential to the way *Peanuts* functions as a space for thought. A *Peanuts* strip, even one seemingly packed with goings-on, unfolds patiently. The strip from Sunday, April 18, 1965, depicts a disagreement (sparked by Lucy, of course) on the pitcher's mound. An argument about morality ensues: Charlie Brown's moral qualms about throwing a beanball make him a world-historical hypocrite. "What about the way the early settlers treated the Indians? Was that moral? How about the Children's Crusade? Was that moral?" Each new panel brings a fresh participant and perspective to the mound, and accusations become colloquy. By the penultimate panel, ten players stand on or around Charlie Brown's perch (a pulpit overrun by parishioners), and five speech balloons, thick with philosophical reasoning ("Define morality!"), fill the sky over their heads. But Schulz makes order out of this chaos, arraying his characters in a single line (the panel is unambiguously *Last Supper*–ish, with characters, except for Charlie Brown, grouped in threes). One reads the scene from right to left, both together with and independent of the dialogue—a tidy progression that can be taken in with a serene sweep of the eye. (*Peanuts*'s thoughtful pacing is reminiscent of that other Midwestern export, *Mister Rogers' Neighborhood*. The two also share a rejection of the violence and manic energy that characterize their contemporaries.) The larger Sunday strips are particularly adept at the doling out of time, as they have more space in which to work. But the same effect plays out on a smaller scale in the dailies. In the four-panel baseball strip from August 5, 1972, Lucy harangues Charlie Brown from left field. The entire top half of the second panel is tightly packed with her rant, rendered in a thicket of bold type and punctuated at the end with an eye-catching, electrifying "BOOOOOOO!!" Her energy is palpable, but it cannot last. In the next panel, Lucy sits on the ground, alone and silent, like a calm ocean, and the reader's eye rests on her form and the open white space surrounding it for a surprisingly long moment before moving on to the last, bitterly self-reflective panel.

NO COMIC STRIP may feel more like a series of vignettes than *Peanuts*, especially when the already minimal backgrounds disappear in favor of empty white or monochrome backdrops, as though a thick curtain has descended to further pull a character out of time and into some more concentrated realm of feeling. The generous allotment of white space in the daily strips originated not by design but out of necessity. As David Michaelis details in his biography of Schulz, *Peanuts* began life in pinched dimensions and was sold as a potential space-filler for any section of a newspaper, even the classifieds. To draw the reader's eye, Schulz opted for the less-is-more approach, "fighting back" with white space to echo what he once called the strip's "very slight incidents."[4] The simplification of his character design and their situations grew beyond the strip's early run: "the more they developed complex powers and appetites while staying faithful to their cut-out, shadow-play simplicity," Michaelis writes of Charlie Brown and the gang, "the easier it would be for Schulz to declare the hard things he was set on saying."[5] Had Schulz filled his panels with visual distractions, the business of examining interior problems might have proved less successful.

Peanuts's formal qualities made it an outlier. As a boy, Schulz read comics that incorporated tight crosshatching, deep vanishing points, and thread-like lines, as well as the masterful modernism of Frank King's *Gasoline Alley*. But such visual enrichment didn't appeal to him as a practicing cartoonist—he was, by his own admission, "a great believer in the mild in cartooning." What of *Peanuts*'s contemporaries? Mort Walker's *Beetle Bailey* and Hank Ketchum's *Dennis the Menace* began around the same time as *Peanuts*. *Beetle Bailey* is an uncomplicated gag-dependent strip drawn with what Michaelis calls "elastic visual exaggerations,"[6] and *Dennis the Menace* relied on a wealth of visual detail to deliver its absurdist, situational humor. Both grew faster than *Peanuts* in readership and recognition, but neither has attained *Peanuts*'s broad cultural impact.

It's easy to forget how unlikely this cultural ascendency might have seemed. Schulz created an oddly shaped boy, an anthropomorphized dog, and a host of children who don't behave or speak as children do, and he placed them in an efficient, nondescript setting—only on the *surface* of reality, you might say. The reader should be skeptical of this setup. And yet, Charlie Brown's emotional struggle is familiar, and the reader is roused by it. Bertolt Brecht would have approved of *Peanuts*. He sought this same "partial" illusion for the theater "in order that it may always be recognized as an illusion."[7] Too complete an impression of naturalness, and one forgets this isn't reality but art. Brecht would have us read not literally, but critically and interpretively. Though *Peanuts* does not have all the same aims as a piece of didactic political theater like *Mother Courage*, it, too, is meant to be engaged with, not skimmed over. The strip "deals in intelligent things," Schulz once said, "things that people have been afraid of."[8] He did not consider *Peanuts* a children's comic; even in Snoopy, his most kid-friendly character, Schulz created a self-willed, occasionally anxious fantasist. I wonder if Brecht would have loved Lucy best, as I do. Born into *Peanuts* as a "fussbudget," she soon becomes a prime mover behind the strip's conflict and Charlie Brown's feelings of disillusionment. Lucy is assertive, nervy, confident, stubborn, and manipulative; she can moon over a beau and still excoriate him for his inattentiveness. And despite her near-constant bluster, she is a person who feels profound pain. In the Sunday strip for June 30, 1963, she feels low and rages, "I've never had anything, and I never will have anything!" Linus patiently replies, "Well, for one thing, you have a little brother who loves you." And Lucy, her reserves spent, cries in his arms. Her modernity is best on display in her psychiatrist booth, which offers a kind of glimpse behind the scenes—that break with illusion that Brecht insisted upon. A parody of the semiseriousness of a kid's lemonade stand, Lucy's booth calls itself a psychiatrist's practice but offers none of its customary trappings other than its desk—but this pared-down presentation (including, perhaps, Lucy's confident authority) allows Charlie Brown to recognize its purpose.

The reader recognizes it, too, but sees what Charlie Brown does not (or chooses not to): it is a façade, in construction and intent. Unlike the naïve young analysand, we won't be beguiled by Lucy's blunt advice. Still, we turn it over in our minds as we read, struck by some bigger truth in counsel we know to be ill-advised.

Yet another defining visual feature of *Peanuts* for me is the low wall at which the characters sometimes pause for conversation. Some daily strips take place entirely behind this wall, like the one from Tuesday, May 6, 1958, which has Charlie Brown and Lucy leaning on its even stonework, facing out at the reader, in all four panels. The wall strikes me as a decidedly theatrical element, as makeshift as any that could be wheeled out onto a stage. The panels' lines make a neat proscenium arch. (It is so obvious a device that when I see it I think of Snout in *A Midsummer Night's Dream*, who, playing the part of a wall in the play within a play, insists, "This loam, this roughcast, and this stone doth show / That I am that same wall. The truth is so.") If Lucy's booth divides characters, with one on each side of the desk, and gives her an air of dialogic authority, then the wall is more Socratic, a site that encourages deliberation and reflection. In the strip for Monday, March 17, 1969, Linus and Lucy are at the wall. "I have a lot of questions about life, and I'm not getting any answers!" she complains, adding over the next two panels, "I want some real honest-to-goodness answers . . . I don't want a lot of opinions . . . I want answers!" In the last panel, Linus offers an answer that isn't an answer, one that is itself a question and can only elicit further questions: "Would true or false be all right?"

Through *Peanuts*, Schulz wanted to tell hard truths about,

as he said, "intelligent things." But the main truth he tells is that there are no answers to the big questions. In the long run, no one wins and no one loses; this isn't drama, it's life. The strip's solace is that the reader isn't alone in facing these fraught issues, and its gift is a space in which she is invited to think, to contemplate the big picture on a small scale, like soaking in the emotional ambience of a Rothko painting. It's tempting, and desirable perhaps, to think of *Peanuts* as a mirror in which the reader sees and is absorbed by her own reflection, but that view undermines the elegant simplicity of Schulz's creation: powerfully complex characters, who, together, represent the constituent parts of humanity and who operate in a "shadow-play" (to borrow from Michaelis's keen observation), or what is only a workable representation of the world. In and through this setting, Schulz created in Charlie Brown "a man who reflects about his part,"[9] as Benjamin writes of the actor in Brecht's concept of epic theater. (And here again we are not so far from Hamlet.) The irony of *Peanuts*'s visual flatness and economy is that they engender a capacious space—room enough both for Charlie Brown's reflection on Schulz's hard truths and for the reader's own consideration of these big ideas. The strip's achievement, and a significant reason for its longevity, is in its creation of a space of inquiry that is never closed off.

VERY EARLY IN *Peanuts*'s history, Schulz doesn't fully know his characters, in the way a novelist or a playwright can invent a character but then must follow that character's lead to know where they are meant to go and what they are meant to do. One strip of *Peanuts* can be satisfying in the way a single, shining sentence of a novel can be satisfying; we pin it on the wall as a reminder of an idea or a feeling, and it can stand on its own in that way, but it is also always only a fragment of a more expansive tale. It isn't enough to see Lucy pull the football out from under Charlie Brown once; the point is that she does it again and again and again. The repetition of the act, from strip to strip, autumn to autumn, produces the same question anew each time: why does she do it and how does he respond? And each time, the answer is different. (Charlie Brown "loses in so many miserable ways," Schulz observed in an interview with Al Roker on *Today* in 1999.)

The thoughtfulness with which Schulz examines humanity does not expire and does not cease to provoke astonishment (much like Lucy's ongoing football charade). In the Sunday strip from November 26, 1961, Snoopy spends a dozen wordless panels bounding through curtains of rain that slash vertically and violently through each scene. Schulz punctuates the beagle's short bursts of speed, rendered on monochromatic backgrounds, with tenuous moments of peace, as he pauses in doorways and under umbrellas—small moments of reprieve amid a visual cacophony. The final panel finds him recumbent atop his doghouse: the rain still falls in brutal torrents, but he is able to cope with it, a tender body at rest in a familiar landscape at last.

Notes

1. Benjamin, ever aware of the force of history at his back, fled the Nazis across Europe and eventually committed suicide in a Spanish border town in 1940 rather than be turned over to them.

2. Luc Sante, "The Human Comedy," introduction to *Peanuts Every Sunday: 1961–1965* (Seattle: Fantagraphics Books, 2015), 5.

3. Charles M. Schulz, *My Life with Charlie Brown*, ed. M. Thomas Inge (Jackson: University Press of Mississippi, 2010), 165.

4. Quoted in David Michaelis, *Schulz and Peanuts: A Biography* (New York: Harper, 2007), 207.

5. Ibid., 211.

6. Ibid., 271.

7. Bertolt Brecht, "From the *Mother Courage* Model," in *Brecht on Theatre: The Development of an Aesthetic*, ed. and trans. John Willett (New York: Hill and Wang, 1964), 219.

8. Quoted in Michaelis, 278.

9. Walter Benjamin, "What Is Epic Theater?" in *Illuminations: Essays and Reflections*, ed. and with an introduction by Hannah Arendt, trans. Harry Zohn (New York: Schocken Books, 1988), 153.

Why I Love *Peanuts*

Joe Queenan

In my favorite installment from *Peanuts*, the famous comic strip that debuted in U.S. newspapers on October 2, 1950, the character Snoopy receives a rejection letter from a New York publishing house to which he has been submitting his work. The letter says that it has been quite some time since the publishing house has received any submissions from the ambitious dog, who, in one of many alter-egos, has now fancied himself a canny wordsmith. The final panel, which I used to carry around in my wallet, until it finally disintegrated, shows Snoopy reading the words, "This suits our current needs."

Any young writer submitting unsolicited manuscripts to publishing houses in the 1960s or '70s would have felt a chill run down his spine as he read the words, "This suits our current needs." No matter what you submitted, and no matter what publishing house, within a few weeks you would receive a cold, impersonal note reading: "Thank you for your submission.

Unfortunately, your work does not suit our current needs."
Charles M. Schulz, whose work would earn him hundreds of
millions of dollars over his half-century career, had never lost
touch with the aspiring cartoonist whose early work had been
rejected, manhandled, or ignored. It was this human quality,
this compassion for the young and the powerless, that made *Peanuts* what it was. Schulz had the common touch.

Peanuts, which grew out of earlier work Schulz had done in
a column called *Li'l Folks*, debuted around the time the U.S. became embroiled in the Korean War. It was a time of genuine political hysteria, with Americans terrified that the communists
in the Soviet Union and China would overrun the world, and,
if this failed, unleash a nuclear holocaust as a kind of consolation prize. *Peanuts*, so endearing, so harmless, so good-natured,
was a daily antidote to this atmosphere of fear and loathing, in
the same way that the arrival of the Beatles in the U.S. a few
months after John F. Kennedy's assassination helped to bring
young people back to life. Throughout the Red Scare of the
'50s, the desegregation wars in the deep south, the Kennedy
assassinations, the murder of Martin Luther King, the war in
Vietnam, the hostage crisis in Iran, and—well, you get the
idea—*Peanuts* was always there as a touchstone and a balm. Unlike so many other venerated objects in U.S. pop culture, it was
sweet without being stupid, reassuring without being infantile.
In the dark era in which it began, it served much the same function as *I Love Lucy*. The difference was it had brains.

THE COMIC STRIP ran for almost fifty years, the last original
panel being published on February 13, 2000, the day after its
creator died. The strip ran in many countries and was translated

into many languages, even though fans in foreign countries might not have fully grasped its decidedly American sensibility. The premise, after all, is a bit of an inside joke: the central character in *Peanuts* is the hapless, downbeat Charlie Brown. Americans do not ordinarily take much of a shine to hapless losers. But they took a shine to Charlie Brown.

It is generally agreed that Schulz's heyday was in the '60s and '70s, that toward the end the strip became a bit too saccharine and predictable. That said, it had a nice run before it became little more than a merchandising vehicle, the marketing arm of a much larger empire. The strip first saw the light of day one month before I was born. So it was always there, and seemed like it had always been there.

It was like the sky: pleasant, visually appealing, reliable. *Peanuts* had a *Picture of Dorian Gray* quality; you kept getting older and more decrepit and more cynical, but it didn't. By the time you started reading it, you were already older than the characters in the strip, so it immediately made you nostalgic for childhood. Not necessarily for your childhood, but for the childhood Lucy and Charlie and Linus were having.

The name *Peanuts* is derived from the term "peanut gallery," which describes the cheap seats in a theater. The name was assigned to the strip by the syndicate that began to run it in 1950; Schulz himself hated it. Yet in retrospect, it seems altogether perfect in the same way that *The Great Gatsby* is a far better book title than F. Scott Fitzgerald's original suggestions: "Trimalchio in West Egg," "The High-Bouncing Lover," "On the Road to West Egg," "The Gold-Hatted Gatsby." Unlike many of the famous comic strips that preceded it—*Tarzan, The Phantom, Brenda Starr, Mark Trail*—*Peanuts* did not belong to any one character. Though the perpetually downbeat Charlie Brown was the emotional center of the strip's universe, few identified with him. He was very much like the essential loser friend that so many of us have, the harmless, hapless, but ultimately lovable one who never gets anything right. His haplessness was an inspiration to us all; no matter how bad things got in our daily lives, they would get much worse for Charlie Brown. But never worse in a horrible way. Just . . . worse.

The other characters were all foils to Charlie Brown. Peppermint Patty, the tomboy par excellence, was the one who was game for anything. Snoopy was the quirky canine who was off in his own world. Linus was the quintessential weird younger brother, who never quite fit in. Of all the characters, Lucy, the feisty little girl who liked to mix it up with the boys, was the closest to reality. I grew up with girls who seemed to have patterned their personality around Lucy, never giving an inch, always willing to give you an earful. But I never met anyone who shaped his personality after Charlie Brown.

You didn't have to like all the characters in *Peanuts* to enjoy the strip. I never quite got Marcie or Franklin, mid-'60s additions who seemed to serve an ancillary function. Woodstock, the lovable little bird who became Snoopy's protégé, annoyed me. Schroeder's Beethoven fixation I found tiring. But Lucy, Chuck, Peppermint Patty, and Snoopy were fine.

From the very beginning, *Peanuts* had an elegiac quality. It made Americans pine for an earlier, more innocent time that had never actually existed. In this sense, *Peanuts* occupied a place in the American consciousness that was a bit like that occupied by Sir Walter Scott's novels in Victorian times, evoking a time and place where life was simpler and easier to understand, and therefore entirely illusory. Though Schulz would sometimes make satirical allusions to events of the day, the adult world never really intruded. Physically, he did not allow adults to enter the strip. Nor did he allow senseless cruelty. Pratfalls, yes, but not cruelty. The world of *Peanuts* was hermetically sealed, in the way that children at play have always wanted their cosmos hermetically sealed.

Peanuts did not look like the comic strips that had preceded it. Many of these were incredibly busy and complicated, and sometimes grotesque. They were stylish and beautiful, but inaccessible; the artist did not invite his audience in. *Peanuts*, by contrast, was deceptively simple in design and very accommodating to the viewer. There was usually not much more than the characters' expressions, perhaps a doghouse or a playing field. This graphic approach didn't change much over the years; it was not broke, so there was no reason to fix it.

People often enjoy something without knowing why. This is why those audio guides you find in art galleries are so stupid: no one can explain to you why Bellinis are beautiful, and no amount of curatorial gas-bagging can make you like Renoir unless you are already the type of person who is predisposed to like Renoir. It probably never occurred to most people who liked *Peanuts* that its graphic ingenuity and deceptive elegance was a large part of its appeal. But it was. Before *Peanuts*, the most famous comic strips were arty. *Peanuts* was not arty.

Eventually, it became fashionable to find more in *Peanuts* than was really there. American academics are always offering courses in such things as the philosophical subtexts implicit in *The Simpsons*, or what *Mad Men* says about the American psyche because academics can never leave well enough alone. I find this sort of stuff first-class bilge, an inability to accept a popular art form on its own terms. No amount of blather can turn U2 into Bach, and the fact that Charles Schulz produced a larger body of work than Rimbaud doesn't put him in Rimbaud's weight class.

Everything about *Peanuts* flew in the face of such pretentiousness; it was a comic strip that never took itself seriously. It was a lighthearted little set of four panels you could look forward to every day, no matter where you were, if only to follow the exploits of a silly dog who imagined himself a dog-fighting aviator in the First World War. Nobody ever knew where the idea for Snoopy and the Red Baron came from. Nobody knows why Peppermint Patty had so much trouble cracking the mystery of Snoopy's identity. Nobody knows why the hapless Charlie Brown was so hapless. It did not matter. The ideas came from somewhere. And when they got here, they were more than welcome to pull up a chair and stay a while. Fifty years, in fact.

Nonsense!

Peter D. Kramer

Lucy van Pelt first played psychotherapist on March 27, 1959. In the seminal strip, she sits behind a box labeled "Psychiatric Help 5¢." Charlie Brown takes a seat on the low chair provided for clients. "I have deep feelings of depression . . ." he says, and then, "What can I do about this?" Lucy puts a finger to her chin. Then she leans on folded arms and delivers her considered opinion, "Snap out of it! Five cents, please." It is a perfect joke.

Note regarding sources: I don't pretend to be a *Peanuts* expert. In thinking about the psychiatry booth routines, I have relied on David Michaelis's *Schulz and Peanuts*; *Peanuts: The Art of Charles M. Schulz*; Rheta Grimsley Johnson's *Good Grief: The Story of Charles M. Schulz*; the website of Schulz biographer Michael Schuman; the Peanuts Wiki *Fandom*; and various Pinterest collections of old strips. I want also to acknowledge Anna Creadick's *Perfectly Average: The Pursuit of Normality in Postwar America*, and the essay "Baffling Search for the Normal Man," by Peggy and Pierre Streit, from the June 3, 1962, number of *The New York Times Magazine*. Leston Havens's book on Harry Stack Sullivan is *Participant Observation*. Thanks to the Brown University Libraries for obtaining Lucy-centric *Peanuts* collections for me, including *Lucy: Not Just Another Pretty Face* and *How to Be a Grrrl! By Lucy van Pelt*.

Perfect jokes are meant to be built on. Charles Schulz will fiddle with this one endlessly. The consultation box will grow a signboard and a second tagline, "The Doctor is In." Snoopy will compete with Lucy from behind a board that advertises, "Friendly Advice, 2¢," or "Hug a Warm Puppy, 2¢." Lucy will use the booth for a travel agency. She will dispense valentines from the booth, and a dish called goop, also five cents. These versions are funny, when they are, because they play off the original, where Lucy offers dismissal in the guise of treatment.

Most of the series will involve psychiatric care. Lucy will tell Charlie Brown to stop his silly worrying. When he asks how, she'll say, "That's your worry! Five cents, please!" Charlie Brown will complain that people talk over him and go on and on. In response, Lucy will do just that. Charlie Brown will achieve the long view: "I've been coming to you for some time now, but I don't really feel that I'm getting any better." Is he any worse? No? Five cents!

The jokes gain from their constant elements. Charlie Brown feels unease. Lucy fails to provide what he's come for. The billing is relentless. Finally, the assemblage, the theme and variations, become the work of art, a grand commentary on the impossible relationship among need, trust, help, and character.

In this way, the doctor-is-in collection parallels Schulz's most famous running gag, the one with the football. Here, the script is more uniform. Lucy places the ball. Charlie Brown runs toward it. While he's in the act of kicking, she pulls it away. He should have learned his lesson, but he hasn't. Each time, he's wary. Each time, Lucy convinces him to rely on her despite all. The result is another pratfall.

The first football-gag cartoon involving Lucy appeared in

1952, in a Sunday strip with ten frames, enough space for her to fool Charlie Brown twice. The doubling is necessary, because the poignancy is in reiteration. The joke is about ignoring experience. The joke is about who each one is. Charlie Brown is trusting to a fault—or a virtue. He prefers to trust, however often his faith is betrayed. Giving fellow humans the benefit of the doubt is a fine if painful way to live. "Don't! Don't!" we cry to Charlie Brown, and then we're glad he does.

We, too, take pratfalls. We, too, may be the better for taking them. There's solace in that observation, and food for thought, too, about what's right for us. If betrayal is the way of the world, how should a person live?

At first glance, the doctor gag runs on the same principle. Repeatedly, Charlie Brown exposes himself to ridicule by baring his soul. Repeatedly, Lucy brings him up short. But after that, the two jokes differ.

To understand the football joke, you don't need to know much about football. The joke is not about football. It's about human nature. The doctor-is-in gag is less classic, less essential, because it's more specific. It comments on character, to be sure. But it's also about psychotherapy. Say, "The doctor is in," and everyone gets the reference. It's about not just any doctor but this kind, the sort who listens attentively—or not.

For a joke to work, we need to know and expect something and then to have that expectation upset or else fulfilled in an all-too-characteristic way. To understand what's wrong with what Charlie Brown gets, we need to know what he should get, that is, to have a prior concept of psychotherapy, how it is done. The doctor-is-in jokes comment on the relationship between psychiatrist and patient.

Schulz was inclined to throw this perspective into question. When a biographer, Rheta Grimsley Johnson, asked him about his critique of psychiatry, or (as another biographer has written) child psychology, Schulz said that he was just playing with a standard cartoon setup, the kid with the lemonade stand.

The answer is partly plausible. Before we get to the dialogue, what's funny about the psychiatric care booth is that its product is so different from what kids ordinarily sell for a nickel. But that is also to say that Lucy and Charlie Brown—dispensing and consuming psychotherapy—are unusual kids, wise and tuned in beyond their years, kids speaking like grown-ups. In interviews, Schulz liked to appear uncomplicated and uncalculating, but he was neither. There is something disingenuous in his ducking the conclusion that when a character offering psychiatric care hosts a character complaining about deep depressive symptoms, psychiatry is at issue. Although the presentation is compact, diverse aspects of the profession seem to be in play: therapists, therapy, and the business of psychiatry.

We have an impression of therapists. They will be empathetic, thoughtful, subtle, intuitive, slow to judge, and slow to speak—intent on throwing the questioner back on himself. That's the setup for Lucy's punchlines. She's chosen the profession she's least suited to. She has the wrong temperament.

She's also drawing from the wrong repertory. Psychiatrists make interpretations, or they did at midcentury. "Snap out of it!" is not an interpretation. It's like the Ring Lardner line from forty years earlier: "'Shut up,' he explained." The retort is no explanation, but it is how we might, honestly and impulsively, want to answer a child (that's the setup in the Lardner novel) who asks an embarrassing question—just as "Snap out of it!" is what we sometimes feel like saying when people entrust us with an intimate complaint.

Charlie Brown has made himself vulnerable, and he's not getting what he has a right to expect, not getting an interpretation. All the same, he has to pay. "Five cents, please" is the second joke, about how intent psychiatrists are on billing.

In one strip, Lucy admits, shamelessly, "I'll treat any patient who has a problem and a nickel." In another, when Charlie Brown asks whether he will ever become mature and well-adjusted, Lucy demands payment in advance, since he won't like the answer. Working with Snoopy, Lucy spends less time treating his anxiety—fewer cartoon frames, anyway—than collecting her fee.

This theme—cash before all—is also a hoary one. George Gershwin relied on it in his song "Freud and Jung and Adler" for the 1933 musical *Pardon My English*. In a repeated refrain, the doctors sing that they practice psychoanalysis because it "pays twice as well" as specialties that deal with bodily ailments. Therapists are inherently comical *Luftmenschen*, impractical, except on this one front. They like their fees. Lucy's perky insistence about billing gives the five-cents-please strips their final kick.

Snap out of it! works, then, because of general expectations about what constitutes help when we're down and specific ones about how therapists are: empathetic and delicate. *Five cents, please!* works because of a contrasting account of therapists, as ineffectual and venal. But I wonder whether other issues are not active as well, issues even more particular to the time, the late 1950s.

For instance, what does it mean for Charlie Brown to say that he has deep feelings of depression? That last word will sound discordant to anyone familiar with a discussion, about the proper use of antidepressants, that has been current in psychiatry in recent years. It starts with the claim that depression has changed meaning, that it used to refer to very grave conditions—mostly to the depressive phase of bipolar disorder—while lesser conditions, now lumped with depression, went under the heading of neurosis. Charlie Brown's line suggests otherwise. In daily speech, depression, anxiety, and neurosis were all in the same territory, and almost everyone suffered from them.

A second misconception is that today we're at a high point for psychiatric diagnosis. By this account, we have pathologized normality. Who doesn't have anxiety, depression, or an attention deficit? But *Peanuts* became popular at what was arguably the true high-water mark for psychiatric diagnosis. The leading mental health survey of the 1950s was the Midtown Manhattan Study. It judged 80 percent of respondents to have a condition that might merit treatment. A *New York Times Magazine* piece reported that "only 18.5 per cent of those investigated were 'free enough of emotional symptoms to be considered well.'"

That same article reviewed a study from the University of Minnesota based on exhaustive personality testing of especially healthy young men. The research produced a characterization of the "normal man." He turned out to be a rare bird and perhaps a colorless one—"a bit dull" with "limited drives and horizons."

The fifties was, in other words, a time of obsession with and deep ambivalence about normality. In the wake of the Second World War and then the Korean War, people longed for normality and for the chance to be normal. But the condition seemed out of reach and perhaps not fully admirable. *The Man in the Gray Flannel Suit* was a defining work, as a book and then a movie. Was normality possible for those who had endured war? Was normality conformity? Consumerism? Blandness?

When Charlie Brown reveals his feelings of depression— and, on other occasions, anxiety—he is saying that he is like everyone else, like most of Schulz's readers. "My anxieties have anxieties" is a Charlie Brown line, one that became a book title for Schulz. Nor is it clear that Charlie Brown's self-doubt is less admirable or perceptive than Lucy's certainty. We root for Charlie Brown, we want him to have successes, but we may not wish him to be other than as he is, ill at ease.

We understand this much about Charlie Brown's depressive symptoms automatically. They serve as a premise for humor because what he has is what we all have.

It's in our time that depression has a darker meaning. Today, the snap-out-of-it joke might be hard to tell. We'd need to distinguish Charlie Brown's near-universal depression from a serious disorder, one where commanding a sufferer to bootstrap it might not be funny at all.

Psychiatry was in a particular phase in the 1950s as well. The first modern psychotherapeutic medications had just been developed, but they were not in widespread use. Within the profession, orthodox psychoanalysis had spawned alternatives, but they remained outside the mainstream. Freudianism had taken the country by storm in prior decades, clinically and intellectually. Psychiatry was mostly psychotherapy, and psychotherapy was mostly psychoanalysis.

It may be hard to recall how rigid orthodoxy was. Patients came for treatment many times a week, lay on the couch, associated freely, and received in response intervals of silence interrupted by interpretations laced with references to non-intuitive concepts like transference and projection, castration anxiety and penis envy. Implicitly, this complex armature made psychotherapy an apt comic foil.

At the same time, Freudian psychology had become the standard way of viewing mental functioning. Fluency in its tropes was a requirement for making art and literature and sophisticated conversation.

When she says, "Snap out of it," Lucy is rejecting that whole apparatus. Lucy sees the emperor in his nakedness. That's what Schulz later said about her. "She has a way of cutting right down to the truth."

Lucy's way is an American way—pragmatic. I have mentioned alternative schools of therapy. America had adopted or given rise to them, treatments that were less mystical and more directive than the standard version. Alfred Adler, Franz Alexander, Karen Horney, and Harry Stack Sullivan all had their adherents, doctors more attentive to social phenomena and more willing to comment on patients' behavior.

Sullivan in particular had something of Lucy in him, or perhaps it's the other way around. When, in therapy, a young man tried to deny that a love affair had mattered to him, Sullivan interrupted: "Nonsense, you were happy with her." The young man had enjoyed successes in the relationship, and Sullivan did not want them lost. And Sullivan could be directive. On one occasion, Sullivan reported, he interrupted a patient to exclaim, "Merciful God! Let us consider what will follow that!" Engaging in "clumsy dramatics," Sullivan confessed, was part of his method.

Perhaps it's just me, but I hear echoes of Sullivan in certain Lucy vignettes. For instance: Sullivan practiced with his dogs, two cocker spaniels, in the consulting room. The story goes that once a patient, a fellow psychiatrist, protested, "I wonder what would happen if you had to choose between those dogs and me!" Sullivan said, "I could arrange a referral." I mention the legend because of the strip where Lucy asks her beloved Schroeder, "What if I told you that you had to choose between your piano and me?" Schroeder says, "That wouldn't be difficult."

(Here roles are reversed, with Lucy being brought to attention. Schulz made this move regularly. On one occasion, he had Lucy allow as how, in treating Charlie Brown, she has learned about herself. Charlie Brown delivers the punchline, "Five cents, please!" The actors change but the pattern remains: sensitivity comes at a cost.)

Again, Sullivan made a grand statement that gained some currency: "There are few things that I think are so harrowing as the occasional psychiatrist who knows a great deal about right and wrong." *Peanuts* features a theme along these lines when Charlie Brown tells Lucy that he bought Linus a new blanket: "I thought I was doing the right thing." After putting finger to chin, Lucy proclaims: "In all of mankind's history, there has never been more damage done than by people who 'thought they were doing the right thing.'"

Sullivan's therapeutic posture came to be called counter-projective. The patient arrived with expectations about how authority figures act. Sullivan would behave differently. Franz Alexander's variant of psychoanalysis operated along similar lines.

By the 1950s, alternative, more vigorous approaches to

patients were very much in the air. Perhaps Schulz was making fun of them, too, so that Lucy's sharpness—her counterprojective technique—cuts both ways, as a critique of both Freudianism and its critics.

His denials notwithstanding, Schulz seems to have been conversant with the psychotherapies of his day. Famously, he coined the phrase "security blanket," as the demotic equivalent of the British psychoanalyst Donald Winnicott's "transitional object." Schulz played contract bridge regularly with a neighbor, Fritz Van Pelt, whose family name, with the *v* made lowercase, had become Lucy's. The story goes that Van Pelt had taken a psychology course that covered Winnicott. When Schulz teased Van Pelt's daughter by hiding her special bunny, the father warned Schulz off, explaining how an object halfway between toy and parent afforded a child a sense of security. Next, Linus got his blanket.

Internal evidence, in the cartoons, reveals facility with psychotherapy. When Lucy treats Snoopy for a phobia—he has become fearful of sleeping outdoors at night—she suggests that guilt (over his inadequacies as a watchdog) may be at the root. Exploring the problem, she asks Snoopy whether he was happy at home and whether he liked his mother and father. On another occasion, she tells Linus, "The fact that you realize you need help, indicates that you are not too far gone." There's no way that these routines are not *about* psychotherapy, about psychotherapy as something funny and not a little suspect.

In practice, it was impossible to be attuned to cultural trends at midcentury without being aware of psychoanalysis, pro and con. I can say a word about my own exposure. In 1959, I was in grade school. I don't recall reading the *Peanuts* strip, although it appeared in our local paper. I mostly came to Schulz later, in the *Happiness Is a Warm Puppy* era. (It was Lucy, in a soft moment, who spoke that line.) I was likelier to be conversant with Sullivan and Alexander. My mother had read them during World War II, when she trained as an occupational therapist. Their texts featured prominently on the family's bookshelves.

I had been exposed to the methods. Joan Doniger, a family friend who had trained with my mother in occupational therapy, was a babysitter in my early childhood. Donny, as Joan was mostly called, went on, in 1958, to found Woodley House, one of the first psychiatric halfway houses, serving people with serious mental illness. The residents were required to be in psychoanalysis, but Donny was a counterweight. She had a good deal of Lucy in her. Donny would tell residents, "I understand that you're hallucinating, but you need to get along with your roommate—and sweep out your room."

Perhaps it is not coincidence that, in medical school, I sought out Leston Havens as a mentor. Les was a Sullivan scholar known for his ability to surprise patients and catapult them into new levels of honesty and openness.

Here's a Havens moment I recall from my first psychiatry rotation. A patient enters the room, charms the trainees with offhand chatter, and begins to reminisce about his pleasant childhood. Havens reaches into his pocket, whips out a bill, and says, "Five bucks says your old man was a son-of-a-bitch." The patient, a sociopath, gets down to business.

Later, I would study schools of family therapy that were similarly confrontational.

After training, I dropped those methods. I did not often bring a patient up short, at least not intentionally. I was concerned about patients' fragility. Perhaps I was in rebellion as well, against the dramatic techniques that had achieved prominence by the late 1970s. My, and my generation's, version of *Snap out of it!* was prescribing. We used medicines to free a patient from circular thinking so that the work of self-examination could proceed.

Considering talk therapy alone: were my patients the worse for my reticence? Perhaps. We are free to imagine that Charlie Brown gains something from Lucy's brusque response. He is being thrown back on his own resources, with the message that they may be more substantial than he believes. Lucy as therapist, I am suggesting, does not go entirely against the grain.

That's the genius of a perfect joke, isn't it, to encapsulate every aspect of a complex ambivalence? "Snap out of it! Five cents, please" captures and exposes contradictory feelings, of awe and contempt, toward psychoanalysis and its alternatives.

That said, it would be wrong to reduce the doctor-is-in routine to its premises. The genius of Schulz is in coaxing transcendent results from everyday material. The subject is the human condition. The humor in that perfect strip—"Snap out of it!"—is bittersweet: we feel blue, we expose our feelings, we get a bracing dismissal, and we pay for the privilege. Life's like that. Good grief!

Even this scope is too narrow. As his fellow cartoonist, Jules Feiffer, was known to insist, Schulz was intensely modern, aware of the absurdity of our existence and the self-referential nature of art.

Late in the *Peanuts* canon, Schulz contributed a highly *meta* strip that suggests that he was continuing to puzzle out this matter of the psychiatry stand, what it was or had been about, and how seriously its content should be taken. The cartoon's dialogue would not be out of place as a coda to a Woody Allen movie, like that routine at the end of *Annie Hall* about needing the eggs.

Franklin, a new character—new in the strips and new in town—asks Lucy how the lemonade business is going. Lucy corrects him: "This is a psychiatric booth." Puzzled, Franklin asks Lucy whether she's a real doctor. Lucy answers the question with a question: "Was the lemonade ever any good?"

Percy Crosby and Skippy

The Aesthetic Ancestors of
Schulz and Charlie Brown

David Hajdu

It was *so Peanuts*. A lonesome small-town boy, the main character of the strip, sat by himself on a street curb. He was resting his head on the palm of one hand, his elbow propped on one knee. His eyes, though they were drawn simply as two little circles, somehow looked achingly sad. There was no background or environmental detail—just white space and a few scribbly pen lines to suggest shadows, as if this kid were literally as alone in the world as he seemed to feel. Talking aloud to himself, he said, in the second panel, "For no reason at all I catch myself feelin' happy—"

In the third panel, he finished the thought: "—an' it's all I can do to steer my mind back into things that worry me."

The strip, named for its beleaguered young star, Skippy, was syndicated in thousands of newspapers around the United States, including the *Minneapolis Tribune*, which the family of Charles M. Schulz received at home in St. Paul. On the date this curbside episode was published, July 15, 1935, Schulz was twelve years old. As he would recall years later, when he was famous for a newspaper strip of his own, *Skippy* was one of his favorites.

There's no knowing how deeply Schulz was influenced by *Skippy* when he was still a child with artistic talent and Skippy was a mammothly popular phenomenon in America, omnipresent through not only the comics pages but also movie spin-offs, hardcover books, a radio series, a popular song, and countless tie-in products from *Skippy* dolls and *Skippy* games to Skippy peanut butter. (Yes, *that's* where the brand that's practically a synonym for peanut butter got its name, as a licensee of the comic strip.) *Skippy* was, in multiple ways, the *Peanuts* of its day.

Schulz, in an address given at an event for the National Cartoonists Society in 1994, made a point to bring up the artist and writer responsible for *Skippy*, Percy Crosby, as a model of cartooning mastery. "If you're a young person and you haven't studied Percy Crosby," Schulz said, "you'd better get down and find some books and see how Percy Crosby drew."

What you would discover in the panels of Crosby's signature project is a world that largely foreshadowed the aesthetic and philosophical spheres that Charlie Brown and his friends (and associated beagles and sparrows) would begin to occupy five years after the final *Skippy* strip was published. At the same time, *Skippy*, in its overt politicking and occasional outright weirdness, was something other than a beta version of *Peanuts*, and Percy Crosby and Charles Schulz were as different as men as Snoopy and Spike differ as anthropomorphic cartoon dogs.

Skippy was introduced in 1923 (a few months after Charles M. Schulz was born) in *Life* magazine, for which Crosby had been contributing illustrations and single-panel gag cartoons. Moving to newspaper syndication in 1925, *Skippy* might have appeared at first to be yet another entry (and a relatively late one, at that) in the tradition of features with kiddie characters that had begun in the first days of the comic-strip medium. The earliest funny pages were overpacked with young people, most of them troublemakers or unruly objects of adult ire—roustabouts, urchins, truants, and brats like the Yellow Kid, Happy Hooligan, the Katzenjammer Kids, Little Jimmy, and Buster Brown. Young readers would relate to them for their age and prankstery attitudes, and older people in the booming population of immigrants who made up the bulk of early comics readers would relish them for their anarchic mockery of American rules and manners.

"There were some other wonderful strips with little kids in them," Schulz would recall in an interview. "Of course, *Skippy* would be the best example."

Like *Peanuts*, which Schulz had originally wanted to call *Li'l Folks*, *Skippy* was a cartoon about young characters who were anything but cartoonish. Skippy and his friends were small kids living in a small town in the early twentieth century, and their activities were grounded intimately in the smallness of that experience. They went to school, grudgingly; they played ball, not too well; and they hung around together—a lot, idling the seemingly endless hours of childhood in the days before American parenting and elementary education turned into synchronized machines for micromanaging kids' out-of-school hours with homework, lessons, and organized sports. In *Skippy*, as later in *Peanuts*, the characters walked about and sat around and talked to one another—and to themselves—at a pace that was truer to life than the chaotic frenzy in the back alleys where Happy and his gang engaged in their hooliganism; yet it was ultimately less like the tempo of life than the rhythm of the mind.

Crosby, like Schulz, conjured the experience of childhood with exquisite sensitivity and veracity, depicting the lives of Skippy and his friends from their own point of view. We see few adults in *Skippy*, though some appear now and then—teaching class, running the ice-cream shop, checking report cards, or otherwise embodying adult authority—in contrast to the wholly adult-free landscape of *Peanuts*. Still, Skippy isn't exactly a realistic child, any more than Charlie Brown is. They're both deeply astute and introspective figures who speak with unrealistic, or anti-realistic, maturity and sophistication. They live like kids, but think like philosophers.

There were strains of spirituality in *Skippy*, much as there would be in *Peanuts*. (When I was a kid and obsessed with *Peanuts*, I read the two books by Robert L. Short that connected the strip to Christian scripture, *The Gospel According to Peanuts* and *The Parables of Peanuts*, and showed them off to grown-ups as ostensible proof of Schulz's seriousness.) We see Skippy kneeling at his bed at night, praying for God to relieve his mother's headache and give it to him. The mode of thought most deeply wrought in *Skippy*, however, was political; and, in this, Crosby took his strip to a realm where Schulz was never comfortable.

Skippy and Charlie Brown were, like the main characters of many other comic strips that absorbed cartoonists for most of their lives, projections of their creators' self-images. Both the boys and the men who made these strips were bookish, reflective, socially insecure, and inclined to melancholy. Otherwise, they could hardly have been more different. Crosby, unlike Schulz, was a fiercely political creature, at one time associated with socialism (as a young staff artist for the *New York Call*, a daily newspaper supported by the Socialist Labor Party of America), later an ardent anti-Communist. "Communists absolutely have no sense of humor," Crosby complained.

Over the course of *Skippy*'s twenty-two-year run, Percy laced the strip with political messages that grew more forceful with the years. In a strip from 1927, the ideology came gently and with humor. Two youngsters argue while Skippy listens in from his perch on the curb. "I'll have youse know my mother's a better washwoman than yourn," one says.

"My mother is no washwoman—she's a washlady," the other replies.

"Here! Here!" Skippy interjects. "None o' your class hatred."

Before long, the tone of the strip would begin to harden. In a strip from 1928, Skippy strolls with a little girl dressed in what seems like a Latin American shawl, and she asks him, "What's all this Pan American stuff I see in the papers?"

Skippy answers, "The Pan America stuff started off 'n Vesey Street by your belittlin', and now it's takin' aviators an' warships to press out the wrinkles."

The girls responds, "Congress can't bluff me."

In the third and final panel, the kids walk away, their backs to the reader, and Skippy says, "The map o' the United States is like an open hand, ready to shake with South America; but it's guys just like you that's tryin' to make a fist out of it."

Through the 1930s and into the early '40s, *Skippy* became an increasingly erratic and decreasingly popular outlet for Crosby's volatile psyche. The panels of some strips would be filled with nothing but text—no sign of Skippy at all; just the venomous, hard-to-follow rants of a cartoonist unraveling in the panels of the funny pages.

Overwhelmed by a conspiracy of problems—mental illness, a rough divorce, alcoholism, tax trouble—Crosby lost the fortune he had amassed from *Skippy*'s success and ended up institutionalized for psychiatric care. The last *Skippy* strip was published on Crosby's fifty-fourth birthday, December 8, 1945. Charles Schulz had just finished his wartime military service and was working his first job as a professional artist, lettering for a Catholic comic book called *Timeless Topix*.

Percy Crosby died, penniless and largely forgotten, in the psych ward of King Park's Hospital—on his birthday, again: December 8, 1964. It was the year Charles Schulz would become the first cartoonist ever to receive two Reuben Awards from the National Cartoonists Society. Within a year, the characters of *Peanuts* would be on the cover of *Time*, and *A Charlie Brown Christmas* would make its TV premiere.

Schulz would continue writing and drawing *Peanuts* to growing acclaim for another thirty-five years, even as his once-assured ink lines grew ever shakier with age. "I used to have a great pen line, you know," he said in 1986. "I had a pen line which I would match to Percy Crosby's anytime, but that was a long time ago."

On *Krazy Kat* and *Peanuts*

Umberto Eco

George Herriman's *Krazy Kat* came into existence around 1910–1911 and ended in 1944 with the death of the author. The dramatis personae were three: a cat of unspecified sex, probably female; a mouse, Ignatz; a dog acting as policeman, Offissa Pupp. The drawing was remarkable, with certain surrealistic inventions, especially in the improbable lunar landscapes, deliberately intended to divorce the events from any verisimilitude. The plot? The cat madly loves the mouse, and the wicked mouse hates and tyrannizes the cat, preferably by hitting him on the head with a brick. The dog constantly tries to protect the cat, but the cat despises this unrestrained love; the cat adores the mouse and is always ready to excuse him. From this absurd situation without particularly comic ingredients, the author drew an infinite series of variations, based on a structural fact that is of fundamental importance in the understanding of comics in general: the brief daily or weekly story, the traditional strip, even if it narrates an episode that concludes in the space of four panels, will not work if considered separately; rather it acquires flavor only in the continuous and obstinate series, which unfolds, strip after strip, day by day.

In *Krazy Kat* the poetry originated from a certain lyrical stubbornness in the author, who repeated his tale ad infinitum, varying it always but sticking to its theme. It was thanks only to this that the mouse's arrogance, the dog's unrewarded compassion, and the cat's desperate love could arrive at what many critics felt was a genuine state of poetry, an uninterrupted elegy based on sorrowing innocence. In a comic strip of this sort, the spectator, not seduced by a flood of gags, or by any realistic or caricatural reference, or by any appeal to sex and violence, could discover the possibility of a purely allusive world, a pleasure of a "musical" nature, an interplay of feelings that were not banal. To some extent the myth of Scheherazade was reproduced: the concubine, taken by the Sultan to be used for one night and then discarded, begins telling a story, and because of the story the Sultan forgets the woman; he discovers, that is, another world of values.

The best proof that the comic strip is an industrial product purely for consumption is that, even if a character is invented by an author of genius, after a while the author is replaced by a team; his genius becomes interchangeable, his invention a factory product. The best proof that *Krazy Kat*, thanks to its raw poetry, managed to overcome the system is that at the death of Herriman nobody chose to be his heir, and the comic-strip industrialists were unable to force the situation.

Now we come to Charles Schulz and *Peanuts*, which belongs to the "lyric" vein of *Krazy Kat*. Here, too, the cast of characters is elementary: a group of children, Charlie Brown, Lucy, Violet, Patty, Frieda, Linus, Schroeder, Pig-Pen, and the dog Snoopy, who is involved in their games and their talk. Over this basic scheme, there is a steady flow of variations, following a rhythm found in certain primitive epics. (Primitive, too, is the habit of referring to the protagonist always by his full name— even his mother addresses Charlie Brown in that fashion, like an epic hero.) Thus you could never grasp the poetic power of Schulz's work by reading only one or two or ten episodes: you must thoroughly understand the characters and the situations, for the grace, tenderness, and laughter are born only from the infinitely shifting repetition of the patterns, and from fidelity to the fundamental inspirations. They demand from the reader a continuous act of empathy, a participation in the inner warmth that pervades the events.

The poetry of these children arises from the fact that we find in them all the problems, all the sufferings of the adults, who remain offstage. These children affect us because in a certain sense they are monsters: they are the monstrous infantile reductions of all the neuroses of a modern citizen of industrial civilization.

They affect us because we realize that if they are monsters it is because we, the adults, have made them so. In them we find everything: Freud, mass culture, digest culture, frustrated struggle for success, craving for affection, loneliness, passive acquiescence, and neurotic protest. But all these elements do not blossom directly, as we know them, from the mouths of a group of children: they are conceived and spoken after passing through the filter of innocence. Schulz's children are not a sly instrument to handle our adult problems: they experience these problems according to a childish psychology, and for this very reason they seem to us touching and hopeless, as if we were suddenly aware that our ills have polluted everything, at the root. But still more: the reduction of adult myths to childhood myths (a childhood that no longer comes "before" our maturity but "after") shows us the cracks in an adult mythology and allows Schulz a way out of it. These monster children are capable suddenly of an innocence and a sincerity that call everything into question, sift out the detritus of the grown-up world, and give us back a world that is still and always very sweet and soft, tasting of milk and cleanliness. Thus in a constant seesaw of reactions, within a single story, or between one story and another, we never know whether to despair or to heave a sigh of optimism. But, in any case, we realize that we have emerged from the banal round of consumption and escapism, and have almost reached the threshold of meditation. The most amazing proof of this is that while distinctly "cultivated" comics, like *Pogo*, appeal only to intellectuals (and are consumed by the mass audience only through distraction), *Peanuts* charms both sophisticated adults and children with equal intensity, as if each reader found there something for himself, and it is always the same thing, to be enjoyed in two different keys.

Peanuts is thus a little human comedy for the innocent reader and for the sophisticated. In its center is Charlie Brown: ingenuous, stubborn, always awkward, and doomed to failure. Requiring, to a critical degree, communication and popularity, and repaid by the matriarchal, know-it-all girls of his group with scorn, references to his round head, accusations of stupidity, all the little digs that strike home, Charlie Brown, undaunted, seeks tenderness and fulfillment on every side:

in baseball, in building kites, in his relationship with his dog, Snoopy, in playing with the girls. He always fails. His solitude becomes an abyss, his inferiority complex is pervasive—tinged by the constant suspicion (which the reader also comes to share) that Charlie Brown is not inferior. Worse: he is absolutely normal. He is like everybody else. This is why he is always on the brink of suicide or at least of nervous breakdown: because he seeks salvation through the routine formulas suggested to him by the society in which he lives (the art of making friends, culture in four easy lessons, the pursuit of happiness, how to make out with girls—he has been ruined, obviously, by Dr. Kinsey, Dale Carnegie, Erich Fromm, and Lin Yutang).

But since he acts in all purity, without any guile, society is prompt to reject him through its representative, Lucy, treacherous, self-confident, an entrepreneur with assured profits, ready to peddle a security that is completely bogus but of unquestioned effect. (Her lessons in natural science to her brother Linus are a jumble of nonsense that turns Charlie Brown's stomach. "I can't stand it," the unfortunate boy groans, but what weapons can arrest impeccable bad faith when one has the misfortune to be pure of heart?)

Charlie Brown has been called the most sensitive child ever to appear in a comic strip, a figure capable of Shakespearean shifts of mood; and Schulz's pencil succeeds in rendering these variations with an economy of means that has something miraculous about it. The text, always almost courtly (these children rarely lapse into slang or commit anacoluthon), is enhanced by drawings able to portray, in each character, the subtlest psychological nuance. Thus the daily tragedy of Charlie Brown is drawn, in our eyes, with exemplary incisiveness.

To elude this tragedy of nonintegration, each psychological type has its strategies. The girls escape it thanks to an obstinate self-sufficiency and haughtiness: Lucy (a giantess to be admired with awe), Patty, and Violet are all of a piece; perfectly integrated (or should we say "alienated"), they move from hypnotic sessions at the TV to rope-skipping and to everyday talk interwoven with sarcasm, achieving peace through insensitivity.

Linus, the smallest, on the other hand, is already burdened with every neurosis; emotional instability would be his perpetual condition if the society in which he lives had not already offered him the remedies. Linus already has behind him Freud, Adler, and perhaps also Binswanger (via Rollo May); he has identified his baby-blanket as the symbol of a uterine peace or a purely oral happiness—sucking his finger, blanket against his cheek (if possible, with TV turned on, in front of which he can huddle like an Indian; but he can also be without anything, in an oriental sort of isolation, attached to his symbols of protection).

Take away his blanket and he will be plunged once more into all the emotional troubles lying in wait for him day and night. Because, we must add, along with the instability of a neurotic society he has absorbed all its wisdom. Linus represents its most technologically up-to-date product. While Charlie Brown is unable to make a kite that will not get caught in the branches of a tree, Linus reveals suddenly, in bursts, dazzling skills: he performs feats of amazing equilibrium, he can strike a quarter flung in the air with the edge of his blanket, snapping it like a whip ("the fastest blanket in the West!").

Schroeder, on the other hand, finds peace in aesthetic religion. Seated at his little toy piano from which he draws the tunes and chords of transcendental complexity, slumped in total worship of Beethoven, he saves himself from everyday neuroses by sublimating them in a lofty form of artistic madness. Not even Lucy's constant, loving admiration can budge him. (Lucy cannot love music, an unprofitable activity, whose reason she doesn't comprehend: but in Schroeder she admires an unattainable higher being. Perhaps she is stimulated by the adamantine shyness of her pocket Parsifal, and she stubbornly pursues her work of seduction without making a dent in the artist's defenses.) Schroeder has chosen the peace of the senses in the delirium of the imagination. "Do not speak ill of this love, Lisaweta: it is good and fertile. It contains nostalgia and melancholy, envy and a bit of contempt, and a complete, chaste happiness"—this is not Schroeder speaking, of course: it is Tonio Kroeger. But this is the point; and it is no accident that Schulz's children create a little universe in which our tragedy and our comedy are performed.

Pig-Pen, too, has an inferiority to complain about: he is irreparably, horrifyingly dirty. He leaves home neat and spruce, and a second later his shoelaces come untied, his trousers sag over his hips, his hair is flaked with dandruff, his skin and clothes are covered with a layer of mud. Aware of his vocation for the abyss, Pig-Pen turns his plight into a boast; he speaks of the dust of centuries, an irreversible process: the course of history. It might almost be a Beckett character speaking.

A constant antistrophe to the humans' sufferings, the dog Snoopy carries to the last metaphysical frontier the neurotic failure to adjust. Snoopy knows he is a dog: he was a dog yesterday, he is a dog today, tomorrow he will perhaps be a dog still. For him, in the optimism of the opulent society in which one moves upward from status to status, there is no hope of promotion.

Sometimes he essays the extreme resource of humility (we dogs are so humble, he sighs, unctuous and consoled); he becomes tenderly attached to those who promise him respect and consideration. But as a rule he doesn't accept himself and he tries to be what he is not: a split personality if ever there was one, he would like to be an alligator, a kangaroo, a vulture, a penguin, a snake . . . He tries every avenue of mystification, then he surrenders to reality, out of laziness, hunger, sleepiness, timidity, claustrophobia (which assails him when he crawls through big grass), ignorance. He may be soothed, but never happy. He lives in a constant apartheid, and he has the psychology of the segregated; like an Uncle Tom, he has finally, *faute de mieux*, a devotion, an ancestral respect, for the stronger.

In this encyclopedia of contemporary weakness, there are, as we have said, sudden luminous patches of light, free variations, allegros, and rondos, where all is resolved in a few bars. The monsters turn into children again, Schulz becomes only a poet of childhood. We know it isn't true, and we pretend to believe him. In the next strip he will continue to show us, in the face of Charlie Brown, with two strokes of his pencil, his version of the human condition.

What Charlie Brown, Snoopy, and *Peanuts* Mean to Me

Kevin Powell

I was born and raised in an American ghetto. I have no direct memory of the Civil Rights Movement, of Dr. King, Dolores Huerta, Fannie Lou Hamer, Bobby Kennedy, Yuri Kochiyama, or Malcolm X. I also have no direct memory of what life was like in America before the 1960s. What I did know was my single mother, my absent father who never married my ma, horrific poverty, violence, abuse, rats, roaches, and much sadness and loneliness as an only child. What I am convinced saved my life was the vision of my mother—in spite of having only an eighth-grade education—to instill in me from the time I could form and comprehend words a love of learning. Even at age three I was already questioning the world, and my place in it: this I do recall.

Apart from reading, which my mother pushed hard and is the reason why I am a writer today, I had a bottomless love for television as a kid, particularly cartoons. I believe, truthfully, that these animated images represented both a feeding of my imagination and an escape, at least temporarily, from our very dire and unpredictable living conditions. We moved much, as poor people often do, but there was always a television, a black-and-white television, with a hanger on top serving as a replacement for the antennae, and a thick line often running through it, distorting the images at times. But I did not care. I loved animation, and I watched them all, *Bugs Bunny*, *Tom and Jerry*, *The Flintstones*, *The Jetsons*. But then there was Charlie Brown, Snoopy, and the entire *Peanuts* gang. I do not remember if I first saw the comic strip in our local Jersey City newspaper, the *Jersey Journal*, or if it was one of the TV specials that hooked me. No matter, hooked I was, and I absorbed *Peanuts* in every imaginable way as a boy.

My earliest memory was of Charlie Brown trying to kick a football and Lucy always removing it just as he was about to do so. That image served as a metaphor for my own tough life. How can we ever *not* be poor? Will we ever be able to leave this ghetto life? Why do I feel so close yet so far from relief, from hope?

There was also a certain kind of melancholy that permeated Charlie Brown that I related to instinctively, a loner mentality in spite of his being a part of a community of other quirky children. I likewise related profoundly to how Charles Schulz rendered the voices of adults, parents, teachers, authority figures as, well, inaudible. My mother was a mighty yeller, doing the best she knew how to raise me, a man-child, but there was an unfettered pleasure I took in how the youngsters of *Peanuts* had their adult yellers speaking what seemed to be a foreign language. Youth do not want to be yelled at or talked down to; they, we, want to be spoken with, and heard.

I can say now I have battled depression much of my life, and I can say with certainty that *Peanuts*, the comic strip, the television programs, the characters, remain one of the things that still brings me tremendous happiness to this very day. I had a framed image of Snoopy on my wall for many years, and only in storage now because I am married, and space is at a premium. This is how deeply connected I am to these characters, even as a grown man.

For sure it has been in my adult years that I have come to love and appreciate *Peanuts* in a very different way. One of the ways I have dealt with the traumas of my past has been years upon years of therapy. One of the counselors said to me, a while back, "Find the things that actually made you happy as a child, and keep those things close for the rest of your life." Almost immediately I went out and purchased *A Charlie Brown Christmas*, sat there and watched it alone, and I cried, profusely, as all the memories came flooding back to me.

On another occasion, while I was doing a speech at a historic all-black private boarding school in Mississippi, it blew my mind to learn that Charles Schulz had donated money to this institution, and there on campus was the Charles M. Schulz "Snoopy" Hall. My hosts told me that Schulz, a very shy man, had once been scheduled to come speak at the school, but he called the school's president and said that he would just like to send a check instead. Those funds built Snoopy Hall, the girls' honors dormitory. Mr. Schulz also lent his name to the Charles

M. Schulz Scholarship Fund, which still provides tuition for student leaders to this day.

I am someone who has spoken at well over a thousand institutions at this point, has been to all fifty American states and many places overseas, too—me the poor boy from the American ghetto. But whenever I think of my fondest memories of my speeches and my travels, my mind and soul forever return to that Mississippi dorm named after Snoopy. This, to me, is the essence of *Peanuts*, of the impact it has had and will continue to have on generations of people of all backgrounds. It is the reason why I find myself, even in middle age, posting *Peanuts* quotes and images across social media platforms whenever the mood hits me, whenever I do not have the words myself to express a feeling, any feeling.

I have escaped the worst of what I experienced as a child, this I know. But what I will never escape, what I do not ever want to escape, is the incredible innocence and joy I feel whenever I see or think about Charlie Brown, Snoopy, all the *Peanuts* characters, and the freedom they gave me then, that I still have with me now, to be all of who I am, quirks and all.

Charlie Brown, Spider-Man, Me, and You

Ira Glass

Recently, I ran into my best friend from junior high school. He'd been living in New York for years. "Lemme ask you something." He drew in close as he said it; his voice was low. "Every girlfriend I've had in New York has asked me what my favorite books were growing up. Did you *read*? Did anyone ever tell us to *read* back in Baltimore?"

We weren't dumb kids. We were expected to get As and go to college. But reading was something you did for school. You plowed through the novels, figured out the themes and ideas as a way to answer questions on a test. It was like math, just another puzzle to solve. The idea of reading a book for pleasure, of taking a book personally—I didn't discover that until well into college.

Except when it came to cartoons. Somehow they slipped under the radar, because they didn't seem like reading. When I was little, I had books of *Peanuts* cartoons that I re-read constantly. I don't remember ever thinking they were funny. Who ever laughed at *Peanuts*? I just liked the mood of them. I was a sulky little kid, easily upset, didn't play sports, didn't like playing outside at all. I had a few years when I was obsessed with getting sent to Vietnam and dying, starting around the time I was six and my Uncle Lenny went to the war. I had friends but I was closer to my mom than to my friends. I thought of myself as a loser and a loner and *Peanuts* helped me take comfort in that. Maybe to my detriment. One of my oldest, most solid feelings is the feeling of preferring to be on the bottom, dejected and apart from others. It's still there today, waiting for me if I have a bad week, like a bad robot ready to come to life. That's the dark-but-happily-dark feeling I got reading Charles Schulz's strip. "All the loves in the strip are unrequited," he said in 1985. "All the baseball games are lost, all the test scores are D-minuses, the Great Pumpkin never comes, and the football is always pulled away." Even after I managed to get some friends, somehow I held on to all that feeling.

There's not a lot of art for kids that's so drenched in sadness. Or if there is, I didn't know about it. It's comforting to have something that so thoroughly lets you wallow. I definitely took it too far. My mom sometimes scolded me, "You're not Charlie Brown!" I was undeterred. In grade school, I and some friends staged our own bastardized production of that musical about Charlie Brown. We sang the songs from a book we got at the music store, and performed scenes we remembered from seeing the touring company at the Morris Mechanic Theater downtown. There was choreography, I remember, which mostly involved marching around. Because I organized the show, I got to play the lead. Which is pretty much how I ended up hosting a national radio show years later.

Once I got older, a friend introduced me to Spider-Man, which was basically the same loser feeling as *Peanuts*, but staged with a teenager in a superhero costume. Spidey was enormously competent in some ways—as was I, with my good grades and my weekend business doing magic shows for kids' parties—but he still managed to live under a cloud. Persecuted. Misunderstood. A failure even when he was a success. And of course, most important of all, very sad.

I love that these two melancholic glumsters might be the most popular characters in comics. That they're iconic figures in our culture, known to most everybody. I don't have anything against winners. Winners are fine. Good-looking, brilliant, rich super-achievers have their place. I suppose. But they don't offer much comfort to the lonely. For that, you need someone as misunderstood and alone as you feel. You need Charlie Brown. His very existence makes you feel understood and less alone.

Nice that he's still around, years after he was conjured into existence, to perform this pen-and-ink voodoo.

Drawing Empathy

A Cartoonist's-Eye View

Chris Ware

A s a kid, I spent a lot of time alone. Because my mother was single and worked all day long, my grandparents' house became a sort of second home where, if I wasn't being monitored directly, I occupied myself drawing or reading while my grandmother and grandfather tended to their yard and housework. My grandfather had been a sports editor (and, later, managing editor) for the *Omaha World-Herald*, where, in this latter role, he assumed the makeup of the daily and Sunday comics pages. For him, this task was a vestigial pleasure because as a boy he'd wanted to be a cartoonist, though providence and necessity (he had been booted from college for stealing university stationery and sending a forged letter to all the fraternities mandating they appear Sunday morning for VD testing) had willed otherwise.

As a perk of his role as comic-strip decider, he'd received, and kept, the published collections of the various comic strips the *World-Herald* contracted on a shelf in his basement office, which I was free to peruse in my housebound afternoon wanderings while he and my grandmother raked, mowed, and sprayed DDT on their lawn outside. He had been among the country's earlier managing editors to add a strange, iconographic, and purposefully designed "space-saving" strip to the *World-Herald*'s pages named *Peanuts*—my grandmother told me once how she and he had sat at their kitchen table reading the syndicate pitch samples together while "howling with laughter." The earliest *Peanuts* paperback collections published by Rinehart and Co. were my favorites among these books, a welcoming world into which I regularly lost myself.

To say that the *Peanuts* characters were real to me would be an understatement. As I familiarized myself with the strip's cast via these 1950s and 1960s collections and the 1970s newspaper page my grandfather had edited—to say nothing of the broadcast specials which marked the fall and winter seasons for my TV-addled generation—Charlie Brown, Linus, and Snoopy became more than just a diversion; they became my friends. In fact, at one point, after reading an especially upsetting 1970s Valentine's Day strip where, as usual, Charlie Brown received no cards, I crafted an awkward valentine and demanded that my mother mail it directly to the newspaper (where I knew she had an "in") and where, somehow, I hoped it might find its way into his tiny, stubby-fingered hands.

What kind of artist, through his simple newsprint drawings, could break the heart of a child like that?

*   *   *

EVEN THE LEAST critical reader or viewer can sense falseness and fakery on the part of an unskilled (or worse, a dishonest) cartoonist. And because the comic strip is a valueless throwaway, the cartoonist must win the reader's trust without benefit of critical backing, museum walls, and monied collectors. The comic strip is the cartoonist laid bare on the page, a condensed sum-uppance of the artist's notions, ideally, of what it is that not only makes life funny, but also what makes it worth living. This artistic effort has to occur not just over the course of a life's work on a handful of masterpieces, but every single day. Every day, the skeptical reader arrives cold to a little slice of comic-strip newsprint and gives the cartoonist four, maybe five seconds: "Okay, make me laugh." It's no wonder that Schulz woke up feeling "funereal," or like he "had a term paper due every morning." Or as he also said, "In a comic strip, yesterday doesn't mean anything. The only thing that matters is today and tomorrow."[1]

It's not the drawing, or the lines, or the lettering, or the funny words that make a comic strip work. "Timing" is the life force of comics: beyond the mastery of drawing skills, writing, and design tricks, without a sensitivity to the rhythms and the music—a.k.a. the reality—of life, a comic strip will arrive DOA, nothing more than a bunch of dumb pictures. When the comic-strip reader (a couple of hundred million of them in Schulz's case) threads through those four panels containing those little repeating hieroglyphs, the characters must come alive on the page with as much ferocity and reality as the people in one's own life and memory. Timing is the undergirding, the ever-running engine of this narrative visual language, and Charles Schulz shaped and formed it as his artistic medium. The reader doesn't just look at Charlie Brown, Linus, Lucy, and Snoopy, but reads them, almost as musical notes in a silently heard composition of hilarity, cruelty, and occasional melancholy.

Schulz's earliest experiments in the form were not, however, so sophisticated. Struggling in his twenties at night at a basement laundry table on a foreign legion–themed adventure strip while working days at the Minneapolis mail-order educational company Art Instruction, Inc. (née The Federal School of Cartooning—where he'd found his first encouragement), he pursued aims that were squarely in keeping with the fashion for features like Roy Crane's *Captain Easy* and Milton Caniff's *Terry and the Pirates*. Such illustrated adventures eschewed the vaudevillian origins of the comics (think *Mutt and Jeff* or *Krazy Kat*) and paralleled the ascent of talkies and the Second World War, introducing a cinematic approach to comics that reconceived the theatrical cartoon-strip panel as a camera viewfinder, introducing close-ups, long shots, and dramatic lighting to the language and all but recasting comics as "movies on paper." Taking the reader out of the heart of the comic strip to an observed viewpoint might have worked for war and detective stories, but it couldn't have been more anathema to what was necessary for *Peanuts* to blossom. (Imagine Charlie Brown as a realistically drawn eight-year-old boy, his face half blackened in dramatic shadow.)

It wasn't until Schulz started submitting filler "gag" one-panels for the Catechetical Guild Educational Society of St. Paul that he inched back toward something of the comic strip's iconic, native beginnings. *Just Keep Laughing*, drawn for Topix Comics,[2] pictured semirealistic kids, but ones who slouched under the graphic influence of Percy Crosby's *Skippy*, a free, loose brush line following falling-down socks, neighborhood curbs, and tousled hair. It was (now, famously) *Li'l Folks*, gag panels about kids drawn for local Minnesota papers, as well as some even more simplified single-panel cartoons submitted to the *Saturday Evening Post*, which eventually morphed into *Peanuts*. Whereas many comics in 1950 were cluttered frames of discursive dialogue and illustrations, some of these earliest strips are surprisingly spare—the kids zigzagging up and down through tall grass on a diagonally tilting seesaw, a simple flower growing to the height of the panel—but Schulz was not alone in this "minimalist" approach. A host of strips (the disquietingly scrotal *Henry*, Otto Soglow's telegraphic *Little King*, Crockett Johnson's subdued masterpiece *Barnaby*, and Ernie Bushmiller's frozen *Nancy*) worked from a similarly distilled visual language. *Peanuts*, however, was the first to be designed to be printed the size of a postage stamp. In 1950 the comics page was a more or less settled territory into which few new features could be shoe-horned, and from the get-go *Peanuts* was marketed as a space-saver. The strip's characters had inflated heads and shrunken bodies, and the simple, almost typographical reduction of the strip's characters not only saved editorial column inches, but was simply requisite for the strip to be read. It also, near al-chemically, enabled the transplanting of its "children" out of a seen, external world to a remembered, internal one. Who would've thought that such a hard-nosed commercial decision would catalyze the greatest works of popular art of the twenti-eth century?

Indeed, the earliest *Peanuts* strips almost seem to take smallness as their peeved raison d'être, a sort of humiliation that the "li'l folks" must suffer in a space unaccommodating to their bigger ideas, urges, and emotions. These proto-*Peanuts*, little pancaked planaria with Sumerian eyes and tiny bodies, evolved rapidly—right before readers' eyes during the first two years of the 1950s. Instinctively allowing just the tiniest bit of realism back into their proportions and postures, and somehow, I think, ineffably shaping them within the idiosyncrasies of his own handwriting, by 1954 Schulz was so masterfully intuiting and internalizing his characters that they seemed to burn the page, modulating between whispers to cataclysmic eruptions so violent the panels could barely contain their fury. (It also helped that the preponderance of exclamation points in the earliest strips gave way to ellipses, allowing for a greater range of "volume" when needed.) The blank everyman Charlie Brown of the earliest strips gave way to a self-doubting loser, Lucy developed into a tormentor, her younger brother Linus eventually into the strip's philosopher, etc. Schulz poured himself into these various molds, like molten metal flowing into an empty form.

Whereas the haiku daily strip enabled the characters' personalities to mature, the Sunday—double the size and number of panels, and in color—allowed for an expansion of the strip's time and space. Here, Schulz drew what, by contrast, were redolently realistic suburban settings, a stark contradiction to the abbreviation of his characters. This longer form also allowed him to develop his "music," orchestrating more complex extended moments than the shorter daily strip permitted. A fine example of a finely tuned, melodically ferocious and forceful *Peanuts* Sunday strip might be the March 20, 1955 episode (Schulz had added in the larger Sunday page in January 1952, a little over a

year after the daily strip's introduction in October 1950) where
Charlie Brown and Schroeder are playing marbles and Lucy
invades their game, getting angrier and angrier at her missed
shots ("rats . . . Rats! RATS!") and then, wholly improbably and
violently ("What a STUPID GAME!") multiple-exposurely
stomping all of their marbles flat (STOMP! STOMP! STOMP!
STOMP! STOMP!), with a penultimate panel of her angrily
stalking away, a scribbled skein of lines in a balloon above her
head—a skein that the reader "hears" as the end note of the zig-
saggy musical composition that precedes it.[3]

By contrast, just nine months earlier, in May 1954, Schulz
had produced a multipart Sunday sequence that is one of the
weirdest hiccups of the strip's development, and one that points
right back in the direction of the adventure strips that Schulz
had abandoned: Lucy, with Charlie Brown's encouragement,
enters an adult golf tournament. Now it's odd enough that these
kid characters would even play golf (which they had now and
again in earlier strips), let alone play in a tournament, to say
nothing of Schulz deciding to stretch such an implausible story
line over four weeks (he ends each episode with a cliffhanger
"continued" rather than with a punchline), but the fact that
he'd place Charlie Brown and Lucy next to adults—yes, actual
adults appear in the strip—feels very, very wrong.[4] Compared
with the marble-stomping melody mentioned above, this sequence is full of clinkers and disharmonies, producing a queer
sense of dislocation and falseness. It's almost like the strip has
the flu. Indeed, even Schulz seems to be aware of the problem,
one panel showing Charlie Brown and Lucy through a forest of
adult legs, he admonishing her to "just try to forget about all
these people . . . just forget about 'em." While the experiment

proves Schulz's willingness to test his strip's limits, it cemented the primary rule of the *Peanuts* cosmos: adults might be talked about (sports legends, presidents, Charlie Brown's father) or even soliloquized (Linus's infatuation with Miss Othmar) but they must always, quite literally, be out of the picture.

Peanuts increasingly became a strip where the children acted like adults (unlike the very earliest newspaper comics in which adults had acted like children). For a strip, and a nation, riding a postwar economic euphoria, such psychological inversion seems all too appropriate for the baby-booming readers of its heyday. In the 1950s and early 1960s Schulz had written and penciled a second feature with adults for United Features, *It's Only a Game*, as well as fashioned teenage cartoons for a religious periodical, so the grown-up world was certainly within drawing range of his table; it just didn't belong in *Peanuts*. In the same way that architecture seems to both contain and affect our memories, something about *Peanuts*'s synthetic psychological landscape seems to capture the peculiar timelessness by which we imagine and embody our sense of self. To loosely quote Vladimir Nabokov, we all have children buried alive inside us somewhere. "You have to put yourself, all of your thoughts, all of your observations and everything you know into the strip," said Schulz in 1984. *Peanuts* could even be tartly described, as Art Spiegelman once did to me in a phone call, as "Schulz breaking himself into child-sized pieces and letting them all go at each other for the next half-century."

Caught up in remembrances of age-old wrongs and slights, Schulz seemed to have well-worn ruts in a road that led backward, the gates of injustice opening on his drawing table with every new strip. Rejections, dismissals, and disappointments

flooded into the story lines of *Peanuts* just as fluidly as ink from
his pen. So accessible and immediate were these memories that
after the end of twenty years of his first marriage he apparently
thought it okay to pay a visit to his old girlfriend Donna Johnson Wold, a.k.a. "the Little Red-Haired Girl," who had rejected
him at least as many years before and was by all accounts perfectly happily married to someone else. Toward the end of his
life he regularly noted in his school yearbook (from which his
drawings had been rejected, incidentally) when his classmates
died, one by one. It's no wonder that he disliked breaking his
routine; the drawing table was his whole world, his hopes, and
his memories. I'll corroborate: in my own life as a cartoonist
I've made similarly ill-advised personal decisions, and sometimes a vicious word spoken by a mean kid to me forty years
before will surface while I'm working and I'll say something
back to him at the drawing table, out loud. There's definitely
something very weird about this profession, and my simply typing "the Little Red-Haired Girl" and not having to explain it
demonstrates Schulz's genius at harnessing it. We all have our
own little red-haired girl.

Cartoonists, like dog owners, tend to look like their work,
but Schulz somehow skirted that rule, the parenthetical closely
spaced eyes in the middle of Charlie Brown's fat bald head appearing nothing like Schulz the man, who had widely spaced
eyes, a strong, long nose, and an enviable thatch of hair to the
very end. But that's part of Schulz's genius: Charlie Brown
looks less like Schulz than, one must suppose, he feels like him.
From the Yellow Kid to Barnaby to Henry to Tintin to Charlie
Brown, there's a long history of large, bald, white male faces
through which the reader may "see" their various comic-strip

worlds. This is no accident; the less the specificity to a character, the more he (or maybe she—where are our shes?) becomes the strip's protagonist, or "everyman." Culturally, and however unfairly, the pink disc of Charlie Brown's big baby face is about as blank and everyman as one can get.

For white American males, at least. But Schulz did try: in answer to certain readers feeling "left out" of the strip, the introduction of Franklin in 1968 came with a rightful dose of dread on Schulz's part about seeming condescending to African Americans. He needn't have worried, though, because unlike the golfing adults, Franklin felt real—or at least felt respected—as a kind kid on the beach with whom Charlie Brown plays in the sand. ("Whites Only" pools were not uncommon in 1968.) Though Schulz may have lived a quiet remote life in his California studio, he was woke enough to realize that all one had to do was care enough about a character for him or her to "work," even if the shell of the character wasn't his own. Despite the overall racial imbalance of the *Peanuts* cast, this caring is really the secret, mysterious power of Schulz's entire strip. Charlie Brown, Lucy, Linus, Snoopy, Schroeder, Franklin, and everyone came alive on that page because of Charles Schulz's ability to make you care about, feel for—and, in Charlie Brown's case at least, feel through—nearly every one of them.

There is a translucency, if not a transparency, to Schulz's drawing that allows for such sympathy. It's not diverting or virtuosic—it's direct and humble. (He described it as "quiet.") One almost looks through the drawings rather than at them. From the drafted discs of the early 1950s to the doodled masses of the 1990s, the simple act of looking from one drawing to the next animates the essential rhythm of their movements, our unconscious comprehension of the defining lines of the characters' bodies and movements echoing, somehow, our own distillation of experience. Due to an essential tremor in Schulz's hand as the result of a 1981 quadruple bypass, this distillation felt shakier in later years; he sometimes even steadied his drawing arm with the other to reduce it to a minimum. Though a technical frustration that may have slightly changed the "look" of Schulz's strip (my art teachers would've mistaken it for "expression"), it didn't change the strip's essence, or Schulz's devotion to drawing it:

> I am still searching for that wonderful pen line that comes down—when you are drawing Linus standing there, and you start with the pen up near the back of his neck and you bring it down and bring it out, and the pen point fans out a little bit, and you come down here and draw the lines this way for the marks on his sweater, and all of that . . . this is what it's all about—to get feelings of depth and roundness, and the pen line is the best pen line you can make. That's what it's all about.[5]

Schulz's mind, and then hand, transmuted the *Peanuts* characters onto the paper and then into the eyes and minds of millions of readers, and he knew those readers trusted him to "make the best he could make." He never gave up on them. Besides, no one else could have done it; despite their deceptive simplicity, faking a *Peanuts* drawing—let alone four of them in a row—is impossible. The comic-strip language was taken back to its origins and into the realm of the read and the remembered, and for half a century readers of the strip felt *Peanuts* through the singular hand and handwriting of Charles Schulz. In fact, if there is one accomplishment in the art of cartooning for which Schulz should be credited, it's that he made comics into a broader visual language of emotion, and most importantly, of empathy. For this, all cartoonists—especially those of us who have attempted "graphic novels"—owe Schulz, well, everything.

AS I'VE SAID elsewhere, Charles Schulz is the only author whom I've been reading my entire life. From my very earliest attempts to understand text on a page to my own half-century mark as a pink, balding cartoonist, Schulz's work still provides something calming, gentle, sad, funny, biting, honest—and, most of all, real. And at this moment in our country's still-newish century when we seem to be sifting through the remains of our last to decide what to keep, I don't think it's any accident that Charles Schulz and Fred Rogers are enjoying something of a renaissance, as it would be difficult to think of men more different than the one we now have in the White House. I've often paired Rogers and Schulz in my mind for their shared versions of male vulnerability, their Christian generosity, and, most of all, their sincerity. Fred Rogers once referred to the air between a child's eyes and the television screen as a "sacred space," and I'm pretty sure Charles Schulz felt similarly about his comic strip and his readers. Every year my generation marked the passage of the two biggest holidays with two television specials: one, *A Charlie Brown Christmas*, in which Linus quotes the gospel of Luke to movingly invoke the true spirit of the holiday; the other,

It's the Great Pumpkin, Charlie Brown, countervailingly parodies the perception-damaging effects of overzealous faith—again, via the revelations of Linus. Both were written by Charles M. Schulz. A devout Christian at least earlier in his life who led Bible study groups and deeded his vast Sebastopol, California, home and property to the Church of God, Schulz was an unquestionably, seriously religious man.

I was born an atheist and I've never believed in God, but I did believe in Santa Claus. That faith was broken the spring day I discovered, in a desk drawer, the sealed and stamped letter I'd given my mother to send to the North Pole five months before. Confronted by the evidence, she admitted her complicity, involuntarily participating in the follow-up rite of shattering a child's trust in magic, one's parents, etc. (a rite through which every American boy and girl must, apparently, pass).

However, when I made that valentine for Charlie Brown, I knew he wasn't real—I wasn't that dumb. I knew full well he was a drawing made by an artist. Sending him a valentine was just the only thing I could think of doing to alleviate the profound, gnawing sadness I felt for him. I really wanted to make him, and me, feel better. Putting it simply, I never had any crisis of faith about Charlie Brown. I always knew that I liked him—and that maybe, just maybe, he might like me, too.

Notes

I would like to gratefully acknowledge David Michaelis's inspiring biography of Charles Schulz as invaluable to the writing of this essay.

1. Gary Groth, "Schulz at 3 O'Clock in the Morning" (1997 interview), in *Charles M. Schulz: Conversations*, ed. M. Thomas Inge (Jackson: University Press of Mississippi, 2000), 223.

2. Chip Kidd, *Only What's Necessary* (New York: Abrams, 2015), n.p.

3. The strip is in all sorts of compilations, but the original art appears in Kidd, *Only What's Necessary*, n.p.

4. Charles M. Schulz, *Peanuts Every Sunday: 1952–1955* (Seattle: Fantagraphics Books, 2013). The sequence was left out of every strip collection until this appearance, however.

5. Charles M. Schulz, "Address to the National Cartoonists Society" (1994), in *My Life with Charlie Brown*, ed. M. Thomas Inge (Jackson: University Press of Mississippi, 2010), 130.

II

Characters

To the Doghouse

Ann Patchett

My mother's parents once lived in Paradise, California, the tiny town in the foothills of the Sierra Nevada mountains that was erased by fire in the fall of 2018. When I was very small, my parents would drive my sister and me up from Los Angeles to visit. In 1969, the year Snoopy went to the moon, our parents divorced, and my mother and sister and I moved to the other side of the country. The only good part of this arrangement was that my sister and I got to spend our summers back in Paradise. Our father would again drive up from Los Angeles to meet us at the home of his ex-wife's parents, who still loved him. Those were the happiest times of my childhood. California was in every sense the Golden State: the land of our birth and our father and our beloved grandmother, as well as Lake Shasta and the giant redwood forests and the Orville Dam, all a car ride away. The town was perfectly named. *We're on our way to Paradise*, we would say, and, *We've been in*

Paradise all summer. Paradise was also the place I first found Snoopy. I found Snoopy in Paradise the way another kid might have found God.

The sharp detail with which I can remember my grandparents' house is overwhelming to me now. The layout of the garden, the neighbors' cherry trees, the line of quail that crossed the back lawn in the morning to the ground-level birdbath my grandmother kept full for them, the little bottles of enamel paint she kept in a shoe box beneath the kitchen sink so that we could paint rocks, *Family Affair* and the Watergate hearings on television in the evenings, all of these things are so vivid in my mind that it's painful to look at them again. Every single thing in that house, everything about those summer days, is tattooed on my brain. If it happened in Paradise, it stayed. Children's brains are more easily and permanently imprinted upon than the brains of adults. And upheaval in childhood, be it from divorce or death or repeated moves, serves to reinforce memory. I was an introverted kid, and not a strong reader. My grandmother had a stock of mass-market *Peanuts* books she'd bought off a drugstore spinner. Titles like *You've Had It, Charlie Brown* and *All This and Snoopy, Too* were exactly my speed.

People always like to know a writer's influences. I imagine that for Henry James, the extended European tour he began with his parents at the age of twelve led him to settle in England and write about American expatriates. I went to Paradise and read about Snoopy, often while lying in the grass near the birdbath. Influence is a combination of circumstance and luck: where we are taken and what we are shown and what we stumble upon in those brief years when the heart and mind and eyes are fully open and capable of being amazed. When the morning newspaper came to my grandparents' house my sister and I read the funnies together, always *Peanuts* first. Would I have been a different person, a different kind of writer, had I, like James, learned Latin and French? Instead I learned the Happy Dance and mine has been a joyful life, in part because joy was the direction Snoopy pointed me in. Even when I was old enough to know better, I was more inclined toward "To the Doghouse" than *To the Lighthouse*. I was more beagle than Woolf. My formative years were spent in a Snoopy T-shirt, sleeping on Snoopy sheets with a stuffed Snoopy in my arms.

"Theoretically, my older brother should be my role model," Linus's brother Sidecar said. "But that blanket business takes care of that . . . / Which forces me to look elsewhere, and maybe ask the question . . . / Can the neighbor's dog be a role model?" The answer is yes.

One day Snoopy slept on his back with his head in his water dish, and the thought bubble said, "Psychiatrists will tell you that there's no better way to relax than to lie with your head in your water dish!" Two months later, Charlie Brown and Linus and Lucy and Schroeder were all resting blissfully with their heads in water dishes. It's amazing to me that I didn't just roll over and stick my head in the birdbath. Such was the cult of Snoopy. I was not a cool kid, and Snoopy was a very cool dog. I hoped the association would rub off on me.

Which is pretty much the whole point of Charlie Brown's relationship with Snoopy: the awkward kid's social value is raised by his glorious dog. Anyone could see what Charlie Brown got out of Snoopy, even when Snoopy was blowing him off—he raised Charlie Brown's social stock. But what did Snoopy get out of it? I'm guessing it was the loyalty, the doglike consistency that people want in a pet, which of course makes Charlie Brown the dog. I had no problem with this. I would have been thrilled to be Snoopy's dog. I was already his student. Snoopy was a writer, and it was my intention to follow in his path.

Did I become a novelist because I was a loser kid who wanted to be more like the cartoon dog I admired, the confident dog I associated with the happiest days of my otherwise haphazard youth? Or did I have some nascent sense that I would be a writer, and so gravitated toward Snoopy, the dog novelist? It's hard to know how influence works. One thing I'm sure of is that through Snoopy, Charles Schulz raised the value of imagination, not just for me but for everyone who read him.

Not only was Snoopy a famous World War I flying ace who battled with the Red Baron and quaffed root beer in the existential loneliness of the French countryside, he was also Joe Cool on campus. He pinched Charlie Brown's white handkerchief to become a soldier in the French Foreign Legion and was a leader of the Beagle Scouts: a motley flock of little yellow birds. He was a figure skater and hockey player in equal measure, an astronaut, a tennis star, a skateboarder, a boxer, and a suburban pet whose doghouse contained oriental rugs, a pool table, and a Van Gogh. This wasn't just a dog who knew how to dream, this was a dog who so fully inhabited his realities that everyone around him saw them, too. Snoopy heard the roar of the approving crowd as clearly as he heard the bullets whizzing past his Sopwith Camel. Having ventured fearlessly into the world, he could come back to the roof of his doghouse and sit straight-backed in front of his typewriter, to tap out the words that began so many of his stories: "It was a dark and stormy night."

Wait, am I seriously discussing Snoopy, a cartoon dog, as a writer? Am I believing in him as he was drawn to believe in himself?

I am. I did. I do.

I once published a long essay in *The Atlantic* and found myself at the mercy of a smart, zealous young copy editor who told me that it went against the magazine's manual of style to use "it" as a syntactic expletive that has no meaning.

"Are you telling me Dickens wouldn't have been allowed to say, 'It was the best of times, it was the worst of times'?"

"That's what I'm telling you," he said.

"You wouldn't let Snoopy say, 'It was a dark and stormy night'?"

"Not if he was writing for *The Atlantic*."

Speaking of literature, I didn't mention that the first time I'd ever heard of *War and Peace* was when Snoopy performed a six-hour version with hand puppets, just like the first time I heard of Christo was when Snoopy wrapped up his doghouse.

Snoopy worked hard up there on the roof of the doghouse. He saw his own flaws. He typed, "Those years in Paris were to be among the finest of her life. / Looking back, she once remarked, 'Those years in Paris were among the finest of my life.' That was what she said when she looked back upon those years in Paris / where she spent some of the finest years of her life." Which was followed by the thought bubble, "I think this is going to need a little editing. . . ."

"You sure have become a loner," the girl with the naturally curly hair said to him. "You're always by yourself!" To which Snoopy's thought bubble replied, "I can't help it. I've become allergic to people!"

I don't know a writer who hasn't said the same thing at some point in her career.

Snoopy didn't just write his novels, he sent them out. In those dark days before electronic submissions, he taught me what it would mean to stand in front of a mailbox, waiting to hear from an editor. He taught me—I cannot emphasize this enough—that I would fail. Snoopy got far more rejection letters than he ever got acceptances, and the rejections ranged (as they will) from impersonal to flippant to cruel. Later, I could see we'd been building up to this. It wasn't as if he'd won all those tennis matches. The Sopwith Camel was regularly riddled with bullet holes. But he kept on going. He was willing to lose, even in the stories he imagined for himself. He lost, and he continued to be cool, which is to say, he was still himself in the face of both failure and success. I could have skipped those two years at the Iowa Writers' Workshop and relied on what I'd learned from *Peanuts*, because the whole writer's life had been mapped out for me.

First there was the importance of critical reading:

Charlie Brown to Linus: "I'm sorry . . . Snoopy can't go out to play right now . . . he's reading."

Linus: "Dogs can't read."

Charlie Brown: "Well, he's sitting in there holding a book."

Snoopy in his chair: "There's no way in the world that Anna Karenina and Count Vronsky could ever have been happy."

There was imagination, work, rewriting, being alone, realizing that all the good titles had already been taken—*A Tale of Two Cities*, *Of Human Bondage*, *Heart of Darkness*, Snoopy came to all of them too late—sending your work out into the world, and facing rejection, which Snoopy internalized and used to his own advantage.

Linus rings Charlie Brown's doorbell and says, "Ask your dog to come out and play 'chase the stick.'"

Snoopy comes out and hands him a note: "Thank you for your offer to come out and play . . . We are busy at this time, however, and cannot accept your offer . . . We hope you will be successful elsewhere."

Snoopy taught me that I would be hurt and I would get over it. He walked me through the publishing process: ignoring reviews, being thrilled, and then realizing the thrill doesn't last:

"It's from your publisher," Charlie Brown tells Snoopy. "They've printed one copy of your novel . . . / It says they haven't been able to sell it . . . / They say they're sorry . . . Your book is now out of print. . . ."

Snoopy knew there was more work to do, there were other books to write. He taught me to love my job.

"Joe Ceremony was very short," Snoopy typed. "When he entered a room, everyone had to be warned not to stand on Ceremony." At which point Snoopy falls off his doghouse backward, cracking himself up, only to climb up again and look at his typewriter lovingly. "I'm a great admirer of my own writing."

What I needed to know in order to survive and make art, I learned as a child reading comic strips. I was so impressionable you can probably still find the paw print pressed into the soft folds of my brain. When I didn't get into the MacDowell Colony, I remembered Snoopy telling Woodstock, "I think it's an illusion that a writer needs a fancy studio / A writer doesn't need a place by the ocean or in the mountains / Some of our best books have been written in very humble places." It was enough to send Woodstock back to his nest to type, and to send me back to my kitchen table to work.

Snoopy dedicated his first book to Woodstock, "My friend of friends."

"Snoopy is kind of frightening because he's so uncontrollable," Charles Schulz wrote. "And he's a little selfish, too. He really isn't all he claims to be."

I probably would have been a writer without Snoopy, though it would have taken so much longer to learn every hard lesson for myself. I know without a doubt I would have loved dogs. What I don't know is if my love of writing and my love of dogs would have been so intertwined. Snoopy wasn't just my role model, he was my dream dog. He showed me that dogs had inner lives, and so I ascribed an inner life to all the dogs I knew, and they proved me right. I have lived with many dogs I thought of as my equals, and a couple I knew to be my betters. The times I have lived without a dog, the world has not been right, as if there was something out of balance about the days.

"You know what my grandfather says?" Linus told Sally. "He says every child should have a dog . . . / He says that a child who does not have a dog is like a child deprived." To which Snoopy, lying on his doghouse, adds, "The actual term is 'Living without benefit of beagle.'"

I've never been able to name a dog Snoopy, in the same way I couldn't name the pig I got for my ninth birthday Wilbur. It would have been asking too much of the pig, and would have seemed obvious to the farm girl I had become, who compulsively reread *Charlotte's Web*, another book with a great set of lessons about writing. To name a dog Snoopy was to set up the dog for failure, because no matter how great your dog is, his ears will never turn him into a helicopter. Still, the dog I have now is Sparky, named for Charles Schulz, who was known only by his nickname. Sparky has exceeded every expectation. He comes with me to the bookstore I co-own in Nashville and stands straight up on his back legs to greet customers. Surely he has the talent and the patience to write a novel of his own; I'm just glad he never wanted to. It would take too much time away from our relationship. I have found that happiness is, in fact, a warm puppy.

Life could have been different: my parents might have stayed married, and my sister and I wouldn't have spent those early summers in Paradise. My grandmother could have bought *Archie* comics instead of *Peanuts*, and I might have grown up thinking life was about fighting with another girl over the attention of a boy. But fate and circumstance stacked the deck in my favor, leaving me to be influenced by a cartoon beagle. It turned out to be exactly the guidance I needed.

There's Something Peculiar About Lying in a Dark Room. You Can't See Anything.

Chuck Klosterman

I can't write objectively about Charlie Brown. Any detachment I express is an illusion, or maybe a straightforward lie. My alleged critical distance microscopes to zero. It always feels like I'm pretending to write about a two-dimensional character when I'm really just writing about myself.

This, I realize, is no accident.

I know that Charlie Brown is a literary invention consciously designed to make people feel like they're looking at an image of themselves. If you can't empathize with Charlie Brown, you likely lack an ability to empathize with any fictional character. Here is a child continually humiliated for desiring nothing more than normalcy—the opportunity to kick a football, the aptitude to fly a kite, the freedom to walk down the sidewalk without having a random acquaintance compare his skull to a block of lumber. He wants glory, but not an excessive amount (one baseball victory would be more than enough). He has the coolest dog in town, but that plays to his disadvantage. He's an eight-year-old who needs a psychiatrist, and he has to pay the bill himself (only five cents, but still). Charlie Brown knows his life is a contradictory struggle, and sometimes his only option is to lie in a dark room, alone with his thoughts. He will never win. *He will never win.* Yet Charlie Brown is still happy. He still has friends. He still gets excited about all his little projects that are all destined to fail. Very often, young Americans are simultaneously pessimistic about the world and optimistic about themselves—they assume everyone's future is bleak, except for their own. Charlie Brown is the opposite. He knows he's doomed, but that doesn't stop him from trying anything and everything. He believes existence is amazing, despite his own personal experience. It's the quality that makes him so likeable: he does not see the cruel world as cruel. He believes the world is good, even if everything that's ever happened to him suggests otherwise. All he wants are the things everyone else seems to get without trying. He aspires to be average, which—for him—is an impossible dream.

I suppose nobody feels this way all the time. But everybody feels this way occasionally.

Charles M. Schulz died on February 12, 2000. The final *Peanuts* strip ran the very next day, a coincidence noted by virtually everyone who cared about the man and his work. In the years since his passing, I've noticed a curious trend: for whatever reason, it's become popular to assert that the spiritual center of the *Peanuts* universe is not Charlie Brown. The postmodern answer to that puzzle is Snoopy—dynamic, indefatigable, and hyperimaginative. Perception has drifted toward the qualities that the public prefers to celebrate. It's a little like what happened on the TV show *Happy Days*: by its third season, a sitcom originally focused on milquetoast Richie Cunningham had evolved into a vehicle for the supercoolness of Fonzie. Obviously, this type of paradigm shift is no crime against humanity, and I love Snoopy almost as much as his owner (he's a wonderful dancer and my all-time favorite novelist). But Snoopy is not the emotional vortex of *Peanuts*. That's simply wrong. The linchpin to *Peanuts* will always be Charlie Brown. It can be no one else. And this is because Charlie Brown effortlessly embodies what *Peanuts* truly is: an introduction to adult problems, explained by children.

THE INEVITABLE DEATH of daily newspapers will have a lot of collateral damage, some of which will matter more than others. I don't know where the gradual disappearance of the Sunday comics falls within this continuum, or even if it belongs at all. I assume something else will come to occupy its role in the culture, and the notion of bemoaning such a loss will be categorized as nostalgia for an era when the media was controlled by dinosaurs who refused to accept that the purpose of every news story was to provide random people the opportunity to publicly comment on how they felt about it. But I will miss the Sunday comics. I miss them already. As a kid, I loved the idea that there was at least one section of the newspaper directly targeted at my brain; as an adult, it was reassuring to see something that was still the exact same product I remembered from the past. It was static in the best way possible. Like most people, I moved through incremental adolescent phases when different strips temporarily became my obsession: *Garfield* in fifth grade, *Shoe* in seventh grade, *The Far Side* throughout high school, *Calvin and Hobbes* as a college boozehound. But I always considered *Peanuts* the most "important" comic strip, and the one that all other strips were measured against. The fact that *Peanuts* was the first strip on the very top of the Sunday comics' front page verified this subjective belief—if comics were rock bands, it seemed obvious that *Peanuts* was the Beatles.

In 2014, I was asked to write the foreword to a collection of *Peanuts* strips published by Fantagraphics Books (and the essay you're reading now is, essentially, the essay that became that foreword). The strips in this particular collection stretched from 1956 to 1960. It was a transitional period for *Peanuts*—the characters no longer had the generic, unsophisticated appearance of the early *Li'l Folks* epoch, but their fantasies and dialogue rarely skewed as surreal as they would throughout the mid-sixties and beyond. Snoopy "talks," but not in the way we're accustomed (his concerns are more traditionally doglike). His jowls and his gut look a tad thin. Linus van Pelt—still noticeably younger than all the other kids in '57—eventually became interchangeable with his slightly older peers (Schulz was enamored with Linus during this five-year stretch and placed him at the center of the majority of the offerings, most notably a three-week serial where the boy worries about performing at the Christmas program). Around 1959, readers were introduced to Sally Brown for the first time (still an infant). But the most critical evolution involved the persona of Charlie Brown himself. It is during this five-year stretch that he became "the Charlie Browniest." Throughout the mid-sixties, Charlie Brown was still a remarkably confident dude. On the anthology's second page, we see a boy who believes his snow fort is an architectural masterwork; eighteen pages later, Charlie Brown violently punishes the kite he cannot fly.

He's not arrogant, but he is self-assured. He even has moments as a smart aleck. Yet by the inception of the sixties, all that confidence is dead. From 1960 onward, Charlie Brown is the person we all recognize from all those thirty-minute television specials: the unironic loser with a limitless heart, habitually hammered for caring too much.

"Nobody likes me," Charlie Brown says as he stares into space. "All it would take to make me happy is have someone say he likes me." When Lucy overhears this lament, she's immediately incredulous. "Do you mean to tell me that someone has it within his or her power to make you happy merely by doing such a simple thing?" Charlie Brown assures her that—yes—this simple act is all it would take. In fact, it wouldn't even matter if the sentiment wasn't true. He just wants to know how it feels to be liked. But even this is still too much to ask for.

"I can't do it," Lucy replies. And then she walks away. And this, it seems, is the totality of the joke.

One of the common assumptions about *Peanuts* is that Charlie Brown and Charles M. Schulz were the same person, and that we are able to perceive the personality of Schulz by studying the personality of Brown. Certain similarities are undeniable (both of their fathers were barbers, both were obsessed with red-haired girls they never really knew, etc.). But I don't think this connection is fully accurate. The reflection is not as clear-cut as it seems. I believe the primordial *Li'l Folks* version of Charlie Brown—the slightly more assertive kid from the 1940s—was Schulz crafting a fictional version of his literal childhood. Early Charlie Brown was, at least in theory, who Schulz once was. It was an attempt at veiled autobiography. But the later model of Charlie Brown we recognize and love so much more—the model reinvented at the end of the 1950s—was Schulz crafting a version of how he *felt*, both in his memory and in the present tense. It was the construct of an adult, suffering through problems only an adult can conceive and recognize. It was also a depiction of how he *wanted* to feel: Schulz the man was rumored to be a maniacal grudge holder, unwilling to forget any slight or embarrassment ever leveled against him. His creative boyhood doppelganger is the opposite. Charlie Brown could always wipe the slate clean. And that makes an overpowering difference, both for the character and for everyone else.

"IT'S DEPRESSING TO realize that you're so insignificant you haven't got a chance ever to become president," Charlie Brown tells Lucy on a June Sunday in 1957. "It wouldn't be so bad if I thought I had **some** chance." Like so much of the classic *Peanuts* banter, he makes these remarks apropos of nothing—it's just something he's suddenly worried about, for no clear reason. Lucy, of course, obliterates Charlie Brown for voicing this trepidation, mocking him with a tsunami of faint praise, almost as if he had somehow claimed he was destined for political greatness. Is her response amusing? I suppose it's a little amusing. But it's mostly dark and entirely true. At the age of eight, Charlie Brown is considering a reality that most people don't confront until much later: a realization that the future is limited. It's not that he desperately wants to become Dwight Eisenhower—it's the simple recognition that this couldn't happen even if he did. He's confronting the central myth of childhood, which is that anyone can be anything. Charlie Brown represents the downside of adult consciousness. What does Lucy represent? Lucy represents the world itself. Lucy responds the way society always responds to any sudden insight of existential despair: *how did you not know this already, Blockhead?*

It doesn't matter how many times this sort of thing has happened before. It will never stop happening. Like I said—Charlie Brown knows he's doomed. He absolutely knows it. But a little part of his mind always suggests, "Maybe not this time, though." That glimmer of hope is his Achilles' heel. It's also the attribute that makes him so imminently relatable. The joke is not that Charlie Brown is hopeless. The joke is that Charlie Brown *knows* he's hopeless, but he doesn't trust the infallibility of his own insecurity. If he's always wrong about everything, perhaps he's wrong about this, too. When Charlie Brown mentions the impossibility of his own presidential fantasy, there's a vague sense that he wants Lucy to tell him he's mistaken. And at first (of course), Lucy does exactly that. She says "maybe." And then (of course) she does what she always does. She reminds Charlie Brown that he is Charlie Brown. Which is how I suspect Charles M. Schulz felt about himself, up until the very end: "No matter what I do or what I try, I'm always going to be myself." There's a pragmatism to Schulz's philosophy that's so deep it would likely disturb modern readers, particularly those raised to believe that unmitigated agency over one's personal experience is a human right. My favorite example comes from 1973. Charlie Brown and Linus are walking through a downpour. In the cartoon's second panel, Charlie Brown stoically quotes from the book of Matthew: "The rain falls on the just and the unjust." They trudge through panel three, wordlessly considering the meaning of this passage. And then at the conclusion, Linus remarks, "That's a good system!" This exchange has unconsciously become the center of my entire belief system.

It is totally, irrefutably true. But who still thinks this way? As far as I can tell, almost no one.

In the Fantagraphics anthology that included my foreword, there were four strips where Charlie Brown attempted to kick a football. Unless you're a yet-to-be-conceived archaeologist reading this book one thousand years in the future, the outcome of these attempts will not surprise you. Two of these strips (released roughly a year apart) are so similar they almost suggest a lack of imagination. In one, Charlie Brown expresses his conviction that people have the ability to change and deserve the opportunity to do so (and then he breaks his back). In the other, Lucy compliments Charlie Brown's faith in human nature (moments after his back has been broken). This is the reassuring, quasi-eternal, death-and-taxes aspect to *Peanuts*: the children don't grow up and the conflicts don't change. The pigskin's omnipresent unkickability is the Sisyphean symbol for the whole of Charlie Brown's life and the principal metaphor behind why he matters so much to so many people. It is the apex of his failures. But failing is not what makes Charlie Brown my fictional friend and personal protagonist. It's his reasoning for placing himself in a position where failure is inevitable: "I must be out of my mind," he says to himself. "But I can't resist kicking footballs."

He can't resist kicking footballs.

Even though he never, ever does. He still can't resist.

Resistance is futile.

Je Suis Sally Brown

Elissa Schappell

Charles Schulz once said, "We are all pretty much what we are going to be early in our lives. Our personalities and characteristics are established, usually by the time we are five or six years old, but the lids are on. We are like boiling pots on a stove."

Which means, I suppose, that I have always been Sally Brown. I am aware of how uncool this makes me. Lucy has been given, however reluctantly, a feminist facelift, Pig-Pen isn't dirty he's filth-positive, Woodstock's gender identification is fluid. Schroeder is queer.

Ask people what they remember about Sally Brown, if they recall her at all beyond her role as good ol' Charlie Brown's little sister, and they are likely to say, "Her hair." To be fair, Sally's hair, a rad blond flip with a tempest of curls up front, *is* memorable. Indeed, it was her hair that first captured my imagination. Her surreal coif was so much fun to draw. What's more, I imagined that her hair, like my own (despite mine being long, dirty blond and thick), was just as challenging to brush.

As a I grew older my identification with Sally deepened, far surpassing the physical. I recognized Sally's struggles with math. I could see, in Charlie Brown's hapless attempts to tutor Sally, my courageous and long-suffering father's doomed attempts to tutor me. Neither Sally nor I am any better off for their efforts. Instead, they made each of us loathe math all the more.

My strategy, on those dread occasions when I was called on in Math, was not unlike Sally's. I guessed. However, unlike Sally, who piped up answers with breezy conviction, I shrank. My answers, such as they were, were given in a low, humiliated—slurring-numbers-together-in-the-hope-that-one-might-register-as-correct—sort of way.

We now know that a failure to grasp mathematical concepts can be a consequence of a math disability or lousy teaching methods (I can't understand the teacher, his voice is like bwahbwahbwah . . .). No doubt Sally, like me, suffers from ADD. That aside, it's less easy to explain why you didn't make more of an effort to do your homework properly.

Yes, of course Sally and I would get better grades on our theme papers if we chose to spend the time doing tiresome research, but research is so dreary and time-consuming—time when a girl could be drawing, ice skating, or lazing in a beanbag. Shouldn't creative thinking be privileged over something as base as fact? Honestly, should it really matter if in a five-page research paper on Africa you consistently refer to the continent most glaringly on the cover (decorated with a lion and an elephant and a tiger) as *Afirca*?

It should matter, a little bit, but it should matter a lot more that I drew a tiger on the cover when there *are* no tigers in Africa! That I'd drawn a tiger, knowing this but doing it anyway because I'd just taught myself how to draw realistic-looking stripes! It's all a matter of how you look at things.

Is Ohio waterfall country?

Wouldn't it like to be?

Sally's detractors gleefully make sport of her tendency toward malapropisms, the example most tediously cited, "violins breaking out" instead of "violence breaking out." To the unimaginative, this seems a catastrophic flub, but when you consider that no instrument is more notorious for striking terror in the hearts of humankind, it's fiendishly difficult to play and unsparing in its resistance to being mastered—Sally's statement could not be more apt. "Violins breaking out" means unrelenting torture, agony, it means all hope is lost. Satan, for god's sake, plays the violin. Sally's phrasing makes me inhabit the moment in a much truer way than I would otherwise. It's Beat poetry.

I admire Sally's willingness, despite the ridicule she endures, to keep bashing on ahead, trampling on the English language like so much crepe paper, out of a subconscious desire to name her experience.

Why is it surprising that Sally, when tasked with expressing her personal philosophy, offers, "Who cares" and "Forget it." As she plainly explains to Charlie Brown after another ego-battering day at school, "From now on, nothing bothers me."

As thrilling as it is for me to imagine that Sally's "Who cares" and "Forget it" are the products of indifference, apathy, or a simple-minded giddiness that we ascribe to girls, there is the matter of the line "From now on, nothing bothers me."

I knew this wasn't true. I knew that unlike Charlie Brown—who has a tolerance for humiliation that borders on mental illness—Sally bubble-wraps herself in personal philosophies and clichés, not only as a way to protect herself from the kind of abuse her brother seems to invite, but as a way to stop the conversation.

When I was growing up, "Who cares" was one of my central operating principles. I'd never have said it aloud. My parents would have knocked my block off, metaphorically speaking. Not caring, not engaging, or not being invested was a sin second only to laziness. But it was my fallback. *I'm too dumb to understand math (Who cares). Everyone thinks it's funny when I get mad (Forget it). I was the last one picked in gym class, again (Who cares).*

The fact that Sally, like me, never had a best friend was a comfort.

Sure, there's Eudora whom she befriended at camp, but that wasn't remotely akin to the bond Charlie Brown and Linus share, or Snoopy and Woodstock, both of whom would throw themselves on a grenade to protect the other. Given Marcie's devotion, it's easy to imagine a future where she becomes Alice B. Toklas to Peppermint Patty's Gertrude Stein. Lucy, her oldest friend, is a crabby egomaniac who, when she's not handing out psychiatric advice from her booth like shots of arsenic, is terrorizing the unattainable Schroeder. Beloved as he is, Linus, despite being a blanket-dragging thumb-sucker with thinning hair and a Christ complex and little to recommend him, does not return Sally's affections.

Who else is there? It just makes sense for Sally to choose the brick wall of her school to be her closest confidante. The sublime irony. The brick wall is the only entity she believes can comprehend what she is saying, the only one who listens to her. The wall would never mock her, or pity her, or disappoint her. Far from it. So devoted is Sally's wall it doesn't hesitate to even the score with those who hassle her by dropping bricks on their heads.

When the wall decides one night, having "had all it could take," to give in to the burden of its despair and collapse, I was devastated. Yes, a new school is built, with a brick wall identical to the old one, but of course it's different. Sally and the new wall have a cordial relationship, but the fellowship she'd shared with the old wall is gone. As a girl who couldn't go to bed without making sure that the kitchen appliances on the counter were close enough to talk when the lights went off, this resonated with me.

It is this sensitivity that leads Sally to connect the Little Red-Haired Girl's absence with Charlie Brown's overwhelming sadness at never having expressed his love for her. "Before she moved away," Sally notes, "he never cried out during the night."

A little girl doesn't need to have ESP to pick up on the way others find her anger not only unacceptable, but unnerving— particularly her brother. The expression on Charlie Brown's face as he watches Sally coolly mailing a letter to the North Pole, criticizing Santa for being wishy-washy—"Into the teeth of the storm," she says—is nothing short of blank terror.

Sally can't seem to help being honest. She also knew, like I did, that girls honestly expressing their dissatisfaction aren't frightening to adults, but ugly. If Sally wants to get a good grade on her "If I Had a Pony" report, honestly writing "If I had a pony I'd saddle up and ride so far from this school it would make your head swim" will not only fail to impress the teacher, she will be penalized. "That's a good way to get a D minus," she says as she miserably balls up her report and throws it away. It's not that her teacher couldn't see why a girl like Sally might want to escape school—she knows an honest answer isn't what they're looking for.

The classroom was the stage for most of my favorite Sally cartoons. As a girl torn between seeking my teacher's approval and a hunger to let my freak flag fly, the "Show and Tell" strips were liberating. Even though Sally had to know that showing off her "leaf collection" by dumping it on the classroom floor would earn her an F, she went for it. Forget what other people thought: Sally was committed to her vision, and I admired that.

The most successful of Sally's presentations is a document that she declares, in a voice of a carnival flimflam man, "was written by an actual cave man, and was discovered only recently by a farmer in Iowa." You can sense the teacher reaching for her red pen as Sally's classmates lean forward to listen as she begins to spin, "I came into its possession through the exchange of money and certain bits of valuable information." Afterwards Sally, flush with triumph, addresses the reader, "'Show and Lie' is my best subject."

This episode reminds me of the moment in sixth grade when, caught unaware, I was called upon to deliver an oral book report. Understand, I read all the time, good books, smart books, but the book freshest in my mind that day was a bodice-ripper I'd pinched from a friend's mother. (My own mother would have been appalled by my reading choice, and not just by the atrocious writing but the politics.) It was the classic story of a small-town beauty preyed upon by a ruthless Hollywood producer, the love interest a misunderstood rogue with a Scottish accent and an eyepatch. I knew it was a complete piece of crap, but on I went, chin up. Halfway through my report my teacher stopped me. "Let me guess," she said, clearly annoyed, and then predicted exactly the happily-ever-after ending. I can't tell you the moment I decided to be a writer, but I point to this as the moment I became one.

"No, that's not it," I insisted, heart in my throat. "It goes like this . . ."

I then proceeded to imagine aloud an alternate future for the small-town beauty and the one-eyed Scot. No one was living happily ever after. I don't remember exactly, but I seem to recall a plane crash, or maybe it was a shipwreck. As I spoke I watched the expression of disgust on teacher's face softening into curiosity, and my classmates leaning forward in their seats. For the first time I can ever recall in school, I felt good at something. I felt seen for who I really was. It seems Show and Lie was my best subject too.

Triangle with Piano

Mona Simpson

Charlie Brown pines for the Little Red-Haired Girl with a perennial wistful love. Every year, he hopes he'll receive a valentine from her. He never does. She is so absent from Charlie Brown's life that she never once appears in *Peanuts*. Charles Schulz admitted: "I could never draw her to satisfy the reader's impression of what she's probably like."

Charlie Brown opines, "They say that opposites attract . . . She's really something and I'm really nothing . . . How opposite can you get."

Yet there's a sweetness to his pangs. *Peanuts* is about longing, in a particular register, with a palpable sense of safety in its sorrow.

As a very young child, I tried to like comic books in order to please my best friend, who happened to be a male cousin. I remember the capitalized word "POW" and frames of action, rescue, and flying. They reminded me of the endless chases of Saturday morning cartoons, scored with frenetic classical soundtracks. I preferred the Bobbsey Twins, which I read less for their predictably solvable mysteries but for the—to me, exotic—depiction of stable family life.

My cousin and I both read the funny papers, for *Peanuts*, which centered on relationships and depicted feelings more than action, opening the field for later work like Spiegelman's great *Maus* and the graphic novels such as *Blankets*, *Ghost World*, and *Fun Home*. Love, in various shades of unrequition, figured prominently.

PICTURE LUCY LEANING on Schroeder's piano. It was a new idea to take unrequited love among children seriously because the stakes feel necessarily blunted. Whether or not Charlie Brown receives a valentine from the Little Red-Haired Girl, we know he will go home for supper—to a two-parent, white, middle-class Midwestern house—and hope for another valentine next year.

Schulz's "li'l folks" display the full palette of human emotions, though most adult troubles (which sometimes—open the news—involve children too) are kept out of the frames. "There was no room for adults," Schulz said. The only parents who appear in the strip are Snoopy's.

Ballgames take the place of careers. Jobs feel like callings (Lucy's psychiatric advice, Snoopy's novel-writing, Schroeder's music). Though two characters live in single-parent households, no financial hardship is suggested. Schulz introduced a black character, Franklin, with the suggestive line, "Is that your beach ball?" (Beaches and swimming pools, with their tendency toward dishabille, were among the most nationally contentious spaces, prompting the Title II public-accommodation provision of the 1964 Civil Rights Act, which among other things prohibited private beach clubs from exercising racial discrimination.) But no racial conflict arises in *Peanuts*. There is no bankruptcy or serious depression. However extreme the suffering of the characters, their sorrows have a quality of timelessness and, ultimately, safety.

PART OF THE fun of *Peanuts* is the sense that Schulz was dipping in and out of his life for inspiration, and the drawings have that just-dry quality. In *Peanuts: The Art of Charles M. Schulz*, edited by Chip Kidd, Kidd discusses the original Little Red-Haired Girl, a woman named Donna Mae Johnson, who worked in accounting at the Department of Art Instruction, Inc., where Schulz was first a student and later a teacher.

In life, the artist and the art-school accountant were involved for three years, from 1947 to 1950. He proposed and she refused him, and soon after married a fireman named Allan Wold. Though Schulz was devastated, he and Mrs. Wold remained friends for the rest of his life. These few facts could also delineate the emotional tone of *Peanuts*.

In explaining a sketch Schulz once gave her, Mrs. Wold said, "This is a cartoon Sparky drew and left at my desk at Art Instruction."

The drawing shows an unhappy, perhaps angry little girl facing a boy who is offering her a bouquet of flowers she clearly does not want. The upside-down half circle of her refusing frown implies a vivid and complex tangle of emotions.

Near the time of Schulz's retirement, Mrs. Wold said, "I'd like to see Charlie Brown kick that football and if he gets the Little Red-Haired Girl, that's fine with me."

Of course, Charlie Brown never "gets" the Little Red-Haired Girl.

"The Little Red-Haired Girl has moved away and I'll never see her again," Charlie Brown laments, with infinite sorrow. And Schulz—ever the romantic realist—never let him kick the football either.

On Valentine's Day 2011, however, the Schulz Museum gave free admission to all red-haired girls.

SCHROEDER AND LUCY, whom I remembered as a template for extremely unrequited love, turn out actually to be in a relationship. Theirs is not unrequited love so much as complicated love. They are in a triangle, a threesome with Schroeder's toy piano.

It could be argued that Schroeder's essential relationship is to the toy piano, an instrument to which Charlie Brown introduces him. Charlie Brown announces that the toy piano is a beautiful instrument if played properly and proceeds to produce the sounds "plink plink plink." Of course when Schroeder sits down, tongue out of mouth in characteristic concentration, he produces virtuosic classical chords.

It's significant that Schroeder plays on a *toy* piano. The piano is smaller than he is, and yet his idol is Beethoven. Schroeder's dad buys him a recording of Beethoven's String Quartet no. 4. Schroeder had loved Beethoven even before he began playing the piano. In an earlier sketch, he holds a violin and bow and says to a Lucy-like girl, "I dread the day when I have to meet Beethoven face to face."

From his first appearance in the strip in September 1951, Schroeder plays classical music (Schulz drew all the sheet music in the strip by hand, never using assistants, and described the transcription of notes as "extremely tedious").

Charlie Brown decides Schroeder has no sense of humor because he doesn't laugh at a Handel joke. (One musician asks another if he can play the Hallelujah Chorus, see? And this guy says, "Oh, I guess I can handel it!")

Of course Schroeder has perfect pitch. In another strip, Schroeder plays all forty-eight preludes and fugues from Bach's *Well-Tempered Clavier* in an amateur musician's contest and loses to a quick-fingered accordionist. Charlie Brown hasn't cornered the market on failure.

Once, Charlie Brown tried to introduce his friend to a REAL piano. "C'mon Schroeder, we'll see how good you are on a REAL piano!"

Shoved onto the bench of a full-size adult instrument, Schroeder emits a loud "WAH!" flexing his feet in resistance as tears shoot out of him. (The difference between "WAH" and "POW" says something about where Schulz brought the form.) By the end of the strip, Schroeder returns to his toy piano where he plays prodigiously again.

(In this regard, Schroeder differs from his maker. Schulz's professional life began with rejection—his strips were turned down by *Collier's* and the *Saturday Evening Post* and even his high school yearbook; he was told by Disney he was unqualified to be an animator and he supported himself as an art instructor for the correspondence course Art Instruction Inc. before selling *Li'l Folks* to the *Star-Tribune*. But once his work was syndicated Schulz did not freeze and scream "WAH!" In fact, he even worked on the adaptations for television.)

Schroeder likes to be left alone to play his toy piano, though he rarely is alone. Many of the characters lean on Schroeder's instrument, most frequently Lucy.

She was always leaning on his piano.

"I'll bet if we were to get married someday, Schroeder, we would be very happy . . . / While you were practicing the piano, I'd be in the kitchen making your breakfast . . . / Then I'd bring it in like this and set it all out nice, and prop up your favorite newspaper, and pour your coffee . . . / Wouldn't that be romantic?"

For years he is banging the keys NO! in answer to her seductions.

"You and your ol' Beethoven! He wasn't so great."

Lucy breaks his Beethoven bust. She breaks his piano. (But Schroeder is indefatigable and unbreakable. He has a closet full of Beethoven busts and a store of toy pianos.)

Kidd's remarkable cache includes photographs of the Esterbrook 914 Radio pen Schulz used, with the thrilling detail that he relied on these pen nibs "so much that when the company announced it was going out of business, he bought the entire remaining stock. The hundreds of boxes saw him through the rest of his career."

When Lucy becomes dejected, her refrain is "I'll probably never get married."

But a few times, over their fifty years together, Schroeder concedes that there is a relationship.

Lucy says, in another of her characteristic fantasies about an adult life she and the other *Peanuts* characters will never achieve, "Say we've been married for about six months . . . / And let's say

I've made a beautiful tuna casserole for dinner . . . / You walk into the kitchen, and you say, 'What, tuna casserole again?'"

"I'd never say that," Schroeder says.

But she misses his kindness. She's too inside her own rant. "Then I say, 'I worked hard making this casserole, but all you care about is that stupid piano!'"

When Schroeder arrives at the ball field later, he says, "Sorry I'm late . . . I got involved in a marital dispute."

THEN, WHEN LUCY'S father gets transferred and she tells Schroeder the terrible news that she'll be moving, they both cry.

Schroeder has a John Marcher "Beast in the Jungle" moment, realizing he loves Lucy only after she is gone. In a strip from 1966, Schroeder sees a truck driving away. Charlie Brown tells him that it is a moving van. Lucy's family has moved away.

"But I thought she was just kidding! I didn't think they'd really go!"

"Well, what do you care? You never liked Lucy anyway! You were always insulting her."

"But I didn't understand . . . I mean, I . . ."

"Oh, stop making excuses. Go on home and play your ol' Beethoven."

BUT SCHROEDER CAN'T. He sits at his piano and remembers Lucy saying, "Schroeder, what if you and I got married someday, and . . ." He realizes, "I never even said good-bye."

But unlike the Little Red-Haired Girl, the Van Pelts don't stay away. Lucy returns to Schroeder's piano; he begins to play again and, once more, ignores her. Their dynamic resumes.

Still, in a panel drawn late in Schulz's life, Schroeder

promises to kiss Lucy if she hits a home run. She hits the home run, runs the bases, but then refuses his kiss, if it is only because of a bet.

She insists, in the end, on reciprocity.

On Unhappiness, Friendship, and Charlie Brown

Clifford Thompson

During the cold months of the 1971–72 school year, when I was in third grade, my father brought home a cat that one of his buddies didn't want or couldn't keep. My family was soon to make the connection between animal hair—particularly cat hair—and my periodic bouts of asthma; but that hadn't happened yet, which was why, on the day I am recalling, I was home from school, propped up in my parents' bed and struggling for breath. For part of the day I was alone with my grandmother, who was seventy-seven or seventy-eight and who could hear you only if you stood next to her ear and spoke as if to someone a block away. At one point, while she was doing laundry or something in the basement, my breathing went from bad to worse—my lungs, which already felt as if they had shrunk to the size of thimbles, seemed to be shutting down altogether. I shouted for my grandmother, but she couldn't hear me. Then my parents walked in, took one look at me, and whisked me off to the hospital. I came home that evening, my breathing restored (I never saw the cat again), and returned to my parents' bed. Beside me was a stack of my older brother's *Peanuts* books, collections of comic strips from years past. I was comfortable after a day of misery; there was no place I had to go; and my favorite items in all the world were next to me. It was the happiest moment of my childhood.

You don't always need to identify with a character to enjoy a book or movie or TV show or comic strip, but it can certainly help, and my day of adversity helped me to appreciate Charlie Brown, the hero of *Peanuts* and the alter ego of its creator, Charles M. Schulz. Neither my adversity nor my affinity for *Peanuts* was limited to that day. As I am hardly the first to point out, many, many children have identified with Charlie Brown's perennial feelings of disconnectedness from the world around him, and the kinship I felt with Charlie Brown went a long way toward explaining my love of the strip. Charlie Brown was a loser, in both the original sense of the word—he simply lost in a lot of situations—and the modern sense: he seemed to have inherent qualities that made life more difficult for him than it was for other people. Yet those qualities were not of the kind that prevented anyone from feeling kinship with him, since they often seemed to amount to no more than bad luck—and who wouldn't rather blame his failures on his luck than on himself? (The fault, dear Snoopy, lies not in our selves . . .) True, his falling—literally—for Lucy's offers to hold the football while he ran to kick it, despite her having tricked him innumerable times in the past, suggested a trust that bordered on stupidity; but is trusting people the worst sin there is? True, the baseball team of which Charlie Brown was pitcher and manager was routinely slaughtered; but that was hardly his fault alone, even if he did always shoulder the blame. Unlike, say, Lucy, he at least knew there was a game in progress. (Charlie Brown's being the team manager, which I found puzzling as a boy, now makes perfect sense to me. Managing people, as anyone who has done it knows, is an inexhaustible source of headaches, and who would be more likely to find himself in that role?)

There were a couple of differences between Charlie Brown and me. One was skin color. The other was that Charlie Brown experienced things that, most of the time at least, I feared rather than suffered. But the first difference was unimportant to me, and I wasn't even aware of the second, because, as I realize now, the thought of suffering Charlie Brown–like disasters was as big a drag as the disasters themselves. As a boy I had a mortal fear of being laughed at, and my school life—which is most of a child's life—was filled with events designed, it seemed to me, to bring about that result. I hated the tumbles we were made to do in gym class; I was afraid of doing them wrong, not because I might snap my scrawny neck but because there was a roomful of kids ready to laugh at any mistake. There were sometimes dances in the auditorium during school hours, and I would rather have lost a toe than set one on the dance floor. When other kids laughed at Charlie Brown, he seemed like my fellow soldier, taking a bullet that could just as easily have hit me. And his suffering, I thought, made him noble.

I also found *Peanuts* uproariously funny. I often ran to read them to my parents and older siblings, sometimes barely able to get the words out because I was laughing so hard. One strip in particular struck me, when I was in second grade, as the height of sophistication and wit. Charlie Brown and Linus stand at the wall where they often hang out together; Linus tries to assure Charlie Brown that he is not alone in having places where he doesn't feel he fits in, and asks if any place in particular makes him uncomfortable. In the last panel, Charlie Brown replies, "Earth!" I was inspired to create my own strip, "Jerome," which was basically *Peanuts*, except that it was not drawn particularly well, even by the standards applied to eight-year-olds, and it wasn't very funny—I looked at the strips again several years later, and even I didn't get the jokes. (There was one exception: I drew a strip in which a girl, sad that her dress has shrunk in the washing machine, decides to get in the machine herself. Sometime afterward Carl Anderson, the cartoonist who drew *Henry*, had the exact same idea.)

OUR TASTES CHANGE as we grow older, of course, as does the way we think about human relationships. Among the hard truths we eventually learn are that suffering does not necessarily make people noble, that people's misfortunes do not cause us to love them (often they have the opposite effect), and that shared misery is not by itself a basis for lasting friendship. Charlie Brown's feeling of disconnectedness, even if it was not his fault, was the salient feature of his life; as a boy I identified with that feeling, but isn't the idea, eventually, to find like-minded people with whom one has more in common than chronic unhappiness, and then to leave such unhappiness behind? Does anyone really want to be friends with a grown-up Charlie Brown? What would you talk about besides his screwed-up life, and how long would it be before you ran out of consoling words? My now-grown older daughter, who was a much more socially adept child than I ever was and who thus had no use for Charlie Brown, once pronounced him to be "depressed and depressing"; she preferred the title character of *Garfield*, the sarcastic but contented cat who gets the two things he wants in life—inordinate amounts of food and sleep—largely through the force of his sense of entitlement (which is how a lot of humans operate, too). I remember being a pretty serious *Peanuts* fan through my junior high school years, which were the worst years of my youth, probably of my life thus far. Then I went to high school, where suddenly, to my surprise, I was able to relate to my fellow students. Maybe not coincidentally, my ardor for *Peanuts* began to cool. Punchlines such as "Earth!" lost their hold on me, as did Charlie Brown.

In recent years, however, I've picked up a *Peanuts* collection here and there, and in perusing the cartoons I remembered so well, I've had three reactions—all of them pleasant, two of them surprising to me. The first is that rereading the strips is like visiting with long-lost friends; there is the same feeling of affection rekindled, the reasons for the separation forgotten or brushed aside like so much dust. Second, I find that I now respond less to the words—many of the punchlines, as I suspected, aren't very funny to me—and more to the drawings. If *Peanuts* is still being read in decades to come, I predict it will be because of the masterfully rendered expressions on the characters' faces, which are the features of *Peanuts* that still make me laugh. The emotions that, say, Charlie Chaplin or Giulietta Masina or Jim Carrey reflect comically with their eyes and mouths are those that Schulz was able to make funny with a pen: alarm, disgust, impatience, and many more, singly or in combination. Finally, in embracing *Peanuts* during my childhood, then drifting away from it in my adolescence, I had responded to Charlie

Brown alone, as if he were a real kid or had somehow drawn himself. I now saw him for what he was: a drawing, part extension, part creation of Schulz, and I found a new appreciation for him.

It sounds cold to say that friendship, like commerce, is based on mutual benefit; but at bottom, is it not true? Our friends give us something: they make us laugh, or they stimulate us intellectually, or they offer warmth, compassion, and understanding, or, if we are very lucky, they do all of these. To help a friend in need is, in part, to repay such acts, or it is charity. As a being in himself, Charlie Brown has only the fact of his misery to offer, and thus has significant limitations as a friend. But as a gift from a friend, as an offering from Charles Schulz, he is funny, his expressions drawn hilariously, his adventures depicted—I realize now—with an utter lack of sentimentality; he is the medium through which Schulz made many of us laugh while reflecting our fears, through which he conveyed his single greatest gift: his compassion.

The Exemplary
Narcissism of Snoopy

Sarah Boxer

It really was a dark and stormy night. On February 12, 2000, Charles Schulz—who had single-handedly drawn some eighteen thousand Peanuts comic strips, who refused to use assistants to ink or letter his comics, who vowed that after he quit, no new *Peanuts* strips would be made—died, taking to the grave, it seemed, any further adventures of the gang.

Hours later, his last Sunday strip came out with a farewell: "Charlie Brown, Snoopy, Linus, Lucy . . . How can I ever forget them." By then, *Peanuts* was carried by more than 2,600 news-papers in 75 countries and read by some 300 million people. It had been going for five decades. Robert Thompson, a scholar of popular culture, called it "arguably the longest story told by a single artist in human history."

The arrival of *The Peanuts Movie* this fall breathes new life into the phrase *over my dead body*—starting with the movie's title. Schulz hated and resented the name *Peanuts*, which was foisted on him by United Feature Syndicate. He avoided using it: "If someone asks me what I do, I always say, 'I draw that comic strip with Snoopy in it, Charlie Brown and his dog.'" And unlike the classic *Peanuts* television specials, which were done in a style Schulz approvingly called "semi-animation," where the characters flip around rather than turning smoothly in space, *The Peanuts Movie* (written by Schulz's son Craig and grandson Bryan, along with Bryan's writing partner, Cornelius Uliano) is a computer-generated 3-D-animated feature. What's more, the Little Red-Haired Girl, Charlie Brown's unrequited crush, whom Schulz promised never to draw, is supposed to make a grand appearance. AAUGH!!!

Before all that happens, before the next generation gets a warped view of what *Peanuts* is and was, let's go back in time. Why was this comic strip so wildly popular for half a century? How did Schulz's cute and lovable characters (they're almost always referred to that way) hold sway over so many people— everyone from Ronald Reagan to Whoopi Goldberg?

Peanuts was deceptive. It looked like kid stuff, but it wasn't. The strip's cozy suburban conviviality, its warm fuzziness, actually conveyed some uncomfortable truths about the loneliness of social existence. The characters, though funny, could stir up shockingly heated arguments over how to survive and still be a decent human being in a bitter world. Who was better at it— Charlie Brown or Snoopy?

The time is ripe to see what was really happening on the pages of *Peanuts* during all those years. Since 2004, the comics publisher Fantagraphics has been issuing *The Complete Peanuts*, both Sunday and daily strips, in books that each cover two years and include an appreciation from a notable fan.

(The twenty-five-volume series will be completed next year.) To read them straight through, alongside David Michaelis's trenchant 2007 biography, *Schulz and Peanuts*, is to watch the characters evolve from undifferentiated little cusses into great social types.

IN THE STONE age of *Peanuts*—when only seven newspapers carried the strip, when Snoopy was still an itinerant four-legged creature with no owner or doghouse, when Lucy and Linus had yet to be born—*Peanuts* was surprisingly dark. The first strip, published on October 2, 1950, shows two children, a boy and a girl, sitting on the sidewalk. The boy, Shermy, says, "Well! Here comes ol' Charlie Brown! / Good ol' Charlie Brown . . . Yes, sir! / Good ol' Charlie Brown." When Charlie Brown is out of sight, Shermy adds, "How I hate him!" In the second *Peanuts* strip the girl, Patty, walks alone, chanting, "Little girls are made of sugar and spice . . . / . . . and everything nice." As Charlie Brown comes into view, she slugs him and says, "That's what little girls are made of!"

Although key characters were missing or quite different from what they came to be, the Hobbesian ideas about society that made *Peanuts Peanuts* were already evident: people, especially children, are selfish and cruel to one another; social life is perpetual conflict; solitude is the only peaceful harbor; one's deepest wishes will invariably be derailed and one's comforts whisked away; and an unbridgeable gulf yawns between one's fantasies about oneself and what others see. These bleak themes, which went against the tide of the go-go 1950s, floated freely on the pages of *Peanuts* at first, landing lightly on one kid or another until slowly each theme came to be embedded in a certain individual—particularly Lucy, Schroeder, Charlie Brown, Linus, and Snoopy.

In other words, in the beginning all the *Peanuts* kids were, as Al Capp, the creator of *Li'l Abner*, observed, "good mean little bastards eager to hurt each other." What came to be Lucy's inimitable brand of bullying was suffused throughout the *Peanuts* population. Even Charlie Brown was a bit of a heel. In 1951, for example, after watching Patty fall off a curb into some mud, he smirks: "Right in the mud, eh? It's a good thing I was carrying the ice cream!"

Many early *Peanuts* fans—and this may come as a shock to later fans raised on the sweet milk of *Happiness Is a Warm Puppy*—were attracted to the strip's decidedly unsweet view of society. Matt Groening, the creator of the strip *Life in Hell* and *The Simpsons*, remembers, "I was excited by the casual cruelty and offhand humiliations at the heart of the strip." Garry Trudeau, of *Doonesbury* fame, saw *Peanuts* as "the first Beat strip" because it "vibrated with '50s alienation." And the editors of *Charlie Mensuel*, a raunchy precursor to the even raunchier *Charlie Hebdo*, so admired the existential angst of the strip that they named both publications after its lead character.

At the center of this world was Charlie Brown, a new kind of epic hero—a loser who would lie in the dark recalling his defeats, charting his worries, planning his comebacks. One of his best-known lines was "My anxieties have anxieties." Although he was the glue holding together the *Peanuts* crew (and its baseball team), he was also the undisputed butt of the strip. His mailbox was almost always empty. His dog often snubbed him, at least until suppertime, and the football was always yanked away from him. The cartoonist Tom Tomorrow calls him a Sisyphus. Frustration was his lot. When Schulz was asked whether for his final strip he would let Charlie Brown make contact with the football, he reportedly replied, "Oh, no! Definitely not! . . . That would be a terrible disservice to him after nearly half a century."

Although Schulz denied any strict identification with Charlie Brown (who was actually named for one of Schulz's friends at the correspondence school in Minneapolis where Schulz learned and taught drawing), many readers assumed they were one and the same. More important for the strip's success, readers saw themselves in Charlie Brown, even if they didn't want to. "I aspired to Linus-ness; to be wise and kind and highly skilled at making gigantic structures out of playing cards," the children's-book author Mo Willems notes in one of the essays in the Fantagraphics series. But, he continues, "I knew, deep down, that I was Charlie Brown. I suspect we all did."

WELL, I DIDN'T. And luckily, beginning in 1952 (after Schulz moved from his hometown, St. Paul, Minnesota, to Colorado Springs for a year with his first wife, Joyce, and her daughter, Meredith), there were plenty more alter egos to choose from. That was the year the Van Pelts were born. Lucy, the fussbudget, who was based at first on young Meredith, came in March. Lucy's blanket-carrying little brother, Linus, Schulz's favorite character to draw (he would start with his pen at the back of the neck), arrived only months later.

And then, of course, there was Snoopy, who had been around from the outset (Schulz had intended to name him Sniffy) and was fast evolving into an articulate being. His first detailed expression of consciousness, recorded in a thought balloon, came in response to Charlie Brown making fun of his ears: "Kind of warm out today for ear muffs, isn't it?" Snoopy sniffs: "Why do I have to suffer such indignities!?"

I like to think that *Peanuts* and identity politics grew up together in America. By 1960, the main characters—Charlie Brown, Linus, Schroeder, Snoopy—had their roles and their acolytes. Even Lucy had her fans. The filmmaker John Waters, writing an introduction to one of the Fantagraphics volumes, gushes:

> I like Lucy's politics ("I know everything!" . . .), her manners ("Get out of my way!" . . .), her narcissism . . . and especially her verbal abuse rants . . . Lucy's "total warfare frown" . . . is just as iconic to me as Mona Lisa's smirk.

Finding one's identity in the strip was like finding one's political party or ethnic group or niche in the family. It was a big part of the appeal of *Peanuts*.

Every character was a powerful personality with quirky attractions and profound faults, and every character, like some saint or hero, had at least one key prop or attribute. Charlie Brown had his tangled kite, Schroeder his toy piano, Linus his flannel blanket, Lucy her "Psychiatric Help" booth, and Snoopy his doghouse.

In this blessedly solid world, each character came to be linked not only to certain objects but to certain kinds of inter-actions, too, much like the main players in *Krazy Kat*, one of the strips that Schulz admired and hoped to match. But unlike *Krazy Kat*, which was built upon a tragically repetitive love triangle that involved animals hurling bricks, *Peanuts* was a drama of social coping, outwardly simple but actually quite complex.

Charlie Brown, whose very character depended on his wishes being stymied, developed what the actor Alec Baldwin, in one of the Fantagraphics introductions, calls a kind of "trudging, Jimmy Stewart–like decency and predictability." The Charlie Brown way was to keep on keeping on, standing with a tangled kite or a losing baseball team day after day. Michaelis, Schulz's biographer, locates the essence of Charlie Brown—and *Peanuts* itself—in a 1954 strip in which Charlie Brown visits Shermy and watches as he "plays with a model train set whose tracks and junctions and crossings spread . . . elaborately far and wide in Shermy's family's living room." After a while,

> Charlie Brown pulls on his coat and walks home . . . [and] sits down at *his* railroad: a single, closed circle of track . . . Here was the moment when Charlie Brown became a national symbol, the Everyman who survives life's slings and arrows simply by surviving himself.

In fact, all of the characters were survivors. They just had different strategies for survival, none of which was exactly prosocial. Linus knew that he could take his blows philosophically—he was often seen, elbows on the wall, calmly chatting with Charlie Brown—as long as he had his security blanket nearby. He also knew that if he didn't have his blanket, he would freak out. (In 1955 the child psychiatrist D. W. Winnicott asked for permission to use Linus's blanket as an illustration of a "transitional object.")

Lucy, dishing out bad and unsympathetic advice from her "Psychiatric Help" booth, was the picture of bluster. On March 27, 1959, Charlie Brown, the first patient to visit her booth, says to Lucy, "I have deep feelings of depression . . . / What can I do about this?" Lucy replies: "Snap out of it! Five cents, please." That pretty much sums up the Lucy way.

Schroeder at his piano represented artistic retreat—ignoring the world to pursue one's dream. And Snoopy's coping philosophy was, in a sense, even more antisocial than Schroeder's. Snoopy figured that since no one will ever see you the way you see yourself, you might as well build your world around fantasy, create the person you want to be, and live it out, live it up. Part of Snoopy's Walter Mitty–esque charm lay in his implicit rejection of society's view of him. Most of the kids saw him as just a dog, but he knew he was way more than that.

Those characters who could not be summed up with both a social strategy and a recognizable attribute (Pig-Pen, for instance, had an attribute—dirt—but no social strategy) became bit players or fell by the wayside. Shermy, the character who uttered the bitter opening lines of *Peanuts* in 1950, became just another bland boy by the 1960s. Violet, the character who made endless mud pies, withheld countless invitations, and had the distinction of being the first person to pull the football away from Charlie Brown, was mercilessly demoted to just another snobby mean girl. Patty, one of the early stars, had her name recycled for another, more complicated character, Peppermint Patty, the narcoleptic tomboy who made her first appearance in 1966 and became a regular in the 1970s. (Her social gambit was to fall asleep, usually at her school desk.)

Once the main cast was set, the iterations of their daily

interplay were almost unlimited. "A cartoonist," Schulz once said, "is someone who has to draw the same thing every day without repeating himself." It was this "infinitely shifting repetition of the patterns," Umberto Eco wrote in *The New York Review of Books* in 1985, that gave the strip its epic quality. Watching the permutations of every character working out how to get along with every other character demanded "from the reader a continuous act of empathy."

For a strip that depended on the reader's empathy, *Peanuts* often involved dramas that displayed a shocking lack of empathy. And in many of those dramas, the pivotal figure was Lucy, the fussbudget who couldn't exist without others to fuss at. She was so strident, Michaelis reports, that Schulz relied on certain pen nibs for her. (When Lucy was "doing some loud shouting," as Schulz put it, he would ink up a B-5 pen, which made heavy, flat, rough lines. For "maximum screams," he would get out the B-3.)

Lucy was, in essence, society itself, or at least society as Schulz saw it. "Her aggressiveness threw the others off balance," Michaelis writes, prompting each character to cope or withdraw in his or her own way. Charlie Brown, for instance, responded to her with incredible credulity, coming to her time and again for pointless advice or for football kicking. Linus always seemed to approach her with a combination of terror and equanimity. In one of my favorite strips, he takes refuge from his sister in the kitchen and, when Lucy tracks him down, addresses her pointedly: "Am I buttering too loud for you?"

It was Lucy's dealings with Schroeder that struck closest to home for Schulz, whose first marriage, to Joyce, began to fall apart in the 1960s while they were building up their huge estate in Sebastopol, California. Just as Schulz's retreat into his comic-strip world antagonized Joyce, Michaelis observes, so Schroeder's devotion to his piano was "an affront to Lucy." At one point, Lucy becomes so fed up at her inability to distract Schroeder from his music that she hurls his piano into the sewer: "It's woman against piano! / Woman is winning!! Woman is winning!!!" When Schroeder shouts at her in disbelief, "You threw my piano down the sewer!!," Lucy corrects him: "Not your piano, Sweetie . . . / My competition!" Now, that's a relationship!

IN THIS DEEPLY dystopic strip, there was only one character who could—and some say finally did—tear the highly entertaining, disturbed social world to shreds. And that happens to be my favorite character, Snoopy.

Before Snoopy had his signature doghouse, he was an emotional creature. Although he didn't speak (he expressed himself in thought balloons), he was very connected to all the other characters. In one 1958 strip, for instance, Linus and Charlie Brown are talking in the background, and Snoopy comes dancing by. Linus says to Charlie Brown, "My gramma says that we live in a veil of tears." Charlie Brown answers: "She's right . . . This is a sad world." Snoopy still goes on dancing. By the third frame, though, when Charlie Brown says, "This is a world filled with sorrow," Snoopy's dance slows and his face begins to fall. By the last frame, he is down on the ground—far more devastated than Linus or Charlie Brown, who are shown chatting off in the distance, "Sorrow, sadness and despair . . . grief, agony and woe. . . ."

But by the late 1960s, Snoopy had begun to change. For example, in a strip dated May 1, 1969, he's dancing by himself:

"This is my 'First Day of May' dance. / It differs only slightly from my 'First Day of Fall' dance, which differs also only slightly from my 'First Day of Spring' dance." Snoopy continues dancing and ends with: "Actually, even I have a hard time telling them apart." Snoopy was still hilarious, but something fundamental had shifted. He didn't need any of the other characters in order to be what he was. He needed only his imagination. More and more often he appeared alone on his doghouse, sleeping or typing a novel or a love letter. Indeed, his doghouse—which was hardly taller than a beagle yet big enough inside to hold an Andrew Wyeth painting as well as a pool table—came to be the objective correlative of Snoopy's rich inner life, a place that no human ever got to see.

Some thought this new Snoopy was an excellent thing, indeed the key to the strip's greatness. Schulz was among them: "I don't know how he got to walking, and I don't know how he first began to think, but that was probably one of the best things that I ever did." The novelist Jonathan Franzen is another Snoopy fan. Snoopy, as Franzen has noted, is

> the protean trickster whose freedom is founded on his confidence that he's lovable at heart, the quick-change artist who, for the sheer joy of it, can become a helicopter or a hockey player or Head Beagle and then again, in a flash, before his virtuosity has a chance to alienate you or diminish you, be the eager little dog who just wants dinner.

But some people detested the new Snoopy and blamed him for what they viewed as the decline of *Peanuts* in the second half of its fifty-year run. "It's tough to fix the exact date when Snoopy went from being the strip's besetting artistic weakness to ruining it altogether," the journalist and critic Christopher Caldwell wrote in 2000, a month before Schulz died, in an essay in *New York Press* titled "Against Snoopy." But certainly by the 1970s, Caldwell wrote, Snoopy had begun wrecking the delicate world that Schulz had built. The problem, as Caldwell saw it, was that

> Snoopy was never a full participant in the tangle of relationships that drove *Peanuts* in its Golden Age. He couldn't be: he doesn't talk . . . and therefore he doesn't interact. He's there to be looked at.

Snoopy unquestionably took the strip to a new realm beginning in the late 1960s. The turning point, I think, was the airing of *It's the Great Pumpkin, Charlie Brown* in 1966. In this Halloween television special, Snoopy is shown sitting atop his doghouse living out his extended fantasy of being a World War I flying ace shot down by the Red Baron and then crawling alone behind enemy lines in France. Snoopy is front and center for six minutes, about one-quarter of the whole program, and he steals the show, proving that he doesn't need the complicated world of *Peanuts* to thrive. He can go it alone. And after that he often did.

In 1968, Snoopy became NASA's mascot. The next year, Snoopy had a lunar module named after him for the *Apollo 10* mission (the command module was called "Charlie Brown"). In 1968 and 1972, Snoopy was a write-in candidate for president of the United States. Plush stuffed Snoopys became popular. (I had one.) By 1975, Snoopy had replaced Charlie Brown as the center of the strip. He cut a swath through the world.

For instance, in parts of Europe *Peanuts* came to be licensed as *Snoopy*. And in Tokyo, the floor of the vast toy store Kiddy Land that is devoted to *Peanuts* is called Snoopy Town.

To accommodate this new Snoopy-centric world, Schulz began making changes. He invented a whole new animal world for Snoopy. First came Woodstock, a bird who communicates only with Snoopy (in little tic marks). And then Snoopy acquired a family: Spike, a droopy-eyed, mustachioed beagle, followed by Olaf, Andy, Marbles, and Belle.

In 1987, Schulz acknowledged that introducing Snoopy's relatives had been a blunder, much as Eugene the Jeep had been an unwelcome intrusion into the comic strip *Popeye*:

> It's possible—I think—to make a mistake in the strip and without realizing it, destroy it . . . I realized it myself a couple of years ago when I began to introduce Snoopy's brothers and sisters . . . It destroyed the relationship that Snoopy has with the kids, which is a very strange relationship.

He was right. Snoopy's initial interactions with the kids—his understanding of humanity, indeed his deep empathy (just what they were often missing), coupled with his inability to speak—were unique. And that's why whenever Snoopy's relatives showed up, the air just went out of the strip.

BUT FOR MANY fans, it wasn't merely Snoopy's brothers and sisters dragging him down. There was something fundamentally rotten about the new Snoopy, whose charm was based on his total lack of concern about what others thought of him. His confidence, his breezy sense that the world may be falling apart but one can still dance on, was worse than irritating. It was morally bankrupt. As the writer Daniel Mendelsohn put it in a piece in *The New York Times Book Review*, Snoopy "represents the part of ourselves—the smugness, the avidity, the pomposity, the rank egotism—most of us know we have but try to keep decently hidden away." While Charlie Brown was made to be buffeted by other personalities and cared very much what others thought of him, Snoopy's soul is all about self-invention—which can be seen as delusional self-love. This new Snoopy, his detractors felt, had no room for empathy.

To his critics, part of what's appalling about Snoopy is the idea that it's possible to create any self-image one wants—in particular, the profile of someone with tons of friends and accomplishments—and sell that image to the world. Such self-flattery is not only shallow but wrong. Snoopy, viewed this way, is the very essence of selfie culture, of Facebook culture. He's the kind of creature who would travel the world only in order to take his own picture and share it with everyone, to enhance his social image. He's a braggart. Unlike Charlie Brown, who is alienated (and knows he's alienated), Snoopy is alienating (and totally fails to recognize it). He believes that he is what he's been selling to the world. Snoopy is "so self-involved," Mendelsohn writes, "he doesn't even realize he's not human."

Just as some people thought that Charlie Brown, the insecure loser, the boy who never won the love of the Little Red-Haired Girl, was the alter ego of Schulz himself near the beginning of his career, so Snoopy could be cast as the egotistical alter ego of Schulz the world-famous millionaire, who finally found a little happiness in his second marriage and thus became insufferably cutesy. (In 1973, Schulz and his wife divorced, and a month later Schulz married Jeannie Clyde, a woman he met at the Warm Puppy Café, at his skating rink in Santa Rosa, California.) Two-legged Snoopy, with his airs and fantasies—peerless Snoopy, rich Snoopy, popular Snoopy, world-famous Snoopy, contented Snoopy—spoiled it all.

Schulz, who had a lifelong fear of being seen as ostentatious, believed that the main character of a comic strip should not be too much of a showboat. He also once said he wished he could use Charlie Brown—whom he described as the lead character every good strip needs, "somebody that you like that holds things together"—a little more.

But he was smitten with Snoopy. (During one of the Christmas ice shows in Santa Rosa, while watching Snoopy skate, Schulz leaned over and remarked to his friend Lynn Johnston, another cartoonist, "Just think . . . there was a time when there *was* no Snoopy!") Schulz, Johnston writes in an introduction to one of the Fantagraphics volumes, found his winning self in this dog:

> Snoopy was the one through which he soared. Snoopy allowed him to be spontaneous, slapstick, silly, and wild. Snoopy was rhythm, comedy, glamour, and style . . . As Snoopy, he had no failures, no losses, no flaws . . . Snoopy had friends and admirers all over the globe.

Snoopy was the polar opposite of Charlie Brown, who had nothing but failures, losses and flaws. But were the two quite so radically far apart?

SNOOPY'S CRITICS ARE wrong, and so are readers who think that Snoopy actually believes his self-delusions. Snoopy may be shallow in his way, but he's also deep, and in the end deeply alone, as deeply alone as Charlie Brown is. Grand though his flights are, many of them end with his realizing that he's tired and cold and lonely and that it's suppertime. As Schulz noted on *The Today Show* when he announced his retirement, in December 1999: "Snoopy likes to think that he's this independent dog who does all of these things and leads his own life, but he always makes sure that he never gets too far from that supper dish." He has animal needs, and he knows it, which makes him, in a word, human.

Even Snoopy's wildest daydreams have a touch of pathos. When he marches alone through the trenches of World War I, yes, of course, he is fantasizing, but he also can be seen as the bereft young Charles Schulz, shipped off to war only days after his mother died at the age of fifty, saying to him: "Goodbye, Sparky. We'll probably never see each other again."

The final comic strips, which came out when Schulz realized he was dying, are pretty heartbreaking. All of the characters seem to be trying to say goodbye, reaching for the solidarity that has always eluded them. Peppermint Patty, standing in the rain after a football game, says, "Nobody shook hands and said, 'Good game.'" Sally shouts to her brother, Charlie Brown: "Don't you believe in brotherhood?!!" Linus lets out a giant, boldface "SIGH!" Lucy, leaning as ever on Schroeder's piano, says to him, "Aren't you going to thank me?"

But it's Snoopy who is grappling with the big questions, the existential ones. Indeed, by his thought balloons alone, you might mistake him for Charlie Brown. The strip dated January 15, 2000, shows Snoopy on his doghouse. "I've been very tense lately," Snoopy thinks, rising up stiffly from his horizontal position. "I find myself worrying about everything . . . Take the Earth, for instance." He lies back down, this time on his belly, clutching his doghouse: "Here we all are clinging helplessly to this globe that is hurtling through space. . . ." Then he turns over onto his back: "What if the wings fall off?"

Snoopy may have been delusional, but in the end he knew very well that everything could come tumbling down. His very existence seems to be a way of saying that no matter what a person builds up for himself inside or outside society, everyone is basically alone in it together. By the way, in the end Snoopy did admit to at least one shortcoming, though he claimed he wasn't really to blame. In the strip that ran on January 1, 2000, drawn in shaky lines, the kids are having a great snowball fight. Snoopy sits on the sidelines, struggling to get his paws around a snowball: "Suddenly the dog realized that his dad had never taught him how to throw snowballs."

III

Two Poems

A Childhood in
Four Acts

Jill Bialosky

For Charles M. Schulz, our savior

I.

End of October,
days recede
quickly into night. Leaves
fall in slow motion.
It's Halloween.

We rummage
for a mask
to hide behind, a personality
to turn into or become.
Grief has made mother
her own strange bandit.

There are wars that must be won.

The beauty with luminescent
turquoise eyes drapes herself in mother's
pink negligee, short fur sleeping coat.
Dons a crown of plastic flowers. Princess of our desires.

The jester who makes us laugh
if mother is late getting home
paints her face white,
pulls on a stocking cap,
draws a smile turned upside down.

Draped in a white bed sheet,
cut holes for my eyes,
I get my wish.
I'm finally invisible, a ghost of myself.

We are daughters of the night,
dreaming of battles
and good deeds to perform
to trick the gods to release our
father and restore our home.

Following the train of children,
in store-bought Spider-Man, Batman,
Casper the Friendly Ghost,
we trek down the block,
walk up to stoops donned

with creepy hanging bats, skeletons,
ghoully jack-o-lanterns.

Oh no, the dark spook house.
Do we *really* have to dip
our hands into ketchup blood
and cold spaghetti guts?

Warned of razors
planted in apples, poisoned unwrapped candy,
not to be lulled into a stranger's car:
there are men that might snatch
and kill us, suddenly the world
has turned painfully dark.

The sky cracks. Thunder.
Wind rips the trees
and it rains like no other.

Leafless trees twist and rattle,
the moon weirdly orange.
Pumpkins on porch steps smashed.
Hooligans have begun to egg the windows.
It's time to go home.

Rushing past the house deemed
to belong to witches, dark all year round,
one of our brown shopping trick-or-treat bags,
weakened by rain, loses bottom.

The witch's door screeches open.
What is evil if not fear? What is childhood
if not preparation for adulthood? We run.

A monument of greed,
of longing, of desire
to hoard and not squander,
those coveted candies,
left behind and glittering on the walk,
each piece a token of all we desire
and all that will ruin us.

II.

It's the Great Pumpkin, Charlie Brown.
Lucy is the bossy older sister.
She always knows the answers.
I am Linus, the hopeful one, waiting
for the Great Pumpkin to rise.
Maybe he is god, maybe
someone to believe in. Maybe he will save us
from our desires and humiliations.
The youngest is Snoopy,
the World War Bomber fighting the Red Baron.
The girl who climbs to the top of the clubhouse
and beats her chest.
And the boy I love at school,
reincarnated into Schroeder, a beau savant,
soulful and unattainable,
deep into his piano.
Or maybe I'm Charlie Brown

who can't believe he's gotten an invitation
to Violet's party, who cuts too many holes
in his white ghost sheet, having had trouble
with the scissors, and ends up with rocks in his bag.
Why is it that one failure leads to another?
Or perhaps I'm Sally, in love with Linus.
I know I'm not Pig-Pen. Nor
as forthright as Peppermint Patty.
I don't have ringlets like the Girl with Naturally
Curly Hair. Maybe we're all misfits?
Charlie Brown's raking the leaves.
Snoopy dives in. There's Charlie Brown
waiting to kick the football, snatched away
just as he's about to kick,
head in the clouds.
And Linus in the pumpkin patch,
shivering, sucking his thumb,
blanket in one hand, waiting
for the Great Pumpkin
to rise over the pumpkin patch,
like our long-lost father
hoping he will
finally reveal himself to us.

    III.
The day before Christmas
we string popcorn and cranberry.
Hook red and green glass
bulbs and gingerbread decorations
until branches droop under the weight

of our greed for beauty and transformation.
No matter. Who gets to crown the tree
with the satin angel, a jeweled tiara or golden star?
Look. The sun comes through the clouded windows.
Maybe there will be a miracle.

We ride the rapid transit
from the suburbs to downtown's
Terminal Tower to see Mr. Jingaling
and visit the Twigbee shop
where boys and girls line
up to buy gifts. No parents allowed.

Poor Santa. He looks sad. His beard is
drooping. Not one of us
wants to sit on his knee
to ask for what we *really* want.
To want is to tempt ridicule.
Still, it's better to believe.

On the rapid home
our wrapped candle and soaps
suddenly outside the fanciful shop
look pitiful in our laps.

The spectacle of houses
decorated with colored lights flash past.
Each one grander than the other.
It's growing dark.
Snow is slowly covering the lawns

in a white protective
blanket. We are shivering and cold.

Home. We put out our plate of cookies,
glass of milk and ascend
to our rooms to wait.
One of us searches the sky.
Can reindeers fly?

IV.
Charlie Brown is depressed.
No one has sent him a Christmas card.
What is the meaning of Christmas?
Linus begins his soliloquy:
"And there were in the same country shepherds
abiding in the field, keeping watch over their flock by night.
And lo, the angel of the Lord came upon them,
and the glory of the Lord shone round about them,
and they were sore afraid. And the angel said unto them,
'Fear not, for behold, I bring you tidings of great joy
which will be to all people.
For unto you is born this day
in the city of David a savior, which is Christ the Lord.
And this shall be a sign unto you.
Ye shall find the babe wrapped in swaddling clothes
lying in the manger.' And suddenly,
there was with the angel a multitude of the heavenly host,
praising God and saying, 'Glory to God in the highest,
and on Earth peace, good will toward men.'"
Charlie Brown is skeptical.

Lucy has commanded he direct
the school play and buy a Christmas tree.
Does compassion make him choose the saddest;
are we all bound by our own peculiar fate,
minor victories and wish for ballast?
Trimmed with one red bulb
from Snoopy's decorated doghouse,
the branch with barely a needle left
droops to the ground and falls over.
I really am a blockhead, says Charlie Brown.
It is a good tree, Linus says.
All it needs is a little love.
We are all that which we might yet
become. Daughters of the night
commanders of our own legends.
And lo and behold, the gang swaps out the tree
for a better one and hark the angels sing.

Grief

Jonathan Lethem

For Linus van Pelt

I

I saw the children of my neighborhood destroyed by mangle
    comics, disease comics, and gory comics, aggravating
    hysterical fussbudgets,
dragging themselves through the sarcastic streets at dawn
    looking for an angry plaid ice cream,
angelheaded blockheads obligated to play outside whenever the
    starry dynamo in the machinery of night is shining,
who spanking and roughnecked and hollow-eyed and
    high sat up smoking in the supernatural darkness of
    second childhoods floating across the tops of suburbs
    contemplating the chromatic fantasia,
who bared their brains to the Great Pumpkin under the El and
    saw goldfishes or horses or lambs or chipmunks staggering
    on suburban roofs illuminated,
who passed through kindergarten with a piece of candy hidden

in their ear hallucinating caramel and Beethoven among
the scholars of income tax,
who were expelled from the nursery for crazy & publishing
mud pies on the windowsills of the skull,
who cowered in toy rooms in diapers, leaving their candy bars
on the sidewalk and listening to the test patterns through
the wall,
who got busted in their sandboxes for putting their hand into a
glass of milk,
who hit one another with a piece of sod or drank lemonade
in Paradise Alley, or hit their balls in the rough and were
accused of killing snakes,
every winter it's the same thing, girls in stadium boots,
incomparable blind streets of shuddering cloud and lightning
in the mind leaping toward kite-eating trees, illuminating
all the motionless world of Time between,
humiliation of bare soup, backyard green tree cemetery dawns,
balloons supposed to be round, not square, storefront
comic racks of joyride soda fountain blinking traffic light,
oh, you dirty balloon, you better come back here, trash-
can lid rantings, the hustle and bustle of the city,
to me there's nothing more depressing than the sight of an
empty old candy bag,
until the noise of wheels and children brought them down
shuddering mouth-wracked and battered bleak of brain all
drained of brilliance in the drear light of Zoo,
who sat there trying to make people think the wind is blowing,
a lost battalion of platonic tricyclists rolling along the curbs,
whose last pitches flew over the backstop and rolled down
the sewer,

yacketayakking screaming vomiting whispering facts and

memories and anecdotes and eyeball kicks and shocks of

taxes, theology, tadpoles, tamales, time-tables, tea and

Tennessee Ernie,

who sat listening to the ocean roar, supposed to be home

taking a nap, scared of a piece of fuzz on the sidewalk,

suffering Eastern sweats and bubble gum—chewings and

migraines of macaroni under candy-withdrawal on bleak

curbs,

who drew a line clear around the world wondering where to

go, and went, leaving no broken hearts,

who just when you began to learn the technique your parents

took away your blanket,

who studied muskrat or mole? Mackerel? Or maybe mouse?

Magna charts? Mahler telepathy and bop kabbalah because

the cosmos instinctively vibrated at their feet,

who loned it through the streets here on earth among millions

of people, while that tiny star was out there alone among

millions of stars,

who thought they were only aggravating when thirty-three

marshmallows gleamed in supernatural ecstasy,

who was doomed to go through life with nothing but a face face,

who lounged, all nervous and tense, with nothing more

relaxing than to lie with your head in your water dish,

who put the girl in charge of the salt mines leaving behind

nothing but the shadow of dungarees and the lava and ash

of poetry,

whose poem is supposed to have feeling, whose poem couldn't

touch anyone's heart, whose poem couldn't make anyone

cry,

who gets depressed because he doesn't know how to turn the
set on,

who while eating supper was fooling around and was told "try to
act like a human being" and replied "define human being,"

who broke down crying in white gymnasiums naked and
trembling before the machinery of other skeletons,

who bit parents in the neck and shrieked with delight in cribs
for committing no crime but their own wild cooking
pederasty and intoxication,

who was a mess when he ate and a mess when he played and a
mess when just standing still, but was at least consistent,

who let themselves be fucked in the ass by saintly
motorcyclists, now what brought that on? Are you out
of your mind? What are you trying to do, disgrace our
family? Oh, the humiliation of it all, we'll probably have
to move out of the neighborhood.

who went untouched and unmarred by modern civilization,

who hiccuped endlessly trying to giggle but wound up with a
sob handing out lists of people's faults,

who without your blanket would crack like a piece of old
bamboo,

who is just about to starve to death when his grandma comes
up with a baked-bean hot dish! The little kid wonders
where the beans came from . . . then he notices something!
His bean-bag is missing!

who if somebody likes you, he pats you on the head—if he
doesn't like you he kicks you,

who learned in medical circles the application of a spiritual
tourniquet,

who wept at the romance of Halloween with their paper bags

full of rocks and bad music, who said these rocks are
    especially groomed to be hurled in anger!
who sat in boxes breathing in the darkness, always felt sorry for
    amoebas, and in all the excitement forgot to feed the dog,
who wasn't sure whether he was going to end up in an
    orphanage or the humane society under the tubercular sky
    surrounded by orange crate racers of theology,
sometimes I think I'm a kind of vacant lot myself!
who scribbled all night rocking and rolling over lofty
    incantations which in the yellow morning were stanzas of
    gibberish, paypur, dore, howse, welkum, nice, spune!
awl this reeding is hard one mi eyes!
who cooked rotten animals lung heart feet tail dreaming of the
    pure vegetable kingdom, boy, I'm glad I'm not a lizard! I
    wonder if there are any dogs on the moon?
who plunged themselves under meat trucks looking for an egg,
    whose stomach has matured early,
who last year was the only person you knew who had three
    hundred and sixty-five bad days,
who threw their watches off the roof to "see time fly," & alarm
    clocks fell on their heads every day for the next decade,
in all the world there's nothing more inspiring than the sight
    of someone who has just been taken off the hook!
who shot him behind the Davenport this actually happened
    and if that isn't fatal I don't know what is,
who had to erect some sort of mental fence to keep unpleasant
    news out of his mind,
and who therefore ran along the icy sidewalks obsessed with a
    sudden set of flashcards, only three years old and forced to
    go commercial,

who barreled down the sidewalks of the past journeying to each
    other's sandbox-Pig-Pen-solitude or first-leaf-to-die watch,
who tricycled seventy-two hours to find out if I had a vision or
    you had a vision or he had a vision just to find out insults
    seem to travel farther when the air is thin,
who nervous, lacking confidence, stupid and with poor taste
    and absolutely no sense of design,
yet the type of personality that will probably inspire a heroic
    symphony, a personality so simple that it defies analysis,
a fourteen-carat blockhead, a blockhead, a nitwit, a
    numbskull!
I'm only trying to give Charlie Brown a little destructive
    criticism! Did you ever see a thief with such a round head?
I've been confused from the day I was born,
I have never pretended to be able to solve moral issues, I'm
    only human, I was an only dog, maybe I could blame it on
    society!
ah, Linus, while you are not safe I am not safe, and now you're
    really in the total animal soup of time—
you're the only one who will follow me wherever I go!
if I were the only girl on earth, would you like me?
when you're a dog you don't have to worry like
    that . . . everything is clear cut, they're just imitation
    people,
I've never really seen an eclipse, that lemonade is full of weeds,
    what would you do if the moon fell right on your head?
can a person tear aside the veil of the future?
how about a pail of sand, old friend? to re-create the syntax of
    poor human prose and stand before you aggravating and
    doomed and shaking with shame,

putting down here what might be left to say in time come after
   death, the life you save may be a fussbudget,
and rising sort of tender-hearted, unable to bear to see the
   frightened faces of crazy salesmen,
with the absolute heart of the poem of life butchered out of
   their own bodies good to eat a thousand years,
the wrong person fell off that tricycle!

II

What sphinx of tangled kite string and aluminum bashed open
   their skulls and ate up their brains and imagination?
Mahler! Solitude! Murders! Robberies! Automobile accidents!
   Trash-can lids and unobtainable candy bars! Children
   screaming under the stairways! Boys sobbing in the
   outfield!
Don't forget about kicking dogs! People are always kicking
   dogs too!
Mahler! Mahler! Nightmare of Mahler! Mahler the wishy-
   washy! Mental Mahler! Mahler the broadminded!
Mahler the incomprehensible recess! Mahler whose trees are
   judgment! Mahler the vast kite of disappointment! Mahler
   the slow approaching doom!
Mahler whose mind is pure machinery! Mahler that's no bug,
   that's just a mark on the sidewalk! Mahler it says here that
   young people of today don't believe in any cause! Mahler
   the hearing of a great truth always stuns me! Mahler
   there's nothing sacred to songwriters anymore!
Mahler I'll bet you didn't realize that family life was so
   mathematical! Why the theological implications alone are
   staggering!

Mahler whose love is endless oil and stone! Mahler I hear
someone talking but I don't see a soul! Mahler whose
poverty is the specter of genius! Mahler you're the
only person I know who can hear someone eating
marshmallows!

Mahler in whom I sit lonely! Mahler in whom I dream Angels!
Crazy in Mahler! Pneumonia in Mahler! Lacklove and
manless in Mahler!

Mahler who entered my soul early! Mahler in whom I am a
consciousness without a body! Mahler you can't help it if
you play stupidly! Mahler whom I abandon! Wake up in
Mahler! The storm rages as the hundred-foot waves smash
against the ship!

Mahler! Mahler! Robot apartments! invisible suburbs!
Everyone has the potentialities of a hero or goat lying
within them!

They broke their backs lifting Mahler to Heaven! Pavements,
trees, radios, weak ankles!

Rats! Whoosh! Clomp! The whole boatload of sensitive
bullshit! You expect me to believe that the sun is a ball of
fire?

Breakthroughs! over the river! flips and crucifixions! This
is for hot summer nights! And this is for cold winter
mornings! And this is for lies and broken promises!

This peanut butter sandwich has jelly on the edges! You cut my
peanut butter sandwich with a knife that had jelly on it!

Real holy laughter in the river! They saw it all! the wild eyes!
the holy yells! They bade farewell! They jumped off the
roof! to solitude! waving! carrying flowers! Down to the
river! into the street!

If I stood on this chair, do you suppose I could touch the sun?
These rocks are a release for my pent-up emotions!

III
Linus van Pelt! I'm with you in Ace Hospital
   where you're madder than I am
I'm with you in Ace Hospital
   where you'll never be happy until you've won a hundred
      thousand games
I'm with you in Ace Hospital
   where when you play second fiddle too long, it makes your
      stomach hurt
I'm with you in Ace Hospital
   where spite candy never tastes very good
I'm with you in Ace Hospital
   where as long as you've got insomnia you'll never graduate
I'm with you in Ace Hospital
   where we are great writers on the same dreadful typewriter
I'm with you in Ace Hospital
   where you believe in love at twenty-third sight
I'm with you in Ace Hospital
   where your condition has become serious and is reported
      on the radio
I'm with you in Ace Hospital
   where the black keys of your piano are just painted on
I'm with you in Ace Hospital
   where your humor is too subtle for the average reader
I'm with you in Ace Hospital
   Where it must be frustrating to be able to run that fast and
      have no place to go

I'm with you in Ace Hospital

    where you've never heard another song that depresses me
      the way this one does

I'm with you in Ace Hospital

    where there's only one thing more useless than yesterday's
      newspaper

I'm with you in Ace Hospital

    where you keep your pockets full of water

I'm with you in Ace Hospital

    where they're making clouds prettier all the time

I'm with you in Ace Hospital

    where there's no sense in doing a lot of barking if you don't
      really have anything to say

I'm with you in Ace Hospital

    where we both dislike the same thing about Charlie Brown

I'm with you in Ace Hospital

    where some days you think you know

        everything . . . imaginary walls collapse . . . some days
        you think maybe you don't know anything . . . O skinny
        legions run outside . . . some days you know a few
        things . . . O starry-spangled shock of mercy the eternal
        war is here . . . some days you don't even know how old
        you are . . . O victory forget your underwear we're free

I'm with you in Ace Hospital

    in my dreams you try wearing the kite and flying your cap
      across America in tears to the door of my cottage in the
      Western night

Claremont, 2018
All verbiage Ginsberg 1955–56 or Schulz 1952–59

IV

Off the Page

A Charlie Brown
Thanksgiving

Rick Moody

The sweatshirt I wore in the mid-sixties was a Snoopy sweatshirt; Snoopy caught in the act of surfing, and I think the
color of the sweatshirt was a pale blue, and I believe Snoopy was
going from right to left, on a wave that wasn't quite cresting,
and I believe the thought bubble (let us now celebrate Snoopy
and those thought bubbles) said COWABUNGA!

In reproductions I have located online, Snoopy's surfboard
is yellow with a red racing stripe, but my recollection of my
sweatshirt is that it was two- or three-color printing and there
was no yellow, or red. I cannot recall how the sweatshirt came
to me, only that it became well-worn.

Two further items stand out in this matter of the sweatshirt. First, that Snoopy was going from right to left, that is
against a left-to-right Western reading directionality, and, second, that "Cowabunga!" is apparently an expression that owes
its prominence to *The Howdy Doody Show*, a television program

from the 1950s. It was apparently uttered by an indigenous character (played by a white guy), a Native American person, an "Indian," on *The Howdy Doody Show*, and this, it is fair to say, is utterly dubious and politically insensitive. I knew nothing about *Howdy Doody* as a child in the suburbs of Connecticut, although I think I understood that it involved puppets. I probably could not have grasped that Snoopy altered the utterance of Chief Thunderthud of *Howdy Doody*, by altering "Cowabonga!" to "Cowabunga!" No doubt on purpose. (A subtle shade-throwing gesture at Howdy Doody?) I perhaps did not even understand surfing entirely either, as the closest large body of water to my address was the Long Island Sound. It featured ripples, not waves.

I did, however, revere Snoopy. The *Peanuts* story for me commences with the fact that my grandfather was upper-level management at a New York City metro-area newspaper that had a big comics section on weekends. His newspaper, the *New York Daily News*, which was politically objectionable in many ways, was undeniably great in the matter of comics. To my grandfather's credit, even though he was intimidating and much given to opinions of a conservative variety, he really *loved* the comics, or at least paid close attention to them, as he did to everything that ran in the *New York Daily News*.

I began reading *Peanuts,* then, in the comics, along with *Dick Tracy* and some other syndications of the period (*Family Circus*, e.g.), as soon as I could read, which was in the early to mid-1960s. My delight in the anarchy of Snoopy, the unrestrained imagination and acting-out and rising-above of Snoopy, was immediate. Snoopy's anarchic cool was precisely childlike, his refusal to be contained was childlike, his assuming and casting off of identities (World War I flying ace, etc.) was childlike. For me he was easy to love.

Perhaps I liked Snoopy to keep adults from understanding how much I identified with Charlie Brown. All the sad horrible awkwardnesses of Charlie Brown felt like my awkardnesses, namely failure at social engagement, mediocrity at sports, and so on. In other words, having a powerful identification with Snoopy was *aspirational*. The star-crossed depressive cast of Charlie Brown only dawned on me later.

If the apex of the *Peanuts* phenomenon was the late sixties and early seventies, I was perfectly situated for it. The unfurling of the strip into the counterculture, with the addition of the bird named Woodstock, its tentative beginnings with inclusion and diversity (see Franklin, below), these were all happening as my friends were growing up themselves, and commencing into the ferment of the Revolution. We were, in a way, the perfect audience. And perhaps appropriately we helped propel what was the very pinnacle of *Peanuts* as a cultural force: its television specials.

I cannot overstate how important two of these *Peanuts* specials were to me and those I knew well, namely *A Charlie Brown Christmas* (1965) and *It's the Great Pumpkin, Charlie Brown* (1966). They are still classics, these programs, and justifiably so, but they were more than classics to us, they were incredible aesthetic milestones to those of us who beheld them then. They were as important to me as the Beatles.

May I enumerate some of the aspects of greatness to be found in the *Peanuts* television specials? The television shows were important because we finally got to see the *Peanuts* gang move a little bit, and we heard their voices, which, no matter who played them, were always noteworthy for a slight low-affect nasality, and a slowmo line-reading style that defined child actors for decades to come. Also, there was the *music* of the original *Peanuts* television specials. Without Vince Guaraldi, there would be no *Peanuts* in the way that we understand it now. And this is because Vince Guaraldi understood something thematically that was happening in the strips, and managed to convey that in the music. He found the perfect musical analogue for Schulz's incremental narrative development, the spaciousness, the meditative pacing of *Peanuts*, the blue melancholy of Charlie Brown and the gang. Somehow Guaraldi captured all of that. It is in part the open space in his ensemble, the jazz trio sound, the jazz trio of the West Coast variety after Chet Baker and *Birth of the Cool*. This musical space and room to move has to do with Guaraldi's own compositional vocabulary, which is highly melodic, and accessible, and inflected with a lot of different impulses. He seems to have pop, R&B, blues, jazz, and Latin music all readily available to him.

The simplicity of the "Linus and Lucy" musical theme is an indicator of all of this, the fusion of Guaraldi and Schulz into one Wagnerian *gesamtkunstwerk* of cartoon perfection, but you need a larger musical sample, for example, the entirety of the *Charlie Brown Christmas* soundtrack, e.g., to see how incredible was Guaraldi's understanding of the pathos and fragility of Schulz's original. It is still, for me, impossible not to weep over "Christmas Time Is Here," from the *Charlie Brown Christmas* soundtrack. It's chromatic, it's sophisticated, but it's also so open and spare and moving as to be a thing of beauty to children of any age.

The other great development in the cartoon broadcasts of the mid-sixties was the portrayal of adults. The famous *trombone voice* of the teachers and adults in these early *Peanuts* specials said something that all of us growing up then knew and felt—that parent talk was gibberish, alien and laughable—but which had never been spelled out as effectively as here. In the strips, of course, the parents simply didn't exist. But in a more narrative environment it was inevitable that once the storytelling grew more complex, finding a way to render parental gibberish was a necessity, and the *trombone voice* did it in one perfect and unassailable gesture.

Narratively, *It's the Great Pumpkin, Charlie Brown* and *A Charlie Brown Christmas* were excellent and hilarious tragicomedies, too. And we can think of moments like Sally haranguing Linus for making her stay out all night in vain to behold the Great Pumpkin, or Charlie Brown killing his little Christmas sapling—or believing he had killed it—as transformational moments for our understanding of children and holidays generally in the 1960s. Linus's reading aloud from the St. Luke account of the first Christmas in *A Charlie Brown Christmas*—he starts by saying, "Sure, Charlie Brown, I can tell you what Christmas is about"—has in recollection taught me more about what I imagine we're supposed to be doing on that fraught holiday than any other piece of art ever made.

That I felt this enthusiastic about all things *Peanuts* from 1966 to 1973 or so is not terribly unusual, especially given my family's attachment to the Sunday comics. What's more surprising is how much distaste I felt for *Peanuts* as a young adult.

Did Charles M. Schulz fail me, in the late seventies and early eighties? Or did I fail him? Somehow the simplicity of the strips, their often muted punchlines, the repetition of narrative themes—Snoopy and his anarchy, Lucy and her vanity, Charlie

Brown and his never-ending bad luck—these tendencies on the part of the *Peanuts* strip were, it seemed to me, *predictable* in the eighties and were evidence that Schulz was losing his touch, wasn't as fully engaged with the culture as he had been. And so he wasn't talking to me, the recently graduated thrift-store-clothes-wearing, self-inflicted-haircut-wearing, Jacques Derrida– and Roland Barthes–reading, Jean-Luc Godard– and Douglas Sirk–watching, punk- and hardcore-listening college graduate. What a surprise!

But *Peanuts* was just like it was before, back when I loved it. The collected strips of 1979–1980, for example, reveal the same incremental storytelling of before, the same punchlines that feel less like punchlines and more like morsels of spiritual wisdom, and the occasional narrative bomb blast (Peppermint Patty and Pig-Pen share a brief romance in 1980!) rising up out of the reiterations. If anything, Schulz got funnier, and fewer strips felt as though he didn't really know how to *end*.

One feature of the mid-eighties cannot be ignored, however, and that was the beginning of the mass merchandising of the *Peanuts* gang, and in particular their relationship with the corporation known as Metropolitan Life. It is possible that such a decision, a decision to turn over the characters that Schulz worked so hard at to an enormous corporation, was the right thing for Schulz's heirs and for the *brand,* but for an early adherent of the strips, faced with the ubiquity of the Metropolitan Life advertising campaign, it was hard not to feel like what was good about Charlie Brown and his confreres had become a commodity to be bought and sold. And that would perhaps have been how I felt about it in perpetuity, if not for an event in 2009.

Namely, that I became a father.

It is a well-known irony of parenting that children will reject some or all of any legacy material that you send their way. This is especially true with music. For example, I worked very hard to make my daughter aware of the Beach Boys, and, at a certain point in her life, she could name all of the original members of that band and could describe in detail her crush on the drummer. But these days in her world it's all Ariana Grande and Katy Perry. The same proved true with many books of my childhood. My revelatory experience with *Where the Wild Things Are* has never been duplicated in the lives of my two children. And so far no child of mine has ever given a shit about *The Last of the Curlews*. I have attempted to make *Chitty Chitty Bang Bang* and *Oliver!* memorable oldies-programming for my children, but the DVDs, apparently culturally or technologically bypassed, have rarely if ever been watched.

But something happened with my daughter and *Peanuts*. Her first choice for reading is always graphic novels or comics, and so she was already headed in that direction with *Garfield,* e.g. And so at a certain point I started showing her the *Peanuts* television specials. It was an immensely gratifying experience to watch her sink her teeth into those works (and even into *The Charlie Brown and Snoopy Show,* the eighties animated television weekly that has not necessarily been a starting point for anyone), and to take to them completely. As is often the case with my daughter, once she finds a television program she likes, she can watch it innumerable times, to the point of reciting. And thus it came to pass that I saw anew *A Charlie Brown Thanksgiving* and its strange companion piece, *The Mayflower Voyagers*, an episode of a later experiment involving showing events in American history peopled with *Peanuts* characters. In fact, I have now seen these Thanksgiving broadcasts many, many, many times.

As it happens, I once wrote a reasonably well-known Thanksgiving scene myself, in a novel called *The Ice Storm,* which was then made into a rather good scene in a film of the same name. And having accomplished that, I have put Thanksgiving scenes into almost every one of my books (there's a Thanksgiving-in-space passage in my novel *The Four Fingers of Death*). So it was eerie, perhaps, and satisfying that my daughter became so taken with the Thanksgiving episodes of *Peanuts.* But more interesting still is how great these works came to seem to me now.

A Charlie Brown Thanksgiving does touch on many of the classic *Peanuts* themes, but there are several standout passages that should be mentioned in any celebratory account. For example, there is a scene in which Snoopy, at Linus van Pelt's instigation, pulls a lot of junk out of a garage in order to make a table for an outdoor Thanksgiving feast. The sequence lasts for three minutes, and is slugged to a beautiful lazy jazz/soul ballad by Vince Guaraldi called "Little Birdie," whose lyric more or less narrates the action of the sequence. The 1973 amendments to Guaraldi's classic *Peanuts* orchestrations are of note here: *lots of horns.* And Guaraldi sings "Little Birdie" himself, sort of like Bill Withers.

My daughter loved the fight that develops in this sequence between Snoopy and a certain deck chair. A deck chair that Snoopy attempts to set beside the ping-pong table that is to serve for the holiday repast. The deck chair somehow, because of its design, becomes animated, looks human, and it *attacks* Snoopy, who has no choice but to attempt to subdue it. The battle is pitched, the combatants are evenly matched! Snoopy bites the deck chair, the deck chair smacks Snoopy over the head with its canvas seat. They close in for the kill! Eventually, after many twists and turns, and many fine sound effects, Snoopy proves victorious.

A similar later sequence, by which I mean a sequence heavily indebted both to silent film and the Warner Brothers cartoons of the 1930s and 1940s, depicts Snoopy as chef preparing the Thanksgiving feast, which seems to comprise a mere four items: toast, popcorn, pretzels, and candy. The popcorn swells to take up most of the kitchen. The toast stack grows ever taller, wobbling. And at one point, Woodstock accidentally puts Snoopy's ear in the toaster. He tries to butter the smoldering ear.

These passages are classic *Peanuts* television slapstick, and they were enough to capture the attention of my fickle and contemporary daughter, but what of the exceedingly poignant moments that rose up to assault me the middle-aged spectator who resisted *Peanuts* for some thirty years? What are the poignant moments in *A Charlie Brown Thanksgiving*?

It is just after Snoopy's misbegotten culinary efforts, when the whole gang settles down for Thanksgiving (Peppermint Patty, Marcie, and Franklin, et al., having invited themselves over for this purpose, Van Pelts also in attendance), and Peppermint Patty is horrified to behold the menu items that Snoopy has served up. She gives a long, somewhat vindictive speech about how toast, pretzel sticks, and popcorn are not suitable Thanksgiving fare, about how the appropriate items must include *cranberry,* to the immense shame of Charlie Brown. It is then given to Marcie to attempt to cheer him up ("Thanksgiving is more than eating, Chuck"), and to give the traditional *Peanuts* summary of the whole episode: "Those early pilgrims were thankful for what had happened to them, and if they could be thankful, then we should be thankful too."

Not really funny at all, this part of *A Charlie Brown Thanksgiving*, rather tinged with the intense vulnerability of Schulz's protagonist, and not morally prescriptive, so much as involving a recalibration of aspects of holiday living that are shallow, and replacing them, ever so gently, with more emotionally enduring perceptions about gratitude. Thereafter, Charlie Brown secures an agreement from his trombone grandmother to bring all the kids to her house for an actual Thanksgiving meal, featuring, we may suppose, cranberry. Off they go (in a station wagon), leaving behind Snoopy and Woodstock to celebrate together, with turkey, in an end-credit sequence which as others have noted involves avian cannibalism, as Woodstock eats some turkey, too.

On the DVD in question, *A Charlie Brown Thanksgiving* is then followed immediately by the very strange *Mayflower Voyagers*, which is similarly animated (directed by Bill Melendez, who did all the classic *Peanuts* television specials), and which features the *Peanuts* gang wearing pilgrim garb, as well as Renaissance Fair–style arrangements of Guaraldi's "Linus and Lucy." My daughter always wanted to watch this program, too, perhaps for the moment when the pilgrims and the First Peoples get together for their feast. *The Mayflower Voyagers* is turgid and oddly conceived, as it has various *Peanuts* characters getting seasick and nearly dying of starvation, but the whole of these two episodes, taken as one, lobby for a purposeful and intentional Thanksgiving, no matter the contemporary historical anxieties about the origin thereof. They have a cumulative impact that leads one to the very conception of the holiday.

Who was really learning in this experience of beholding anew the *Charlie Brown Thanksgiving* program I'm describing? My daughter who was coming to understand the Schulzian tragicomedy for the first time, with its melancholy echoes of Buster Keaton and W. C. Fields? Was it she who was learning, or was it I, who forsook Schulz and his genius in my callow youth, and who couldn't see the truly human wisdom of the *Peanuts* gang until I could see it through the eyes of my own child? I was the one who knew a thing experientially and then unlearned it in the pursuit of being *modern,* but who can now see again, having been taught by my child. The story I'm telling here has itself the broad outlines of a Schulz narrative, with the poignant part at the end, because it is both gentle and human, and involves humility. The moment of learning, whenever it comes, is a thing to be grateful for, and the pride that precedes it is always worth a sympathetic laugh.

The Gospel
According to Linus (I)

Rich Cohen

Every American generation has its own religion, a common faith made of superstitions, teams, events, jokes, slang, movies—its pop culture. For my father, who was born in 1933, it was a bible written by the two Franks—Sinatra and Capra. In my formative years, which ran from the mid-seventies to the mid-eighties, it included David Letterman and Bruce Springsteen but was centered by *Peanuts*, the world drawn by the cartoonist Charles Schulz: Lucy, Linus, and Charlie Brown, a Job who suffered to soothe our suffering. It was a faith related via parable, the classic text being the TV special *It's the Great Pumpkin, Charlie Brown*.

We think of *Peanuts* as familiar and safe, old hat, but it was cutting-edge for its time. It had grown out of a newspaper comic drawn by a sweet blond-haired genius from Minnesota, home of F. Scott Fitzgerald and Bob Dylan, who turned the quotidian troubles of childhood into a picture poem, an opéra bouffe. What started in *The St. Paul Pioneer Press* as a comic called *Li'l Folks* would, as *Peanuts*, expand across dozens of years and hundreds of papers, the last daily frames running on January 3, 2000, five weeks before Schulz's death. It was fully formed by the 1950s. All those faces, all those idiosyncrasies: Charlie Brown and his expectation of defeat, Lucy and her certitude, Schroeder and his music, Pig-Pen and his dirt. Those angst-ridden characters probably did as much as anything to create the modern American sense of childhood, which, within a generation, would consume the world. The line from *Peanuts* to *The Simpsons* is meandering but not indirect.

The golden age began in 1965, when the first TV special—*A Charlie Brown Christmas*—was broadcast on CBS. Not only was it a success, but it was strange and wildly influential. It was the look of the show, the jazzy score of Vince Guaraldi, how the characters moved, spoke, and danced, and of course the message, which was nakedly religious in a way that's currently unimaginable, all those misadventures—the commercialism, the small tree, the dog—leading to the transcendent moment when Linus recites "The Annunciation of the Shepherds" from the gospel of Luke:

> And there were in the same country shepherds abiding in the field, keeping watch over their flock by night.

> And, lo, the angel of the Lord came upon them, and the glory of the Lord shone round about them: and they were sore afraid.

And the angel said unto them, Fear not; for, behold, I bring you tidings of great joy, which shall be to all people.

For unto you is born this day in the city of David a Savior, which is Christ the Lord.

And this shall be a sign unto you: Ye shall find the babe wrapped in swaddling clothes, lying in a manger.

And suddenly there was with the angel a multitude of the heavenly host praising God, and saying,

"Glory to God in the highest, and on earth peace and goodwill towards men."

When CBS ordered its third *Peanuts* special in 1966—this followed a second special, *Charlie Brown's All-Stars*—producer Lee Mendelson and director Bill Melendez were given something close to total freedom, which they used to invert the medium in all kinds of ways. They chose Halloween over Thanksgiving or Christmas as a subject, then built the story around an oddball of a strip Schulz had written years before. In it, Linus, the most sensitive of the Peanuts, the artist of the group, a searcher with a security blanket which he carries as a preacher carries a Bible, writes a letter, asking for succor from "the Great Pumpkin" as another might ask for succor from Santa or Jesus. Schulz had apparently created this pumpkin deity—he visits children on Halloween—out of thin air, possibly as a parody of Christmas, possibly a metaphor for belief.

And it is a faith. In it, the believer, who seems to be only Linus, seeks to achieve a state of perfect "sincerity"—that word is used again and again; Linus seeks the most sincere pumpkin patch to serve as Gethsemane—which will be rewarded, in the hours before dawn, by a visit from the Great Pumpkin, who will hover over the patch as the Tetragrammaton hovered over the waters. ("Each year the Great Pumpkin rises out of the pumpkin patch he thinks is the most sincere," Linus explains.) It's belief that makes Linus a laughingstock, a figure of pity and contempt. If you believe deeply in anything, you become vulnerable and look foolish—that's what the show would be about. The passion of Linus van Pelt, degradation and humiliation, refusal to submit.

The special aired on October 27, 1966, preempting *My Three Sons,* a great confusing show that deserves its own exegesis. It was a huge hit, earning close to a 50 percent Nielsen share, meaning nearly half the switched-on TVs in America were switched on to *Peanuts.* (The other half were switched to *Bonanza*; additional competition included *Star Trek* and *The Dating Game.*) The show opens with Linus carrying home a pumpkin, which Lucy cuts and guts, causing Linus to scream, "I didn't know you were going to kill it." A festival meant to end with the ascent of a Great Pumpkin has begun with the execution of a regular pumpkin. In other words, Death and Resurrection. From the first, you know the show is different, unique. The art is nearly Expressionist in the way it depicts autumn: the colors and jagged brushstrokes, the vivid October sky, which bleeds like a bruise. Many things that would become familiar made their TV debut on that special. Lucy pulling the football away from Charlie Brown, Lucy bobbing for apples. This is when Snoopy broke out of the strip, when the Beagle became bigger than his show—a trajectory followed by a handful of tangential TV characters. Think Arthur Fonzarelli on *Happy Days*. The background player who becomes the star. The audience cheers whenever he enters. It began when Snoopy turned up costumed as a World War I flying ace, which became an alter ego, a mirror of the aggression and glee inside every fan. That dog touched something in us. It was his split between body and soul, animal and spirit. The key moment comes as he stands beside Schroeder's piano, reacting to marches and waltzes, going from happy to sad. When the music turns especially moody, Snoopy lets out an aching howl, then quickly covers his mouth, ashamed. He's betrayed his hound-dog nature, the animal buried beneath aviator cap and goggles. That's when Snoopy became Fonzie who was really just Elvis. Snoopy was the kid-nation version of the King. And the Great Pumpkin special was the kid-nation version of the King on *The Ed Sullivan Show*. Yes, it would turn hokey later, take up bodysuits and chains and diadems, jump the shark, but the pure thing was still there, even if hidden, right up to the end.

Of course, the center of the show was Linus, mocked as he writes the Great Pumpkin: "Everyone tells me you're a fake, but I believe in you. P.S. If you really are a fake, don't tell me. I don't want to know." When his sister Lucy and the others go off to trick-or-treat, when they go off to Mardi Gras, Linus descends into the wilderness of the pumpkin patch, where he will spend the night in a kind of prayer, seeking to achieve the kind of honest belief that will summon the spirit. Only Sally joins him, but her motive is not pure. She is doing it for Linus, but Linus is doing it for his god. In the end, she too betrays him, leaving him chattering in the cold, waiting for what will never arrive.

Lucy retrieves her brother at 4 A.M., leads him home, and puts him to bed. In one of the most tender moments ever captured on TV, she takes off his socks, for only when the feet are free can the spirit rest. Though Linus has been disappointed and his god has not risen, he sleeps the sleep of the righteous. It's the same sleep as that of the fisherman at the end of *The Old Man and the Sea*. He's spent and the sharks have devoured the tarpon, but the prize was never the catch. It was the quest, the effort and the suffering. In the final frame, Charlie Brown tells Linus that he can shed his embarrassment and shame, the price being only his belief. Linus chooses shame over apostasy.

For many, the special offered a pagan vision. Schulz himself, who taught Sunday school and clearly drew on Christianity in constructing the scenario (Gethsemane, Death and Resurrection), once described the special as "sacrilegious." What is Halloween, after all, if not an idolatrous cult, and what is Linus's letter writing if not a pantheistic prayer made to an old-time nature god? John Updike dismissed the Great Pumpkin as "travesty if not blasphemy." I came across a sermon on *The Entire Gospel* website that used the special to show the fate of those who worship false gods. Linus follows a nature god instead of Jesus, and look where it leaves him. Chattering alone in the cold. "Some believe genuine faith in *anything* is good enough," Emily Jennings writes. "Some Christians believe the key to a successful Christian life is having *more* faith in Jesus. Both are wrong. Faith, as small as a mustard seed, *placed in the right object*, is all the faith God requires. Sitting in a pumpkin patch this Halloween will not produce the Great Pumpkin no matter how sincere you are. We need more than sincere belief—we need the truth. There is only One who is truth."

But to me, the Great Pumpkin *is* about sincerity—that word is key. In the end, it's what you believe but also the sincerity of that belief that can give your life meaning. Sincere belief can order an otherwise formless succession of days, and it is meaningful days, collected together, that add up to a meaningful life.

How Innocence Became Cool

Vince Guaraldi, *Peanuts*, and How Jazz Momentarily Captured Childhood

Gerald Early

I. The Song of Innocence and Experience

> The world's great pop songs burrow into the
> brain like little mind-worms, forever attach-
> ing themselves to a memory of what we were
> doing the first time we heard them: what we
> were eating, smelling, tasting; who we were
> with at that precise moment. Such songs be-
> come a part of the permanent record of our
> lives.
>
> —Derrick Bang, *Vince Guaraldi at*
> *the Piano*, 2012[1]

ENGINEER: Okay, I'm recording. What do
you call it?

VINCE GUARALDI: "Cast Your Fate to the
Wind," take one.

ENGINEER: Cast your what?

—Fabricated dialogue from
the documentary *Anatomy of a Hit* (1963),
about how "Cast Your Fate to the Wind"
became a commercial success

It must have been in November 1962. At least that is the way
I remember it. It was a cold, cloudy Sunday afternoon in Philadelphia and WDAS was on the radio. I had not long before
returned from church and was glad that Louise Williams's gospel show was finally over. On most black AM stations on Sunday, all one heard for a good portion of any Sunday was black
gospel music. I did not hate this music—as an adult I realized
I absorbed enormous amounts of it without knowing, almost
against my will. I was indifferent to it and thought of it as the
music for black religious women who went to Baptist and Pen-
tecostal churches. I was young and, as the young like to think,
different from the others. WDAS's programming had returned
to the black R&B and teen hits of the day. And in the mix of
Chubby Checker, the Orlons, the Marvelettes, Ray Charles,
and Sam Cooke, it was then that I heard for the first time Vince
Guaraldi's "Cast Your Fate to the Wind." I was startled beyond
all telling.

It is true that one rarely heard a jazz instrumental on a

black AM radio station (or a white Top 40 station, for that matter). But jazz was hardly new to me at that time. As a baby boomer I am a member of the last generation of Americans to hear jazz on the radio, as there were still jazz radio stations during my childhood, and to hear jazz casually or subliminally on television in detective shows, such as Blake Edwards's *Peter Gunn* (1958–1961), whose theme, written by Henry Mancini who was in fact more inspired by rock than jazz in writing it, became hugely popular as a hip jazz hook; *M Squad* (1957–1960), starring Lee Marvin, with a theme by Count Basie and often scored by jazz composer and saxophonist Benny Carter; or *Johnny Staccato* (1959), where the detective was a jazz pianist who worked out of a nightclub. (I remember these shows as being particularly popular with the black adults who made up my childhood world; whether their appeal was partly connected to the jazz scoring is something to consider.) I also recall variety shows that had jazz performances (pianist Errol Garner, performing while atop a telephone book, is someone I remember vividly, and of course there was the ubiquitous Louis Armstrong and the regal Duke Ellington appearing on *The Ed Sullivan Show* several times). And of course jazz or something that seemed like it was featured in movie soundtracks, especially crime or noir movies, B movies which were still playing as second features at the movie houses I went to in my youth. (*Murder, Inc.*, a 1960 gangster film that featured Sarah Vaughan as a nightclub singer, comes to mind as an example which I saw four or five times as a kid.) So, growing up, I heard a great deal of jazz, recognized it instantly as jazz when I heard it, but responded to it with considerable indifference. It seemed to be bar music, nightclub music, late-night music, in short, adult music of the worst sort, a kind of abstract series of something approaching sound effects and boring solos, and it meant very little to me.

Nor was I unaccustomed to instrumental music on black and Top 40 radio. Percy Faith's "Theme from *A Summer Place*" from Delmer Daves's 1959 film, Dave "Baby" Cortez's "The Happy Organ" (1959), Duane Eddy's "Rebel Rouser" (1958), The Champs' "Tequila" (1958), and Ferante and Teicher's version of Ernest Gold's "Theme from *Exodus*" from the 1960 Otto Preminger film were all highly successful commercial instrumentals that I heard all the time. My mother loved pianist Roger Williams's highly orchestrated version of "Maria," the song from *West Side Story*, the only musical I know of that she liked. She bought the single and played it all the time for a while. (Williams's rendition reached number 48 on the Billboard Top 100 in 1961.) I experienced my share of pop instrumental music. In fact, when I and another boy were once asked in grade school to bring in a good dance record for the class to dance to during recess, we both brought instrumentals that were popular on black radio at the time: I, with "Wiggle Wobble" by Les Cooper and the Soul Rockers, and my classmate, with "Green Onions" by Booker T. and the MGs (both 1962). But none of the instrumental music I heard on AM radio prepared me for "Cast Your Fate to the Wind," which sounded like nothing I had heard before.

I was so overwhelmed, caught so unawares, when I first heard it that I scarcely believed that I *had* heard it or what I had heard. I did not even hear the title of the record or the name of the artist because of the unexpectedness of it. I immediately wanted to hear it again and knew that if I waited patiently it would be played again within the next two hours. All the songs rotated that way. I suffered through all the R&B hits that I liked just fine before hearing this strange, captivating song but that were now an annoyance. As expected, about ninety minutes later, the disc jockey played it again, and again about two or three hours after that. I learned the song title and the artist, Vince Guaraldi, a strange name. Was he a Negro? It did not sound like a Negro name. It sounded more like the names of the Italians among whom I lived. But because the black people around me liked the tune so much we all thought for a time that Guaraldi must be black. Then I was struck by the possibility that a black radio station was playing a song by a white artist, not unprecedented, but unusual. By the time "Cast Your Fate to the Wind" crested on the charts, at number 22 on the Billboard Top 100 in February 1963 (it first hit the chart on December 8, 1962),[2] I was hearing it on the radio about once an hour or so.

I knew nothing of the song's bossa nova influences or pretensions, never having heard of bossa nova, and I had no idea it was from an album entitled *Jazz Impressions of* Black Orpheus. That would become important later when my older sisters, who like a lot of young people who became involved in the civil rights movement, fell in love with Marcel Camus's 1959 musical film about the Orpheus myth set in Brazil because it had such beautiful black people in it and such lilting music. (Younger, college-educated, more activist blacks certainly liked *Black Orpheus* much more than they did Otto Preminger's big-budget film version of the Gershwin brothers' folk opera, *Porgy and Bess*, which came out the same year, although some argued that a certain kind of exotic primitivism tarnished both films. *Black Orpheus*, for black Americans, did not come with the same political baggage and history as *Porgy and Bess*. And because *Black Orpheus* was foreign, it just seemed hipper.) I did not understand or even recognize the effect the bowed bass had in creating the mood the melody evoked. I did recognize the gospel chords, which is perhaps why I have associated this tune with Black Radio on a Sunday. I did not understand how the middle section of improvisation which I did not like, when the trio went into standard 4/4 jazz swing, intensified the impact of the melody for which I yearned when I heard it. What I knew was that I had never heard any instrumental, any piece of music at all, that touched me so deeply, that seemed to so perfectly *understand* how I felt about life—the agonies and joys of school, the texture of my urban neighborhood, my hopes, my aspirations, my fears, my grief. For the melody struck me as serene, yet melancholy, touching, insouciant, poignant, wistful, and glorious, all at the same time. The song did not at all strike me as happy but rather as optimistic, which meant a lot to me in the working-class world in which I lived. I was paralyzed with delight and heartbreak every time I heard the song on the radio during its run as a pop hit. It was the first piece of jazz I heard that actually *moved* me. It was the first piece of music I heard in my brief life that spoke to me intimately and knowingly as a child, not reaffirming my innocence but somehow conveying the joy and sadness of lost innocence and the inevitability of experience; as if the music knew, without any condescension, what a child was and how a child felt about the lonely crack-up of childhood. I was ten years old.

II. Some Like It Cool

> . . . there's no doubt that the pianist went back
> to "Cast Your Fate to the Wind" when work-
> ing out "Linus and Lucy." Many details are im-
> itated exactly. The main argument of "Fate" is
> a strong, syncopated, even eight-note melody
> harmonized diatonic triads floating over a
> left-hand bagpipe and bowed bass, followed
> by an answering call of gospel chords embel-
> lished by rumbles in the left hand borrowed
> from Horace Silver. This general scheme is
> followed for "Linus and Lucy," even down to
> the same key, A-flat.
>
> —the jazz pianist Ethan Iverson,
> "Deck the Halls with Vince Guaraldi,"
> *The New Yorker*, November 30, 2017

Creation is never quite clear-cut or clean, never quite the spark of sudden genius that one might wish or imagine it to be. Guaraldi claims to have written "Cast Your Fate to the Wind" in 1958, well before its copyright date of 1961. And apparently he did not write it alone.[3] Few pieces of music are written without suggestions or input from other people, who may or may not get credit for it (an especial controversy in the field of jazz and popular music generally). The fact that Guaraldi wrote the piece or conceived of it well before it was recorded by Fantasy Records in February 1962 means that he performed it with his trio in clubs, thus honing the sound and shape of it long before he went into the studio with it. In other words, the song was not simply *composed*, but *crafted*. One of the paradoxes of jazz is that while it is improvised, and a jazz musician may never play the same song the same way twice, jazz is also highly constructed and plotted, designed, you might say. It is not haphazard music. It is the sense that jazz is both overly abstract and haphazard or, worse yet, arbitrary, its insular aims apparent only to the musicians playing it, that makes it unappealing to many people. For many, jazz seems like a cult: music by musicians intended only for musicians. That is why there is such a battle in this cult over commercialism, which is a battle, of course, about nothing more than the modern obsession with authenticity.

WHEN PRODUCER LEE Mendelson decided in 1963 to do a documentary called *A Boy Named Charlie Brown* on cartoonist Charles Schulz and his wildly popular comic strip *Peanuts*, which would feature animation from the strip, he first approached pianist Dave Brubeck and then vibraphonist Cal Tjader to do the score, both of whom turned him down. Then another performer's music came to him.

"I was driving over the Golden Gate Bridge and I had the jazz station on—KSFO—and it was a show hosted by Al 'Jazzbo' Collins," Mendelson remembered. "He'd play Vince's stuff a lot, and right then, he played 'Cast Your Fate to the Wind.' It was melodic and open, and came in like a breeze off the bay. And it struck me that this might be the kind of music I was looking for."[4]

There are two things to note here: Mendelson definitely wanted a jazz score for the documentary despite the fact that Schulz thought jazz was "awful";[5] and he definitely wanted a

West Coast, specifically a Northern California jazz musician to do it. Logistics almost certainly played a significant role as Mendelson was a native San Franciscan. But there was also a certain type of sound or sensibility associated with West Coast jazz that Mendelson, consciously or unconsciously, wanted associated with the film.

A Boy Named Charlie Brown was completed with Guaraldi's music, including the famous theme which would be most identified with the subsequent animated specials, "Linus and Lucy." But the documentary never aired; no network or sponsor showed sufficient interest in it even after it was cut from an hour to thirty minutes. Guaraldi recorded a full jazz treatment of the cues and themes for Fantasy entitled "Jazz Impressions of *A Boy Named Charlie Brown*" in 1964. Nearly all of this music would be used, in various musical guises, lengths, and arrangements, in the animated specials to come. While Mendelson was unable to sell the documentary, Coca-Cola was interested in an animated Charlie Brown Christmas special which Mendelson was able to produce in less than a year. What is interesting here is that Mendelson, who had never planned to make an animated Charlie Brown special which naturally would greatly appeal to children (while of course attracting a sizable adult audience with whom the strip was immensely popular), still wanted to use Guaraldi's jazz as a score. This insistence would suggest he felt the music had some sort of inherent appeal or at least it would not be offputting to children.

The special was aired to a huge audience in December 1965 and thus Guaraldi's *Peanuts* music became widely known to the world, far more so than the jazz versions he had released on Fantasy. Guaraldi added some specific holiday/winter songs to the themes he had already written, including "Skating" and "Christmas Time Is Here," both of which have virtually become holiday standards. The fact that Guaraldi used a children's choir to sing, somewhat out of tune on purpose to give authenticity to the performance, "Christmas Time Is Here" and "Hark, the Herald Angels Sing" for the special intensified the music's connection with children. In 1967, he would record an album with the San Francisco Boys Chorus. "I dig working with kids," Guaraldi said. "They have a sound—a timbre—that's really better than adults doing the same stuff. It's the simplicity that counts. No filigree."[6] The Christmas special, as did all succeeding Charlie Brown television shows, used child voice-actors for the characters, which gave the programs a more child-centric sensibility. (It must be noted that some of the most popular children's television animation at the time did not typically feature children as main characters: this was the case for *The Flintstones* [when Pebbles, Fred and Wilma's daughter, and Bamm-Bamm, Barney and Betty's son, joined the series, they had no lines, only baby sounds which were voiced by adults], *Top Cat, Huckleberry Hound, Yogi Bear, Rocky and Bullwinkle* [with the exception of Mr. Peabody's boy, Sherman], *Magilla Gorilla, Quick Draw McGraw, Tennessee Tuxedo, Hoppity Hooper, Heckle and Jeckle*, and *Mighty Mouse*. Some did, of course, like *Jonny Quest, The Jetsons*, and Harvey cartoons that featured Little Audrey, Baby Huey, Casper the Friendly Ghost, Richie Rich, and Wendy the Witch; these were of course voiced by adults. Famous cartoon characters whose shorts first appeared in movie theaters, like Bugs Bunny, Daffy Duck, Yosemite Sam, Sylvester the Cat, and Pepé Le Pew, rarely had children. Popeye had three nephews who occasionally appeared in his features, as did Walt Disney's Donald

Duck. Animation was certainly considered for and aimed at children but it did not necessarily feature children, probably because the animal and adult characters in most cartoons behave in such a childlike way.) The Charlie Brown specials were different in this regard.

Guaraldi's album based on the Christmas special, *A Charlie Brown Christmas*, released in December 1965, was certified triple-platinum in December 2009, meaning it has sold more than three million copies.[7] Its commercial durability is partly explained by the fact that *A Charlie Brown Christmas* has been broadcast every year without fail since its 1965 premiere.

VINCE GUARALDI'S CAREER was, in the main, that of the typical professional jazz musician in post-World War II–era America. He played as a sideman and as house or intermission pianist in a number of small clubs in his native San Francisco with a variety of musicians and singers—from Stan Getz, Woody Herman, and Benny Goodman to Jimmy Witherspoon and Johnny Mathis—but most notably with vibraphonist Cal Tjader, who was to become one of the leading practitioners of Latin or Afro-Cuban jazz. From the time he left the army in 1948 at the age of twenty, he spent nearly every day playing the piano for hours, making a living somewhere in Northern California, although he did hit the road now and again. Hole-in-the-wall clubs, rather than dance halls or concert stages, had become the last redoubt of the jazz musician as economic and cultural changes, taste changes, were marginalizing jazz, and even these dens were rapidly diminishing in the ferocious onslaught of rock music; the brief period of intense popularity of big band swing, the only time when jazz was the leading popular music in the

United States, ended with the rise of rhythm & blues, rock-and-roll, and the Adult Contemporary and Top 40 markets.

Guaraldi was of course influenced by the revolutionary changes wrought by bebop. He would not have been considered hip or modern by his peers or to himself if he had not been. But he was also influenced by the boogie-woogie of Meade Lux Lewis and Pete Johnson (which eventually earned him the nickname Dr. Funk) as well as by the block chord styling of Miles Davis's pianist Red Garland, a musician he greatly admired and whose influence you can clearly hear on many Guaraldi records, including "Cast Your Fate to the Wind." It was through Tjader that Guaraldi got his Latin kicks and licks, or at least his Latin inclinations, although Guaraldi wound up being more identified with the softer sound of Brazilian bossa nova (which took America by storm through the music of Antonio Carlos Jobim and João Gilberto; Jobim's music, coincidentally, along with Luis Bonfa's, was featured in *Black Orpheus*) than with the hard-driving pulse of Afro-Cuban or mambo jazz. Bossa nova was more melodic, less percussive, more yearning, more "homesick," one might say, than Afro-Cuban music. Bossa nova was cool Latin music. This is clearly evident on the records that Guaraldi made in the 1960s with Brazilian guitarist Bola Sete, which, aside from "Cast Your Fate to the Wind" and the scores of the *Peanuts* television specials, remain his most lasting contributions to jazz. Bossa nova was also one of the three major attempts of the 1960s to make jazz popular or more commercial (the others were soul jazz and jazz-rock fusion). The incredible commercial success of the 1962 Stan Getz/Charlie Byrd album *Jazz Samba*, which reached number 1 on the Billboard Pop charts and spawned the hit single "Desafinado" (number 15 on the Billboard Top 100 in September 1962) and its follow-up album, *Getz/Gilberto*, in 1964, featuring the smash Billboard Top 100 number 1 hit single "The Girl from Ipanema," sung in highly understated fashion by Astrud Gilberto, which reached number 2, testify to the enormous, if fleeting, public interest in this new cool, highly melodic music.[8]

Guaraldi was of the school known as West Coast jazz, and although he was not primarily associated with it or well remembered for being a part of it, as were musicians like Chet Baker, Shelley Manne, Cal Tjader, Howard Rumsey, Paul Desmond, and Dave Brubeck (in his early days especially), Guaraldi's most successful and memorable music shares the sensibilities of this artistic faction. As Ted Gioia in his seminal study, *West Coast Jazz*, writes:

> Critics who pretend that such a thing [West Coast–styled jazz] never existed are practicing an unusual kind of bad faith. Certainly such a sound never accounted for all of the music played at all times on the coast, and maybe not even most of the music played most of the time. But it was prominent enough to demand our acknowledgment. What was this West Coast sound? By and large it has a strong compositional emphasis; it delighted in counterpoint; it had a cooler demeanor than Bird and Dizzy's bebop; the drummers were not so dominating as Roach and Blakey; the horn players were not so heavily rooted in the bebop vocabulary as Stitt and Rollins. The West Coast sound was cleanly articulated, the execution fluid and polished.[9]

In more than one instance, Gioia mentions Guaraldi's music as a typical example of this so-called cool or more subdued school of jazz playing.[10] Certainly, as mentioned above, producer Lee Mendelson recognized something distinctly in the West Coast jazz sound and thought particularly that "Cast Your Fate to the Wind" uniquely captured something fresh in jazz with its gentle yearning melody, its "homesick" beauty. It would be unfair to characterize all of Guaraldi's playing as being in this vein. He was capable of being a very hard-driving pianist, otherwise he would not have heard the name Dr. Funk, and in his later career in the late 1960s and early 1970s he was willing, even eager, to experiment with rock and electronics. Audiences discovered there was nothing cool or subdued about his playing. It was almost unbearably loud. But the lyrical sensibility, the song-like accessibility of "Cast Your Fate to the Wind" (lyrics were, in fact, added to the song), its "cool" nature, which made it sound so fresh, were what made Guaraldi connect with the public as something other than just another working jazz pianist. And it was the characteristics of "Cast Your Fate to the Wind" and of his equally "cool" collaborations with Bola Sete that Guaraldi brought to the music of the *Peanuts* specials: lyrical, highly song-like, soft jazz whose "cool" and playful edge kept them from being "sweet" or merely sentimental. That this music appealed to many adults, especially those who would watch the *Peanuts* specials with their children, would almost go without saying. What attracted them to Charles Schulz's comic strip was how it portrayed the secret child in every adult, for the children in the strip were simply stand-ins for adults. But what is far more important is how appealing this sort of music, the music that grew from the technical and emotional elements of "Cast Your Fate to the Wind," was to children. (And it is a mistake to think that baby-boomer children were not exposed to jazz in animation. The children's programming that featured old movie cartoons exposed us to lots of jazz: old *Betty Boop*, some old *Popeye*, some Warner Brothers and MGM (*Tom and Jerry*), and Walter Lantz. Especially animation that had anything to do with race and black people almost invariably had jazz. Even *The Flintstones* has jazz episodes such as "Hot Lips Hannigan" (1960) and "The Hip Song Writers" (1961) featuring Hoagy Carmichael. The importance of *Peanuts* for the baby-boomer generation was not being exposed to jazz through a children's program but being exposed to a specific type of jazz that was meant to make an emotional appeal to them.)

Guaraldi's "cool" captured perfectly children's sense of romantic disillusionment, their aching for purity as only children can, as it further and further recedes from them. In this sense, growing up is a sort of unremitting form of homesickness. As Charles Schulz wrote, "It is terrible . . . to be a beginner in anything and to feel that you don't know enough about the subject."[11] And that is what the child is constantly reminded of: being a beginner, *in everything*. It is more socially accepted, indeed, socially glorified, in childhood than any other stage in life but it is no easier for that, to live in a world where you are constantly taught, constantly told you do not know enough about anything. The Charlie Brown character captured this existential insecurity with startling poignancy.

For child readers of *Peanuts* like myself, the strip fulfilled our fantasy of a world of marginalized adults, a world essentially without adults. I saw the strip in exactly the opposite way that most adults would: the characters all represented the adult in every child, conveyed that, as children, we were as grown-up as we were ever going to be. Childhood is not about nostalgia merely, as adults tend to see it, but about the joy and frustration of life at a time when one can still believe unconditionally in the wonder of life itself. Childhood was not something apart from real life, as many adults like to think of it, but rather it was real life on another scale, a scale that made up in depth of feeling what it lacked in breadth of experience. Guaraldi's cool themes for the *Peanuts* specials made childhood's innocence not Wordsworth-like, as grandeur fallen, but cool, as in learning how to go on when you blow it, persevering when the gig goes sideways. The optimistic aesthetic of Guaraldi's *Peanuts* music was not that children are good but that children and childhood are expressions of cool.

Notes

1. Derrick Bang, *Vince Guaraldi at the Piano* (Jefferson, NC: McFarland & Company, 2012), 102.
2. Joel Whitburn, *Joel Whitburn Presents Across the Charts: The 1960s, Chart Data Compiled from Billboard's Singles Charts, 1960–1969* (Menomonee Falls, WI: Record Research, 2008), 167.
3. Bang, *Vince Guaraldi at the Piano*, 101.
4. Ibid., 160–61.
5. David Michaelis, *Schulz and Peanuts: A Biography* (New York: Harper, 2007), 348.
6. Bang, *Vince Guaraldi at the Piano*, 213.
7. Joel Whitburn, *Joel Whitburn Presents Top Pop Albums*, 7th Edition (Menomonee Falls, WI: Record Research, 2010), 329.
8. Joel Whitburn, *Joel Whitburn Presents Across the Charts*, 158.
9. Ted Gioia, *West Coast Jazz: Modern Jazz in California, 1945–1960* (New York: Oxford University Press, 1992), 362.
10. Ibid., 362, 368.
11. Charles M. Schulz, *My Life with Charlie Brown*, ed. M. Thomas Inge (Jackson: University Press of Mississippi, 2010), 21.

V

True Stories

You're Weird, Sir

Jennifer Finney Boylan

We were watching a play about infidelity. "He loves me," said Glenn Close, up onstage. "He wants to punish me with his pain, but I can't come up with the proper guilt. It's so tiring and uninteresting. You never write about that, you lot."

"What?" said Jeremy Irons. My girlfriend Beth and I were in the audience, holding hands. The play was Tom Stoppard's *The Real Thing*. We'd been living together for a couple years by then, up on 108th and Amsterdam, one floor above an S&M dungeon.

"Gallons of ink and miles of typewriter ribbon expended on the misery of the unrequited lover!" Close replied. "Not a word about the tedium of the unrequiting."

A year later, in fall of 1985, I was sitting on a couch with an Irish writer named Shannon, listening to a piano piece by Mussorgsky, *Pictures at an Exhibition*. There was a movement called "Catacombs" during which the music grew dark. I looked over at Shannon, and she looked at me, and at that moment we came to an unspoken agreement about all the trouble we were just about to cause.

In weeks to come, I would have to take care to wash my sheets. Because Shannon had a cat, and Beth was allergic. The way I figured, Beth would figure out that something was up, the first time that she sneezed.

I had grown up believing in the transformative powers of love, that a passion for someone outside of myself would change me from the miserable lump I considered myself to be and into someone else: a being of illumination and grace. My parents' adorable marriage had been like that. They were like the Quaker version of Morticia and Gomez Addams.

As a closeted transgender child, I had hoped that a similar love might fall upon me, and in so doing cure me of the unfathomable desire that had secretly dominated my heart since I had been five or six. I had two prayers—one of which was to wake up in the morning mysteriously transformed into the girl I knew myself to be; the other, that an all-encompassing love would erase this desire completely.

It had never occurred to me that, should I manage to trick any unsuspecting woman into falling in love with me, I would be unable, in the long run, to be true to her. My theory was that love would get me outside of myself, and that, once liberated, I would become the best boyfriend in the world, motivated by an all-encompassing gratitude to my lover for having literally saved my life.

As it turned out, this was a false hope. But then the world is full of false hopes, many of them dumber than the hope of being transformed by love.

I likewise did not know, when I was a child, that the

example set by my parents' lovey-dovey relationship was more the exception than the rule.

Still, if I'd been interested in finding evidence for the universality of unrequited love, and the mysteries of queer identity, I wouldn't have had to look much further than the pages of the Philadelphia *Evening Bulletin* brought home by my father each night. The *Inquirer* had good comics too, but the best ones— *Brenda Starr*, *The Phantom*, *Terry and the Pirates*, *Doonesbury*— were in the *Bulletin*.

My favorite strip was *Peanuts*, which, if I'd only been paying attention, contained some pretty powerful lessons for me about the world that lay ahead. *Peanuts* was just one broken heart after another.

Charlie Brown loves the Little Red-Haired Girl, whom we never see. Charlie Brown's little sister Sally is in love with Linus ("Isn't he just the cutest thing?"), whose affections, in turn, are reserved for his blanket. Lucy is in love with Schroeder, but Schroeder is in love with Beethoven. Marcie is in love with Peppermint Patty, but Peppermint Patty is in love with Charlie Brown. And so on.

As a boy, I was a certified goofball—a class clown and a spaz, a melancholy thing whose primary form of self-care was the constant generation of blarney. I did imitations—some of them so good that I could pass for people other than myself on the telephone. I invented satirical songs on the spot, which I performed on the piano or sang *a capella* in my unexpected soprano. I made fake beards out of socks. I buried treasure in the yard and drew up maps that I then hid in places where my sister was likely to find them. The reason why I was so entertaining was no mystery: I was sad.

Good grief.

It was in reading *Peanuts*, lying on the floor beneath the piano in my parents' suburban home in Newtown Square, Pennsylvania, that I first saw evidence of the terrible truth: that my adorable parents resided in a cartoon universe. It was Charlie Brown and his friends—children who lived in a world defined by unrequited love—who resided in the real one.

You can hear the anguish in Charlie Brown's voice as he cries out to the heavens: "Isn't there any one who can tell me what love is all about?"

Ladies and gentlemen, Pig-Pen.

Lights, please.

And there were in the same country scumbags abiding in the sandbox, keeping watch over their slops by night.

Of all the characters in the *Peanuts* universe, Pig-Pen's the one who seems most at peace with the life he has been given. Sure, he's immersed in filth; he can "raise a cloud of dust in a snowstorm." Bullies Patty and Violet are constantly seeking to humiliate him. But Pig-Pen will have none of it. "Aren't you ashamed?" Violet says to him, after making him look in the mirror. "On the contrary," he replies. "I didn't think I looked this good."

In a September 1954 strip, Patty marches along with a bucket, determined to "personally give Pig-Pen a good scrubbing." (In another world, this might be called "reparative therapy.") But when she finds him—sitting, as usual, in a sandbox—he looks clean and shiny. As she departs ("I guess there's some hope for him, after all") you can see that only half of Pig-Pen is clean. The side facing away from Patty is still covered with slime.

While Schulz was said to have grown tired of the character in later years, in part because it was hard to write material for him outside of the one basic joke, it's not hard to understand his enduring appeal (he's number five in the list of favorite characters in one *Peanuts* poll). He's the closest thing the strip has to the spirit of total Zen. "Just think of it," Charlie Brown says to Violet in a strip from November 1959, "the dirt and dust of far-off lands blowing over here and settling on 'Pig-Pen'! / It staggers the imagination! He may be carrying soil that was trod upon by Solomon or Nebuchadnezzar or Genghis Khan!"

"That's true, isn't it," Pig-Pen replies. "Suddenly I feel like royalty!"

It would be nice, I thought, lying there beneath the piano with the Philadelphia *Evening Bulletin*, to live one's life like this.

It gave me *Peanuts* envy.

But still, I wondered: Did Pig-Pen never feel the yearning to be clean? Or was it that he'd come to accept that, whatever purity he'd ever hoped for, was simply not in the cards? Was the secret of Pig-Pen's grace that he lived in a world without desire? Or did he have the same desires as everyone else, but had come, at his very young age, to accept that desire only brings misery, and suffering, and separation from God?

I suspected, even then, that my soul would never be as pristine as Pig-Pen's.

I had not yet cheated on Beth as we sat there in the Plymouth Theatre watching Tom Stoppard's play, at least not if you measure cheating by the fairly high standard of having an actual affair. I was loyal to her in every measure except in my own heart. Which, in its way, was not so unlike Pig-Pen making sure Patty could only see his clean side.

In the mornings I lay there listening to her tender breath taken in sleep. And as I did this I pictured myself knocking on Beth's door *en femme,* the startled expression on her face as she realized that the strange woman before her was someone she already knew. I understood what her response would be, though: *Aren't you ashamed of yourself?* Surely she'd want to give me a good scrubbing.

On the contrary, I might reply. *I didn't think I looked this good.*

If Pig-Pen was an example of making peace with your own weird self, an even better example was Peppermint Patty. She and Marcie attended a different school from Charlie Brown and his friends, on the other side of town. And whatever struggles Charlie Brown's bassoon-voiced teacher provides for him, these pale beside Peppermint Patty's travails. Like me, she got a D minus in almost every subject.

One reason she does so badly in school is that she sleeps through every class. (For my part, I was awake during elementary school, but failed to achieve much in the way of scholarship because all my waking hours were devoted to comic stunts, including one memorable class in which I pretended to have a brain aneurysm.) Whether Peppermint Patty's struggles had anything to do with her home situation wasn't clear—but unlike me, she lived alone with her father, who traveled a lot. Her mother died when she was young.

Unlike the dress-wearing girls at Charlie Brown's school, Peppermint Patty is, well, I guess the euphemism is "tomboy." She wears shirts and pants or shorts. And she's an athlete— virtually every time she plays Charlie Brown's team in baseball, she wins (including one heartbreaking game with the final score of 51–50).

Given her very clear differences from other girls, plus her terrible grades, plus the home situation, you'd think that Peppermint Patty would struggle, that like Charlie Brown she'd find herself in regular need of Lucy van Pelt's Psychiatric Services. But Patty is almost always smiling, upbeat, content. She is, other than Pig-Pen (and maybe Snoopy), the most consistently optimistic member of the cast.

Part of her attitude may be the result of her strange obliviousness to the world around her. My mother had this too—when we merged at seventy miles an hour onto a highway, Mom would generally not look in the side mirror, because she believed, firmly, that "nice people will always just make room." Peppermint Patty believes all sorts of things that appear not to be so: For years she believed that Snoopy was not a dog but "that funny looking kid with the big nose." She believed that Snoopy's doghouse was "Chuck's guest house." She believed that a school for "gifted children" meant a school at which she'd receive a gift for attending; later she attended an obedience training school for dogs.

In her sense of oblivious self-sufficiency, she resembles no one so much as the solitary Pig-Pen, although unlike him, her sense of joy and equilibrium might be the result of the fact that Peppermint Patty is rarely without her sidekick, Marcie, whose love for her is unconditional. Marcie is a strange character, in some ways—she's a good student, unlike the object of her affection. At the same time some of Peppermint Patty's imperviousness seems to have worn off on her. She calls Patty "sir," which might be an honorific, or it might be something else.

My guess is that Marcie, who looks through glasses that make her actual eyes invisible, sees something in Peppermint Patty that no one else can see.

There's a *Family Guy* episode in which Peter (the dad) visits his friend, the grown-up Peppermint Patty, and remarks, "Gee, Patty, the years have been great to you!" And she replies, "Well, I owe that to my better half," and Marcie walks in from stage left and asks, "Who is it, sir?" and plants a kiss on Patty's cheek. It's the happy, twenty-first-century ending that Patty and Marcie deserve, although back when I was reading the strip in the 1960s, it was not the one I would have imagined for her.

It's not the one that Patty imagines for herself, either. In a February 1980 sequence, she finally gets a kiss on a Valentine's Day date from the one person in the *Peanuts* universe—outside of Marcie—who seems to understand her.

It's Pig-Pen, of course.

Later, Charlie Brown and Pig-Pen discuss Peppermint Patty's character. "Patricia is an unusual girl," says Pig-Pen thoughtfully. "Do you know she never once criticized my appearance?"

Patty, for her part, calls up Marcie in the middle of the night. "Hi, Marcie! It's me! I know it's three o'clock in the morning, but I can't sleep . . . You know why I can't sleep? / I'M IN LOVE!"

The last panel of this sequence shows Marcie, flattened in bed, her face exhausted and sad. "I'm sure you'll be very happy, sir," she says, surely one of the most heartbreaking sentences in comics history.

My relationship with Beth didn't last much more than another year after I kissed Shannon. But then, my relationship with Shannon didn't last after I kissed Sandrine, and after her, Samantha, and Nancy, and Nadine. I kissed all of those women, each time knowing that I was betraying the woman before, but also hoping that somewhere, in one of these relationships, I would find the courage to let myself be known.

"I remember how it stopped seeming odd that in biblical Greek," Jeremy Irons says in Stoppard's play, "*knowing* was used for *making love*. Whosit knew so-and-so. Carnal knowledge. It's what lovers trust each other with. Knowledge of each other, not of the flesh but through the flesh, knowledge of self, the real him, the real her, *in extremis*, the mask slipped from the face."

After we broke up, I didn't see Beth again for thirty-three years. Then, in 2017, I was walking around Morningside Heights, heading back to my apartment on Riverside, where my wife was waiting for me. That would be Deirdre, with whom this year I celebrate our thirtieth wedding anniversary—twelve as husband and wife, and eighteen as wife and wife.

A face passed by.

"Beth?" I shouted. "Beth?"

The stranger stopped, and turned back toward me. There I was, the twenty-four-year-old boy she had once loved, now transformed into a fifty-eight-year-old woman. *She seemed so glad to see me I just smiled.*

"You look good," she said, and in reply I said something along the lines of, *Well I owe that to my better half.* Against all odds, my marriage had turned out to be a lot like my parents' after all, vaginas notwithstanding. The transformative power of love had not cured me of the desire to be female—but being fully known, at last, had made it possible for the mask to slip from my face, for me to embark upon the adventure of transition with the knowledge that Deirdre's love for me—like that of Marcie for Peppermint Patty—would endure.

People always want to know how Deirdre adapted to the change. But by coming out as trans, in some ways, I did the opposite of changing; the mysterious self I finally unveiled to my lover turned out, mostly, to be the one she already knew. She is, as Pig-Pen observed, an unusual girl. *She never once criticized my appearance.*

Beth and I stood there on the corner of 116th and Broadway, just shy of the gates of Barnard. We talked about our children. She'd had some trouble with her eyes. I was wearing hearing aids. Columbia students swirled around us as we spoke, not one of them born yet when I'd cheated on this sweet, kind woman a generation before.

Beth and I hugged and then took our leave of each other. My heart felt so full.

I thought about the last time I had seen her, on the day of my father's funeral, the rain coming down upon the urn that contained his ashes.

After Pig-Pen's kiss with Peppermint Patty, he turns to Charlie Brown. The dirt rises from him in waves. An unexpected love has rocked his world.

And yet it has not made him clean.

"I know I'm not very neat," he says. "I can't seem to change."

Bar Nuts

LESLIE STEIN

Working at the bar, I have a lot of the same conversations over and over again...

YUP.

CRAP WEATHER today, eh?

A LONG time AGO, someone GAVE me some GOOD BARTENDING ADVICE:

FIND something you like to talk about, and ENGAGE PEOPLE IN IT! ALL THEY REALLY WANT IS A LITTLE DISTRACTION!

NICE WEATHER today, eh?

WHO's your favorite PEANUTS CHARACTER?

THE CARTOON? WHY?

JUST WONDERING...

A FEW YEARS BACK I WAS on A DATE IN MIDTOWN MANHATTAN... WE HAD WANDERED AROUND ALL DAY WITHOUT MUCH TO DO...
MIND if WE STOP IN this BOOKSTORE?
BO
AH AH!
Peanut
Healt
HEY LES! THEY HAVE some PEANUTS FIGURINES OVER THERE... WANT one?
Peanut
SURE!
WHICH CHARACTER DO YOU WANT?
I DUNNO! YOU PICK!
THIS WAS a total LIE. It WAS A TEST...
If HE Gets Lucy WE'RE through!
Peanuts

Woodstock!

EVER SINCE I WAS LITTLE, I HAVE ALWAYS LOVED WOODSTOCK.

HE WAS the LITTLE BIRD WHO HATCHED in 1967, and, UNABLE to FLY PROPERLY, STUCK AROUND to BECOME SNOOPY'S FRIEND and CONSTANT COMPANION... often LEAVING to HAVE ADVENTURES of HIS OWN...

THE CUTEST and MOST RELAXED of the PEANUTS GANG, HE DID GET INTO FIGHTS with SNOOPY from TIME to TIME... but they ALWAYS ENDED with a **BIG** HUG...

WHAT DO YOU THINK?

DO YOU LIKE IT?

Two Ponies

Jonathan Franzen

In May 1970, a few nights after National Guardsmen killed four student protesters at Kent State University, my father and my brother Tom started fighting. They weren't fighting about the Vietnam War, which both of them opposed. The fight was probably about a lot of different things at once. But the immediate issue was Tom's summer job. He was a good artist, with a meticulous nature, and my father had encouraged him (you could even say forced him) to choose a college from a short list of schools with strong programs in architecture. Tom had deliberately chosen the most distant of these schools, Rice University, and he'd just returned from his second year in Houston, where his adventures in late-sixties youth culture were pushing him toward majoring in film studies, not architecture. My father, however, had found him a plum summer job with Sverdrup & Parcel, the big engineering firm in St. Louis, whose senior partner, General Leif Sverdrup, had been an Army Corps of

Engineers hero in the Philippines. It couldn't have been easy for my father, who was shy about asking favors, to pull the requisite strings at Sverdrup. But the office gestalt was hawkish and buzz-cut and generally inimical to bell-bottomed, lefty film-studies majors; and Tom didn't want to be there.

Up in the bedroom that he and I shared, the windows were open and the air had the stuffy wooden house smell that came out every spring. I preferred the make-believe no-smell of air-conditioning, but my mother, whose subjective experience of temperature was notably consistent with low gas and electricity bills, claimed to be a devotee of "fresh air," and the windows often stayed open until Memorial Day.

On my night table was the *Peanuts Treasury*, a large, thick hardcover compilation of daily and Sunday funnies by Charles M. Schulz. My mother had given it to me the previous Christmas, and I'd been rereading it at bedtime ever since. Like most of the nation's ten-year-olds, I had a private, intense relationship with Snoopy, the cartoon beagle. He was a solitary not-animal animal who lived among larger creatures of a different species, which was more or less my feeling in my own house. My brothers were less like siblings than like an extra, fun pair of quasi-parents. Although I had friends and was a Cub Scout in good standing, I spent a lot of time alone with talking animals. I was an obsessive rereader of A. A. Milne and the Narnia and Dr. Dolittle novels, and my involvement with my collection of stuffed animals was on the verge of becoming age-inappropriate. It was another point of kinship with Snoopy that he, too, liked animal games. He impersonated tigers and vultures and mountain lions, sharks, sea monsters, pythons, cows, piranhas, penguins, and vampire bats. He was the perfect sunny egoist, starring in his ridiculous fantasies and basking in everyone's attention. In a cartoon strip full of children, the dog was the character I recognized as a child.

Tom and my father had been talking in the living room when I went up to bed. Now, at some late and even stuffier hour, after I'd put aside the *Peanuts Treasury* and fallen asleep, Tom burst into our bedroom. He was shouting sarcastically. "You'll get over it! You'll forget about me! It'll be so much easier! You'll get over it!"

My father was offstage somewhere, making large abstract sounds. My mother was right behind Tom, sobbing at his shoulder, begging him to stop, to stop. He was pulling open dresser drawers, repacking bags he'd only recently unpacked. "You think you want me here," he said, "but you'll get over it."

What about me? my mother pleaded. *What about Jon?*

"You'll get over it."

I was a small and fundamentally ridiculous person. Even if I'd dared sit up in bed, what could I have said? "Excuse me, I'm trying to sleep"? I lay still and followed the action through my eyelashes. There were further dramatic comings and goings, through some of which I may in fact have slept. Finally I heard Tom's feet pounding down the stairs and my mother's terrible cries, now nearly shrieks, receding after him: "Tom! Tom! Tom! Please! Tom!" And then the front door slammed.

Things like this had never happened in our house. The worst fight I'd ever witnessed was between my brothers on the subject of Frank Zappa, whose music Tom admired and Bob one afternoon dismissed with such patronizing disdain that Tom began to sneer at Bob's own favorite group, the Supremes; which led to bitter words. But a scene of real wailing and open rage was completely off the map. When I woke up the next morning, the memory of it already felt decades old and semidreamlike and unmentionable.

My father had left for work, and my mother served me breakfast without comment. The food on the table, the jingles on the radio, and the walk to school all were unremarkable; and yet everything about the day was soaked in dread. At school that week, in Miss Niblack's class, we were rehearsing our fifth-grade play. The script, which I'd written, had a large number of bit parts and one very generous role that I'd created with my own memorization abilities in mind. The action took place on a boat, involved a taciturn villain named Mr. Scuba, and lacked the most rudimentary comedy, point, or moral. Not even I, who got to do most of the talking, enjoyed being in it. Its badness—my responsibility for its badness—became part of the day's general dread.

There was something dreadful about springtime itself. The riot of biology, the Lord of the Flies buzzing, the pullulating mud. After school, instead of staying outside to play, I followed my dread home and cornered my mother in our dining room. I asked her about my upcoming class performance. Would Dad be in town for it? What about Bob? Would Bob be home from college yet? And what about Tom? Would Tom be there, too? This was quite plausibly an innocent line of questioning—I was a small glutton for attention, forever turning conversations to the subject of myself—and, for a while, my mother gave me plausibly innocent answers. Then she slumped into a chair, put her face in her hands, and began to weep.

"Didn't you hear anything last night?" she said.

"No."

"You didn't hear Tom and Dad shouting? You didn't hear doors slamming?"

"No!"

She gathered me in her arms, which was probably the main thing I'd been dreading. I stood there stiffly while she hugged me. "Tom and Dad had a terrible fight," she said. "After you went to bed. They had a terrible fight, and Tom got his things and left the house, and we don't know where he went."

"Oh."

"I thought we'd hear from him today, but he hasn't called, and I'm frantic, not knowing where he is. I'm just frantic!"

I squirmed a little in her grip.

"But this has nothing to do with you," she said. "It's between him and Dad and has nothing to do with you. I'm sure Tom's sorry he won't be here to see your play. Or maybe, who knows, he'll be back by Friday and he will see it."

"OK."

"But I don't want you telling anyone he's gone until we know where he is. Will you agree not to tell anyone?"

"OK," I said, breaking free of her. "Can we turn the air-conditioning on?"

I was unaware of it, but an epidemic had broken out across the country. Late adolescents in suburbs like ours had suddenly gone berserk, running away to other cities to have sex and not go to college, ingesting every substance they could get their hands on, not just clashing with their parents but rejecting and annihilating everything about them. For a while, the parents were so frightened and so mystified and so ashamed that each family, especially mine, quarantined itself and suffered by itself.

When I went upstairs, my bedroom felt like an overwarm

sickroom. The clearest remaining vestige of Tom was the *Dont Look Back* poster that he'd taped to a flank of his dresser where Bob Dylan's psychedelic hairstyle wouldn't always be catching my mother's censorious eye. Tom's bed, neatly made, was the bed of a kid carried off by an epidemic.

IN THAT UNSETTLED season, as the so-called generation gap was rending the cultural landscape, Charles Schulz's work was uniquely beloved. Fifty-five million Americans had seen *A Charlie Brown Christmas* the previous December, for a Nielsen share of better than fifty percent. The musical *You're a Good Man, Charlie Brown* was in its second sold-out year on Broadway. The astronauts of Apollo X, in their dress rehearsal of the first lunar landing, had christened their orbiter and landing vehicle Charlie Brown and Snoopy. Newspapers carrying *Peanuts* reached more than 150 million readers, *Peanuts* collections were all over the bestseller lists, and if my own friends were any indication, there was hardly a kid's bedroom in America without a *Peanuts* wastebasket or *Peanuts* bedsheets or a *Peanuts* wall hanging. Schulz, by a luxurious margin, was the most famous living artist on the planet.

To the countercultural mind, the strip's square panels were the only square thing about it. A begoggled beagle piloting a doghouse and getting shot down by the Red Baron had the same antic valence as Yossarian paddling a dinghy to Sweden. Wouldn't the country be better off listening to Linus van Pelt than to Robert McNamara? This was the era of flower children, not flower adults. But the strip appealed to older Americans as well. It was unfailingly inoffensive (Snoopy never lifted a leg) and was set in a safe, attractive suburb where the kids, except for Pig-Pen, whose image Ron McKernan of the Grateful Dead pointedly embraced, were clean and well-spoken and conservatively dressed. Hippies and astronauts, the rejecting kids and the rejected grownups, were all of one mind here.

An exception was my own household. As far as I know, my father never in his life read a comic strip, and my mother's interest in the funnies was limited to a single-panel feature called *The Girls*, whose generic middle-aged matrons, with their weight problems and stinginess and poor driving skills and weakness for department-store bargains, she found just endlessly amusing.

I didn't buy comic books, not even *Mad* magazine, but I worshipped at the altars of Warner Bros. cartoons and the funnies section of the *St. Louis Post-Dispatch*. I read the section's black-and-white page first, skipping the dramatic features like *Steve Roper* and *Juliet Jones* and glancing at *Li'l Abner* only to satisfy myself that it was still trashy and repellent. On the full-color back page I read the strips strictly in reverse order of preference, doing my best to be amused by Dagwood Bumstead's midnight snacks and struggling to ignore the fact that Tiger and Punkinhead were the kind of messy, unreflective kids whom I disliked in real life, before I treated myself to my favorite strip, *B.C.* The strip, by Johnny Hart, was caveman humor. Hart wrung hundreds of gags from the friendship between a flightless bird and a long-suffering tortoise who was constantly attempting unturtlish feats of agility and flexibility. Debts were always paid in clams; dinner was always roast leg of something. When I was done with *B.C.*, I was done with the paper.

The comics in St. Louis's other paper, the *Globe-Democrat*, which my parents didn't take, seemed bleak and foreign to me. *Broom Hilda* and *Funky Winkerbean* and *The Family Circus* were off-putting in the manner of the kid whose partially visible underpants, which had the name CUTTAIR handmarkered on the waistband, I'd stared at throughout my family's tour of the Canadian parliament. Although *The Family Circus* was resolutely unfunny, its panels clearly were based on some actual family's humid, baby-filled home life and were aimed at an audience that recognized this life, which compelled me to posit an entire subspecies of humanity that found *The Family Circus* hilarious.

I knew very well, of course, why the *Globe-Democrat*'s cartoons were so lame: the paper that carried *Peanuts* didn't *need* any other good strips. Indeed, I would have swapped the entire *Post-Dispatch* for a daily dose of Schulz. Only *Peanuts*, the strip we didn't get, dealt with stuff that really mattered. I didn't for a minute believe that the children in *Peanuts* were really children—they were so much more emphatic and cartoonishly real than anybody in my own neighborhood—but I nevertheless took their stories to be dispatches from a universe of childhood more substantial and convincing than my own. Instead of playing kickball and Four Square, the way my friends and I did, the kids in *Peanuts* had real baseball teams, real football equipment, real fistfights. Their relationships with Snoopy were far richer than the chasings and bitings that constituted my own relationships with neighborhood dogs. Minor but incredible disasters, often involving new vocabulary words, befell them daily. Lucy was "blackballed by the Bluebirds." She knocked Charlie Brown's croquet ball so far that he had to call the other players from a phone booth. She gave Charlie Brown a signed document in which she swore not to pull the football away when he tried to kick it, but the "peculiar thing about this document," as she

observed in the final frame, was that "it was never notarized."
When Lucy smashed the bust of Beethoven on Schroeder's toy
piano, it struck me as odd and funny that Schroeder had a closet
full of identical replacement busts, but I accepted it as humanly
possible, because Schulz had drawn it.

To the *Peanuts Treasury* I soon added two other equally
strong hardcover collections, *Peanuts Revisited* and *Peanuts Classics*. A well-meaning relative once also gave me a copy of Robert
Short's bestseller, *The Gospel According to Peanuts*, but it couldn't
have interested me less. *Peanuts* wasn't a portal on the Gospel.
It was my gospel.

Chapter 1, verses 1–4, of what I knew about disillusionment: Charlie Brown passes the house of the Little Red-Haired
Girl, the object of his eternal fruitless longing. He sits down
with Snoopy and says, "I wish I had two ponies." He imagines
offering one of the ponies to the Little Red-Haired Girl, riding
out into the countryside with her, and sitting down with her
beneath a tree. Suddenly he's scowling at Snoopy and asking,
"Why aren't you two ponies?" Snoopy, rolling his eyes, thinks:
"I knew we'd get around to that."

Or Chapter 1, verses 26–32, of what I knew about the mysteries of etiquette: Linus is showing off his new wristwatch to
everyone in the neighborhood. "New watch!" he says proudly to
Snoopy, who, after a hesitation, licks it. Linus's hair stands on
end. "YOU LICKED MY WATCH!" he cries. "It'll rust! It'll turn
green! He ruined it!" Snoopy is left looking mildly puzzled and
thinking, "I thought it would have been impolite not to taste it."

Or Chapter 2, verses 6–12, of what I knew about fiction:
Linus is annoying Lucy, wheedling and pleading with her to
read him a story. To shut him up, she grabs a book, randomly

opens it, and says, "A man was born, he lived and he died. The End!" She tosses the book aside, and Linus picks it up reverently. "What a fascinating account," he says. "It almost makes you wish you had known the fellow."

The perfect silliness of stuff like this, the koanlike inscrutability, entranced me even when I was ten. But many of the more elaborate sequences, especially the ones about Charlie Brown's humiliation and loneliness, made only a generic impression on me. In a classroom spelling bee that Charlie Brown has been looking forward to, the first word he's asked to spell is "maze." With a complacent smile, he produces "M-A-Y-S." The class screams with laughter. He returns to his seat and presses his face into his desktop, and when his teacher asks him what's wrong, he yells at her and ends up in the principal's office. *Peanuts* was steeped in Schulz's awareness that for every winner in a competition there has to be a loser, if not twenty losers, or two thousand, but I personally enjoyed winning and couldn't see why so much fuss was made about the losers.

In the spring of 1970, Miss Niblack's class was studying homonyms to prepare for what she called the Homonym Spelldown. I did some desultory homonym drilling with my mother, rattling off "sleigh" for "slay" and "slough" for "slew" the way other kids roped softballs into center field. To me, the only halfway interesting question about the Spelldown was who was going to come in second. A new kid had joined our class that year, a shrimpy black-haired striver, Chris Toczko, who had it in his head that he and I were academic rivals. I was a nice enough little boy as long as you kept away from my turf. Toczko was annoyingly unaware that I, not he, by natural right, was the best student in the class. On the day of the Spelldown he actually taunted me. He said he'd done a lot of studying and he was going to beat me! I looked down at the little pest and did not know what to say. I evidently mattered a lot more to him than he did to me.

For the Spelldown, we all stood by the blackboard, Miss Niblack calling out one half of a pair of homonyms and my classmates sitting down as soon as they had failed. Toczko was pale and trembling, but he knew his homonyms. He was the last kid standing, besides me, when Miss Niblack called out the word "liar." Toczko trembled and essayed: "L . . . I . . ." And I could see that I had beaten him. I waited impatiently while, with considerable anguish, he extracted two more letters from his marrow: "E . . . R?"

"I'm sorry, Chris, that's not a word," Miss Niblack said.

With a sharp laugh of triumph, not even waiting for Toczko to sit down, I stepped forward and sang out, "L-Y-R-E! *Lyre*. It's a stringed instrument."

I hadn't really doubted that I would win, but Toczko had got to me with his taunting, and my blood was up. I was the last person in class to realize that Toczko was having a meltdown. His face turned red and he began to cry, insisting angrily that "lier" *was* a word, it *was* a word.

I didn't care if it was a word or not. I knew my rights. However many homonyms of "liar" might exist in theory, the word Miss Niblack wanted was clearly "lyre." Toczko's tears disturbed and disappointed me, as I made quite clear by fetching the classroom dictionary and showing him that "lier" wasn't in it. This was how both Toczko and I ended up in the principal's office.

I'd never been sent down before. I was interested to learn that the principal, Mr. Barnett, had a *Webster's International*

Unabridged in his office. Toczko, who barely outweighed the dictionary, used two hands to open it and to roll back the pages to the "L" words. I stood at his shoulder and saw where his tiny, trembling index finger was pointing: *lier, n., one that lies (as in ambush)*. Mr. Barnett immediately declared us co-winners of the Spelldown—a compromise that didn't seem quite fair to me, since I would surely have murdered Toczko if we'd gone another round. But his outburst had spooked me, and I decided it might be OK, for once, to let somebody else win.

A few months after the Homonym Spelldown, just after summer vacation started, Toczko ran out into Grant Road and was killed by a car. What little I knew then about the world's badness I knew mainly from a camping trip, some years earlier, when I'd dropped a frog into a campfire and watched it shrivel and roll down the flat side of a log. My memory of that shriveling and rolling was sui generis, distinct from my other memories. It was like a nagging, sick-making atom of rebuke in me. I felt similarly rebuked now when my mother, who knew nothing of Toczko's rivalry with me, told me that he was dead. She was weeping as she'd wept over Tom's disappearance some weeks earlier. She sat me down and made me write a letter of condolence to Toczko's mother. I was very much unaccustomed to considering the interior states of people other than myself, but it was impossible not to consider Mrs. Toczko's. Though I never met her in person, in the ensuing weeks I pictured her suffering so incessantly and vividly that I could almost see her: a tiny, trim, dark-haired woman who cried the way her son did.

"EVERYTHING I DO makes me feel guilty," says Charlie Brown. He's at the beach, and he has just thrown a pebble into the water, and Linus has commented, "Nice going . . . It took that rock four thousand years to get to shore, and now you've thrown it back."

I felt guilty about Toczko. I felt guilty about the little frog. I felt guilty about shunning my mother's hugs when she seemed to need them most. I felt guilty about the washcloths at the bottom of the stack in the linen closet, the older, thinner washcloths that we seldom used. I felt guilty for preferring my best shooter marbles, a solid red agate and a solid yellow agate, my king and my queen, to marbles farther down my rigid marble hierarchy. I felt guilty about the board games that I didn't like to play—Uncle Wiggily, U.S. Presidential Elections, Game of the States—and sometimes, when my friends weren't around, I opened the boxes and examined the pieces in the hope of making the games feel less forgotten. I felt guilty about neglecting the stiff-limbed, scratchy-pelted Mr. Bear, who had no voice and didn't mix well with my other stuffed animals. To avoid feeling guilty about them, too, I slept with one of them per night, according to a strict weekly schedule.

We laugh at dachshunds for humping our legs, but our own species is even more self-centered in its imaginings. There's no object so Other that it can't be anthropomorphized and shanghaied into conversation with us. Some objects are more amenable than others, however. The trouble with Mr. Bear was that he was more realistically bearlike than the other animals. He had a distinct, stern, feral persona; unlike our faceless washcloths, he was assertively Other. It was no wonder I couldn't speak through him. An old shoe is easier to invest with comic personality than is, say, a photograph of Cary Grant. The blanker the slate, the more easily we can fill it with our own image.

Our visual cortexes are wired to quickly recognize faces

and then quickly subtract massive amounts of detail from them, zeroing in on their essential message: Is this person happy? Angry? Fearful? Individual faces may vary greatly, but a smirk on one is a lot like a smirk on another. Smirks are conceptual, not pictorial. Our brains are like cartoonists—and cartoonists are like our brains, simplifying and exaggerating, subordinating facial detail to abstract comic concepts.

Scott McCloud, in his cartoon treatise *Understanding Comics*, argues that the image you have of yourself when you're conversing is very different from your image of the person you're conversing with. Your interlocutor may produce universal smiles and universal frowns, and they may help you to identify with him emotionally, but he also has a particular nose and particular skin and particular hair that continually remind you that he's an Other. The image you have of your own face, by contrast, is highly cartoonish. When you feel yourself smile, you imagine a cartoon of smiling, not the complete skin-and-nose-and-hair package. It's precisely the simplicity and universality of cartoon faces, the absence of Otherly particulars, that invite us to love them as we love ourselves. The most widely loved (and profitable) faces in the modern world tend to be exceptionally basic and abstract cartoons: Mickey Mouse, the Simpsons, Tintin, and—simplest of all, barely more than a circle, two dots, and a horizontal line—Charlie Brown.

CHARLES SCHULZ ONLY ever wanted to be a cartoonist. He was born in St. Paul in 1922, the only child of a German father and a mother of Norwegian extraction. Much of the existing Schulzian literature dwells on the Charlie Brownish traumas in his early life: his skinniness and pimples, his unpopularity with girls at school, the inexplicable rejection of a batch of his drawings by his high-school yearbook, and, some years later, the rejection of his marriage proposal by the real-life Little Red-Haired Girl, Donna Mae Johnson. Schulz himself spoke of his youth in a tone close to anger. "It took me a long time to become a human being," he told an interviewer in 1987.

> I was regarded by many as kind of sissyfied, which
> I resented because I really was not a sissy. I was not
> a tough guy, but . . . I was good at any sport where
> you threw things, or hit them, or caught them, or
> something like that. I hated things like swimming
> and tumbling and those kinds of things, so I was
> really not a sissy. [. . . But] the coaches were so in-
> tolerant and there was no program for all of us. So
> I never regarded myself as being much and I never
> regarded myself as good looking and I never had
> a date in high school, because I thought, who'd
> want to date me? So I didn't bother.

Schulz "didn't bother" going to art school, either—it would only have discouraged him, he said, to be around people who could draw better than he could.

On the eve of Schulz's induction into the Army, his mother died of cancer. Schulz later described the loss as a catastrophe from which he almost did not recover. During basic training he was depressed, withdrawn, and grieving. In the long run, though, the Army was good for him. He entered the service, he recalled later, as a "nothing person" and came out as a staff sergeant in charge of a machine-gun squadron. "I thought, by golly, if that isn't a man, I don't know what is," he said. "And I felt good about myself, and that lasted about eight minutes, and then I went back to where I am now."

After the war, he returned to his childhood neighborhood, lived with his father, became intensely involved in a Christian youth group, and learned to draw kids. For the rest of his life, he virtually never drew adults. He avoided adult vices—didn't drink, didn't smoke, didn't swear—and, in his work, he spent more and more time in the imagined yards and sandlots of his childhood. He was childlike, too, in the absoluteness of his scruples and inhibitions. Even after he became famous and powerful, he was reluctant to demand a more flexible layout for *Peanuts*, because he didn't think it was fair to the papers that had been his loyal customers. He also thought it was unfair to draw caricatures. ("If somebody has a big nose," he said, "I'm sure that they regret the fact they have a big nose and who am I to point it out in gross caricature?") His resentment of the name *Peanuts*, which his editors had given the strip in 1950, was still fresh at the end of his life. "To label something that was going to be a life's work with a name like *Peanuts* was really insulting," he told an interviewer in 1987. To the suggestion that thirty-seven years might have softened the insult, Schulz replied: "No, no. I hold a grudge, boy."

Was Schulz's comic genius the product of his psychic wounds? Certainly the middle-aged artist was a mass of resentments and phobias that seemed attributable, in turn, to early traumas. He was increasingly prone to attacks of depression and bitter loneliness ("Just the mention of a hotel makes me turn cold," he told his biographer), and when he finally broke away from his native Minnesota he set about replicating its comforts in California, building himself an ice rink where the snack bar was called "Warm Puppy." By the 1970s, he was reluctant even to get on an airplane unless someone from his family was with him. This would seem to be a classic instance of the pathology that produces great art: wounded in his adolescence, our hero took permanent refuge in the childhood world of *Peanuts*.

But what if Schulz had chosen to become a toy salesman, rather than an artist? Would he still have lived such a withdrawn and emotionally turbulent life? I suspect not. I suspect that Schulz the toy salesman would have gutted his way through a normal life the same way he'd gutted out his military service. He would have done whatever it took to support his family— begged a Valium prescription from his doctor, had a few drinks at the hotel bar.

Schulz wasn't an artist because he suffered. He suffered because he was an artist. To keep choosing art over the comforts of a normal life—to grind out a strip every day for fifty years; to pay the very steep psychic price for this—is the opposite of damaged. It's the sort of choice that only a tower of strength and sanity can make. The reason that Schulz's early sorrows look like "sources" of his later brilliance is that he had the talent and resilience to find humor in them. Almost every young person experiences sorrows. What's distinctive about Schulz's childhood is not his suffering but the fact that he loved comics from an early age, was gifted at drawing, and had the undivided attention of two loving parents.

Every February, Schulz drew a strip about Charlie Brown's failure to get any valentines. Schroeder, in one installment, chides Violet for trying to fob off a discarded valentine on Charlie Brown several days after Valentine's Day, and Charlie Brown shoves Schroeder aside with the words "Don't interfere—I'll take it!" But the story Schulz told about his own childhood experience with valentines was very different. When he was in first grade, he said, his mother helped him make a valentine for each of his classmates, so that nobody would be offended by not getting one, but he felt too shy to put them in the box at the front of the classroom, and so he took them all home again to his mother. At first glance, this story recalls a 1957 strip in which Charlie Brown peers over a fence at a swimming pool full of happy kids and then trudges home by himself and sits in a bucket of water. But Schulz, unlike Charlie Brown, had a mother on duty—a mother to whom he chose to give his entire basket. A child deeply scarred by a failure to get valentines could probably not grow up to draw lovable strips about the pain of never getting valentines. A child like that—one thinks of R. Crumb—might instead draw a valentine box that morphs into a vulva that devours his valentines and then devours him, too.

This is not to say that the depressive and failure-ridden Charlie Brown, the selfish and sadistic Lucy, the philosophizing oddball Linus, and the obsessive Schroeder (whose Beethoven-sized ambitions are realized on a one-octave toy piano) aren't all avatars of Schulz. But his true alter ego is clearly Snoopy: the protean trickster whose freedom is founded on his confidence that he's lovable at heart, the quick-change artist who, for the sheer joy of it, can become a helicopter or a hockey player or Head Beagle and then again, in a flash, before his virtuosity has a chance to alienate you or diminish you, be the eager little dog who just wants dinner.

I NEVER HEARD my father tell a joke. Sometimes he reminisced about a business colleague who ordered a "Scotch and Coke" and a "flander" fillet in a Dallas diner in July, and he could laugh at his own embarrassments, his impolitic remarks at the office, his foolish mistakes on home-improvement projects; but there wasn't a silly bone in his body. He responded to other people's jokes with a wince or a grimace. As a boy, I told him a story I'd made up about a trash-hauling company cited for "fragrant violations." He shook his head, stone-faced, and said, "Not plausible."

In another archetypical *Peanuts* strip, Violet and Patty are abusing Charlie Brown in vicious stereo: "GO ON HOME! WE DON'T WANT YOU AROUND HERE!" He trudges away with his eyes on the ground, and Violet remarks, "It's a strange thing about Charlie Brown. You almost never see him laugh."

The few times he ever played catch with me, my father threw the ball like a thing he wanted to get rid of, a piece of rotten fruit, and he snatched at my return throws with an awkward pawing motion. I never saw him touch a football or a Frisbee. His two main recreations were golf and bridge, and his enjoyment of them consisted in perpetually reconfirming that he was useless at the one and unlucky at the other.

He only ever wanted not to be a child anymore. His parents were a pair of nineteenth-century Scandinavians caught up in a Hobbesian struggle to prevail in the swamps of north-central Minnesota. His popular, charismatic older brother drowned in a hunting accident when he was still a young man. His nutty and pretty and spoiled younger sister had an only daughter who died in a one-car accident when she was twenty-two. My father's parents also died in a one-car accident, but only after regaling him with prohibitions, demands, and criticisms for fifty years. He never said a harsh word about them. He never said a nice word, either.

The few childhood stories he told were about his dog, Spider, and his gang of friends in the invitingly named little town, Palisade, that his father and uncles had constructed among the swamps. The local high school was eight miles from Palisade. In order to attend, my father lived in a boardinghouse for a year and later commuted in his father's Model A. He was a social cipher, invisible after school. The most popular girl in his class, Romelle Erickson, was expected to be the valedictorian, and the school's "social crowd" was "shocked," my father told me many times, when it turned out that the "country boy," "Earl Who," had claimed the title.

When he registered at the University of Minnesota, in 1933, his father went with him and announced, at the head of the registration line, "He's going to be a civil engineer." For the rest of his life, my father was restless. In his thirties, he agonized about whether to study medicine; in his forties, he was offered a partnership in a contracting firm which, to my mother's ever-lasting disappointment, he wasn't bold enough to accept; in his fifties and sixties, he admonished me never to let a corporation exploit my talents. In the end, though, he spent fifty years doing exactly what his father had told him to do.

After he died, I came into a few boxes of his papers. Most of the stuff was disappointingly unrevealing, and from his early childhood there was nothing except one brown envelope in which he'd saved a thick bundle of valentines. Some of them were flimsy and unsigned, some of them were more elaborate, with crepe-paper solids or 3-D foldouts, and a few from "Margaret" were in actual envelopes; the styles ranged from backwoods Victorian to 1920s art deco. The signatures—most of them from the boys and girls his age, a few from his cousins, one from his sister—were in the crude handwriting of elementary school. The gushiest profusions came from his best friend, Walter Anderson. But there weren't any valentines from his parents, or any other cards or tokens of their love, in any of the boxes.

My mother called him "oversensitive." She meant that it was easy to hurt his feelings, but the sensitivity was physical as well. When he was young, a doctor gave him a pinprick test that showed him to be allergic to "almost everything," including wheat, milk, and tomatoes. A different doctor, whose office was at the top of five long flights of stairs, greeted him with a blood-pressure test and immediately declared him unfit to fight the Nazis. Or so my father told me, with a shrugging gesture and an odd smile (as if to say, "What could I do?"), when I asked him why he hadn't been in the war. Even as a teenager, I sensed that his social awkwardness and sensitivities had been aggravated by not serving. He came from a family of pacifist Swedes, however, and was very happy not to be a soldier. He was happy that my brothers had college deferments and good luck with the lottery. Among his war-vet colleagues, he was such an outlier on the subject of Vietnam that he didn't dare talk about it. At home, in private, he aggressively avowed that, if Tom had drawn a bad number, he personally would have driven him to Canada.

Tom was a second-born in the mold of my father. He got poison ivy so bad it was like measles. He had a mid-October birthday and was perennially the youngest kid in his classes. On his only date in high school, he was so nervous that he forgot his baseball tickets and left the car idling in the street while he ran back inside; the car rolled down the hill and punched through an asphalt curb, clearing two levels of a terraced garden, and came to rest on a neighbor's front lawn.

To me, it simply added to Tom's mystique that the car was not only still drivable but entirely undamaged. Neither he nor Bob could do any wrong in my eyes. They were expert whistlers and chess players, amazing wielders of tools and pencils, and the sole suppliers of whatever anecdotes and data I was able to impress my friends with. In the margins of Tom's school copy of *A Portrait of the Artist as a Young Man*, he drew a two-hundred-page riffle-animation of a stick-figure pole-vaulter clearing a hurdle, landing on his head, and being carted away on a stretcher by stick-figure E.M.S. personnel. This seemed to me a masterwork of filmic art and science. But my father had told Tom: "You'd make a good architect, here are three schools to choose from." He said: "You're going to work for Sverdrup."

Tom was gone for five days before we heard from him. His call came on a Sunday after church. We were sitting on the screen porch, and my mother ran the length of the house to answer the phone. She sounded so ecstatic with relief I felt embarrassed for her. Tom had hitchhiked back to Houston and was doing deep-fry at a Church's fried-chicken establishment, hoping to save enough money to join his best friend in Colorado. My mother kept asking him when he might come home, assuring him that he was welcome and that he wouldn't have to work at Sverdrup; but I could tell, without even hearing Tom's responses, that he wanted nothing to do with us now.

THE PURPOSE OF a comic strip, Schulz liked to say, was to sell newspapers and to make people laugh. His formulation may look self-deprecating at first glance, but in fact it is an oath of loyalty. When I. B. Singer, in his Nobel address, declared that the novelist's first responsibility is to be a storyteller, he didn't say "mere storyteller," and Schulz didn't say "merely make people laugh." He was loyal to the reader who wanted something funny from the funny pages. Just about anything—protesting against world hunger; getting a laugh out of words like "nooky"; dispensing wisdom; dying—is easier than real comedy.

Schulz never stopped trying to be funny. Around 1970, though, he began to drift away from aggressive humor and into melancholy reverie. There came tedious meanderings in Snoopyland with the unhilarious bird Woodstock and the unamusing beagle Spike. Certain leaden devices, such as Marcie's insistence on calling Peppermint Patty "sir," were heavily recycled. By the late eighties, the strip had grown so quiet that younger friends of mine seemed baffled by my fandom. It didn't help that later *Peanuts* anthologies loyally reprinted so many Spike and Marcie strips. The volumes that properly showcased Schulz's genius, the three hardcover collections from the sixties, had gone out of print.

Still more harmful to Schulz's reputation were his own kitsch spinoffs. Even in the sixties, you had to fight through cloying Warm Puppy paraphernalia to reach the comedy; the cuteness levels in latter-day *Peanuts* TV specials tied my toes in knots. What first made *Peanuts Peanuts* was cruelty and failure, and yet every *Peanuts* greeting card and tchotchke and blimp had to feature somebody's sweet, crumpled smile. Everything about the billion-dollar *Peanuts* industry argued against Schulz as an artist to be taken seriously. Far more than Disney, whose studios were churning out kitsch from the start, Schulz came to seem an icon of art's corruption by commerce, which sooner or later paints a smiling sales face on everything it touches. The fan who wants to see him as an artist sees a merchant instead. Why isn't he two ponies?

It's hard to repudiate a comic strip, however, if your memories of it are more vivid than your memories of your own life. When Charlie Brown went off to summer camp, I went along in my imagination. I heard him trying to make conversation with the fellow camper who lay in his bunk and refused to say anything but "Shut up and leave me alone." I watched when he finally came home again and shouted to Lucy, "I'm back! I'm back!" and Lucy gave him a bored look and said, "Have you been away?"

I went to camp myself, in the summer of 1970. But aside from an alarming personal hygiene situation which seemed to have resulted from my peeing in some poison ivy, and which, for several days, I was convinced was either a fatal tumor or puberty, my camp experience paled beside Charlie Brown's. The best part of it was coming home and seeing Bob waiting for me, in his new Karmann Ghia, at the YMCA parking lot.

Tom was also home by then. He'd managed to make his way to his friend's house in Colorado, but the friend's parents weren't happy about harboring somebody else's runaway son, and so they'd sent Tom back to St. Louis. Officially, I was very excited that he was back. In truth, I was embarrassed to be around him. I was afraid that if I referred to his sickness and our quarantine I might prompt a relapse. I wanted to live in a *Peanuts* world where rage was funny and insecurity was lovable. The littlest kid in my *Peanuts* books, Sally Brown, grew older for a while and then hit a glass ceiling and went no further. I wanted everyone in my family to get along and nothing to change; but suddenly, after Tom ran away, it was as if the five of us looked around, asked why we should be spending time together, and failed to come up with many good answers.

For the first time, in the months that followed, my parents' conflicts became audible. My father came home on cool nights to complain about the house's "chill." My mother countered that the house wasn't cold if you were *doing housework all day*. My father marched into the dining room to adjust the thermostat and dramatically point to its "Comfort Zone," a pale-blue arc between 72 and 78 degrees. My mother said that she was *so hot*. And I decided, as always, not to voice my suspicion that the Comfort Zone referred to air-conditioning in the summer rather than heat in the winter. My father set the temperature at 72 and retreated to the den, which was situated directly above the furnace. There was then a lull, and then big explosions. No matter what corner of the house I hid myself in, I could hear my father bellowing, "LEAVE THE GOD-DAMNED THERMO-STAT ALONE!"

"Earl, I didn't touch it!"

"You did! Again!"

"I didn't think I even moved it, I just looked at it, I didn't mean to change it."

"Again! You monkeyed with it again! I had it set where I wanted it. And you moved it down to seventy!"

"Well, if I did somehow change it, I'm sure I didn't mean to. You'd be hot, too, if you worked all day in the kitchen."

"All I ask at the end of a long day at work is that the temperature be set in the Comfort Zone."

"Earl, it is so hot in the kitchen. You don't know, because you're never *in* here, but it is *so* hot."

"The *low end* of the Comfort Zone! Not even the middle! The low end! It is not too much to ask!"

And I wonder why "cartoonish" remains such a pejorative. It took me half my life to achieve seeing my parents as cartoons. And to become more perfectly a cartoon myself: what a victory that would be.

My father eventually applied technology to the problem of temperature. He bought a space heater to put behind his chair in the dining room, where he was bothered in winter by drafts from the bay window behind him. Like so many of his appliance purchases, the heater was a pathetically cheap little thing, a wattage hog with a stertorous fan and a grinning orange mouth which dimmed the lights and drowned out conversation and produced a burning smell every time it cycled on. When I was in high school, he bought a quieter, more expensive model. One evening my mother and I started reminiscing about the old model, caricaturing my father's temperature sensitivities, doing cartoons of the little heater's faults, the smoke and the buzzing, and my father got mad and left the table. He thought we were ganging up on him. He thought I was being cruel, and I was, but I was also forgiving him.

Lucy Can't See

Lisa Birnbach

In March 1967 the musical comedy *You're a Good Man, Charlie Brown* debuted at Theater 80 in New York's East Village. It ran for four years before moving to Broadway. In advance of it becoming a staple of local theaters and middle schools all over the world, it was cool. Off-Broadway kind of cool. No longer was *Peanuts* just that comic strip your dad saved for you from the evening paper. It had earned downtown cred. The original company included Gary Burghoff (later of TV's *M*A*S*H*) as Charlie Brown, Bob Balaban as Linus, and Reva Rose as Lucy.

That same year, a legally blind third-grader mounted the stage of the auditorium at the Lenox School, a second-tier girls' school on that same city's Upper East Side, to play Lucy in a scene from "The Wonderful World of *Peanuts*," a series of skits without music. It was performed once in a dress rehearsal, and once at a school assembly. It was the first time that girl had gone anywhere outside of her bedroom without wearing her eyeglasses. The audience at Lenox was shocked when they figured out who that somewhat familiar-looking girl was—that shy third-grader who normally wore coke-bottle glasses. It was me.

In the sixties the *Peanuts* gang was the coed group of friends that seemed accessible yet also unattainable. They were sporty. Even if Charlie Brown struck out or Linus was tagged "it." They lived in what we called *the country*. (Their homes were houses, not apartment buildings. They were allowed to walk around their neighborhood without adult supervision.) I lived in the big city and had to be accompanied everywhere. The Browns, the Van Pelts, et al., were also thoroughly American. (My father was born in Germany and spoke with an accent.) They accepted one another even if they didn't always care for one another. They spoke like adults though they lived in small childish bodies. Everyone stood out and no one stood out.

At Lenox, I was the only girl in the Lower School who wore glasses. I was one of the minority who *had* to wear tie shoes. Uniforms were required: a winter jumper, a spring jumper, a tunic and bloomers for gym, and even a specific smock for art class. (They were the French blue painters' smocks our mothers had to purchase at a store called Youth at Play.) We wore them over our other uniforms. This didn't strike anyone as odd at the time, just the usual rigidity of single-sex schools. Naturally, the girls in our school looked more or less alike. Diversity had not yet arrived at the school on East 70th Street.

Glasses weren't cool or retro or indicative of braininess or style in the mid-1960s if you were a kid. There were two styles for girls: cat's-eyes and Clark Kent. There were two colors: pale pink and tortoiseshell.

In the land of *Peanuts*, everyone wore his or her signature look. Lucy's blue dress, Charlie Brown's yellow-and-black zig-zag T-shirt, Schroeder's striped T-shirt, Linus's red shirt and blue blankie, Snoopy's occasional accessories: all provided information about their owners. Our uniforms, on the other hand, only revealed which school we attended. The jumper masked our individual identities in the most efficient possible way. Only through one's socks and coats did anyone have an opinion, or more likely, expressed her mother's point of view. Our own stories were less important.

As one of three kids in my family I was instructed not to be selfish. Selfishness was the worst thing I could imagine; if there were anything more despicable, I hadn't heard of it. I was the only girl in the family so I had less sharing to do if you think about it. I tried not to think about myself too much.

Lucy, on the other hand, enjoyed being self-centered. She was dramatic. She wanted Schroeder's love and respect and had no problem demanding it. She had confidence. She may not have had a guilty bone in her body as she grabbed Charlie Brown's football away from him just as his foot was about to kick it. She could be bad. She could be mean. She didn't really suffer any consequences other than our disdain for her. It was hard for me to feel empathy toward her.

Lucy not only offered advice, she insisted on being paid for it. Lucy was a bossy know-it-all. And this was early on in the comic strip, circa 1952. I recently learned that in 1954 Lucy finally became *Lucy*. (It would take decades—in fact not until well after Charles Schulz's death—but eventually Lucy's big sense of self would be seen as a positive attribute for the modern woman. Was she a little abrasive? *Good grief.* You can't worry about making friends while you ascend your own ladder to success.)

Unlike what I had seen and experienced, the *Peanuts* kids did not run off and tell their parents everything. As a preteen reader of Mr. Schulz's oeuvre, I missed seeing the characters' parents. That was when I considered my parents the heroes of my young life. True, the characters got called in for supper or had to go to school at a certain hour, but they were independent. They solved their own problems. They got on with things. They didn't dwell on hurts or resentments, unlike real kids. Unlike real Birnbachs.

OUR DRAMA TEACHER, Mrs. Brandt, decided I would play Lucy to Karen Klingon's Schroeder. What could she have been thinking?

Offstage, I was more Charlie Brown than Lucy. What those tie shoes and glasses didn't secure, my personality did. Charlie Brown's proving ground was his pitcher's mound. Mine was every day: first the trip in the woody station wagon that was our actual school *bus*, and then the grind of being at Lenox for nine years. I was destined to be unpopular. When your entire grade ranges in size from sixteen to twenty-one girls, most of whom stay put for twelve years, no breaks are given. Every gaffe, every embarrassment, was remembered, catalogued, and indexed. I couldn't really move past my reputation. I was so unpopular *I* wouldn't have befriended me either. My glasses were Charlie Brown's zigzag shirt. Most school days someone would manage to ask me if I were blind. I never could come up with a snappy rejoinder.

My education as a young girl began at this school in the

mid-'60s, but in retrospect it felt like the '40s. (Remember the bloomers we wore for gym? We changed in and out of them in a *cloakroom*.) Most of our teachers remembered the Depression and World War II. They were for the most part in late middle age. They had never wed, or were widows or divorcées; they never had children of their own. Their pride in their students was nominal; many didn't seem to enjoy kids too much. In those days, a job as a teacher was one of the best a college-educated woman could get, after all, especially in a private school. (*These were the years before women wore pants in public in the city.*) Our teachers wore dresses with stockings and heels. They wore lipstick and had their hair done into the fashionable helmet-like hairdos of the 1950s.

We students curtsied. There were guidelines for that, as well as rules for standing up when an adult came into our classrooms. When our headmistress was visible, even out of the most remote corners of our eyes, we were advised to stand up. We recited the Lord's Prayer several times a week. We once received a hands-on lesson on the difference between a ring and a *cocktail ring*. Many of my classmates had old-fashioned names too. In addition to the requisite Karens, Nancys, and Pattys in our grade, there was a Virginia, a Marion, a Frances, a Mary, and a Marguerite. I remember an Alma a few years ahead of us and an Eleanor behind us. Our mothers did not work. At least not when we were in Lower School.

I know this doesn't sound like fun. It wasn't. My best times were when I could read by myself at home in my bedroom. I read both hungrily and lazily. I read books that were "hard" and I read volume after volume of *Peanuts* collections. There was no Facebook then offering photographic proof of other people's good times; this had to be intuited. When my classmates were, I suspected, seeing one another and having fun together, I listened to 45s over and over on my little record player.

I also enjoyed yelling at my brothers whenever they crossed my threshold.

Get out of my room! Get out of my room!

Wait a second! At home, I was Lucy—bossy and smart. At school I was Charlie Brown—pathetic and ineffectual. Now we're getting somewhere.

LUCY WAS THE warrior queen of the *Peanuts* tribe. She was feared. She got her way. She seemed untouched by the sickening desire to be popular, a disease that affected most Americans under the age of twenty throughout the 1960s and '70s. Broadcast television—the only kind that existed at the time—reinforced the urgency of popularity. Any family show pummeled that message home—whether it was learning that the boy who was bullied by the cool kids was actually . . . kind of cool himself, or when someone's big sister loaned her little sibling an outfit that made her the hit of the sock-hop.

As you recall, Lucy was in love with Schroeder. As one of the taller students in the third grade, I had expected to be cast in a male part in "The Wonderful World of *Peanuts*." But if I were going to be one of the three Lucys, couldn't I be "*Therapy 5 cents please*" Lucy? This was going to be awkward since this was a love scene between Lucy and Schroeder, in which I would have to declare my love for him. Since this was in the Dark Ages, the scene would definitely result in teasing against us. Of the two of us, I had the worse gig, since Karen as Schroeder could hunch over her toy piano and try to ignore me.

We rehearsed. I remember nothing about the rehearsals except that I sprawled on the floor, and propped myself up on my elbows, staring into the eyes of Karen/Schroeder. I don't recall it being funny or making anyone laugh. At this point in my *character work*, I still had every intention of performing my Lucy in my own eyeglasses. As we say now, "the optics" were always a risk, but when I had been in the Second Grade Insect Assembly my "Butterfly dancing out of her cocoon" wore glasses, and no one said a word against them. In our First Grade Christmas Pageant, my Joseph wore small cat's-eye-style glasses, and no one complained.

You see where this is headed. In the dress rehearsal, Mrs. Brandt surprised me by telling me I wouldn't be allowed to wear my glasses in performance. I panicked. I was convinced I'd fall off the stage. I pictured it vividly. I'd stumble and roll down the steps. Humiliation was again nearby.

I couldn't shake the fear that I'd end up slipping off the stage in the performance the next day, but I had to commit to becoming Lucy van Pelt. I practiced without my glasses that night. As life became blurrier, I lost mental focus too. I couldn't see—or couldn't see much. From a foot away life for me has always looked like something seen through a frosted bathroom window: colorful mosaics.

But the next day, when I stepped onstage, a funny thing happened. Not being able to see Schroeder or her tiny piano freed me from feeling like my boring, unworthy, Charlie Brownish self. Surrounded by my visual fog, I actually felt like someone else. Not me. Not the little, legally blind, uncool girl who had thrown up (actually twice) at Lenox; the little girl in glasses who was often among the last girls picked for a team; the girl who just wanted someone—anyone—to ask her if she liked *The Man from U*N*C*L*E*, too. All this didn't matter anymore.

Onstage I suddenly felt like an eight-year-old cartoon femme fatale, and I turned to the general vicinity of Karen Klingon's eyes. "Schroeder, look deep into my eyes, and tell me that you love me," I demanded. Whose voice was that? Whose conviction was that? Had I actually turned into Paula Prentiss? (She was the only actress whose name I knew.) Was that sound the audience laughing? At me or with me?

I didn't fall.

The crowd cheered.

READER, MY SUCCESS in "The Wonderful World of *Peanuts*" didn't cause my head to swell. I was still asked daily about my blindness, was still reminded about barfing at chorus, and was still chosen last for volleyball. But I did think of my performance as a victory, and an unseeing Lucy led to more roles at Lenox, including an unseeing schoolgirl (unnamed) in *The Prime of Miss Jean Brodie*, and then a legally blind Sancho Panza in *The World of Don Quixote*. (The latter might have been written by the *Peanuts* playwright.)

I knew I'd never be Paula Prentiss. But I also decided that I didn't have to be Charlie Brown my whole life. I could get contact lenses.

The History of the Twentieth Century, Four Panels at a Time

David Kamp

"WHY COULDN'T McCOVEY HAVE HIT THE BALL JUST THREE FEET HIGHER?"

Wait, who was McCovey? Which particular ballgame was under discussion? And why did this subject so agitate Charlie Brown that his face was tilted skyward, dominated by a black expanse of ink depicting his wide-open mouth, with two tears flying from each of his unseen eyes?

In my elementary-school years—the '70s, basically—I was a dedicated *Peanuts* fan, reading both the daily strip and the paperback collections of Charles Schulz's work that were published every few months. The McCovey strip originally ran on December 22, 1962, four years before I was born, so I must have come across it in an older collection. But Charlie Brown's wail of despair struck a chord across that expanse of time, his bitter longing for a better sports outcome resonating with me. So I had questions.

I also had questions about an uncharacteristic explosion of ire from Schroeder, in a '63 strip in which he exclaimed to Lucy, "Rachel Carson! Rachel Carson! Rachel Carson! / You're always talking about Rachel Carson!" To which Lucy coolly replied, "We girls need our heroines!"

Who was Rachel Carson? Why was she heroic?

In those days, kids didn't have Google or Siri to consult with. For Rachel Carson, I got answers from my mother. This was right in her wheelhouse: an outdoorswoman, activist, and environmentalist, Mom had read *Silent Spring*, Carson's scathing 1962 indictment of Big Chem for the havoc its pesticides were wreaking on the natural world. And as a woman who had dared to become a microbiologist just one generation after Carson had dared to become a marine biologist, my mother was the very embodiment of the kind of girl that Lucy was talking about. So she was nothing less than delighted to tell me all about Rachel Carson.

I can't remember who filled me in on McCovey—that Willie was his first name, for starters, and that he was the San Francisco Giants' power-hitting first baseman, and that in the bottom of the ninth inning in the seventh game of the '62 World Series, against the Yankees, with two men out and two men on, he scorched a line drive that would have won the Giants the championship had it not been hit directly to Bobby Richardson, the Yanks' second baseman.

But I pursued these data about McCovey, and about Carson, solely because Schulz made me want to. His frequent and esoteric name-drops piqued my curiosity, and, in so doing, provided me with an excellent supplementary education about the twentieth century, on subjects that weren't covered in the history and social-studies classes of my otherwise irreproachable public school in central New Jersey. I first heard of Twiggy, and by extension the whole Swinging London scene she represented, because Snoopy announced in a 1967 strip that he thought he was in love with her (a total non sequitur in the context of the Farrah Fawcett '70s, which only made me *more curious*). I first heard of Andrew Wyeth because Snoopy acquired one of Wyeth's paintings in 1966, after he had lost his Van Gogh original in a tragic doghouse fire. (Van Gogh, like Schroeder's beloved Beethoven a canonical dead artist, was someone with whom I was already familiar.)

And from Schulz's ongoing Veterans Day gag in which Snoopy put on his old Army uniform to "go over to Bill Mauldin's house and quaff a few root beers," I was given a non-textbook window into World War II, during which Mauldin, Schulz's pal and contemporary, drew cartoons for *Stars and Stripes*, the U.S. military paper. The Mauldin strips also provided me with useful insight into the secretive bond of war veterans who feel that their experience can only ever be fully understood by fellow war veterans. My father and grandfather were vets themselves, and they never talked to their families about what they had been through. They had their own Bill Mauldins.

Plus, I learned the word "quaff."

PERHAPS I HAVE not adequately conveyed how closely, how Talmudically, I was poring over Schulz's oeuvre back then. *Peanuts* was my joy and my refuge, its magical reconciliation of humor and melancholy simpatico with my own shy, solitary nature as a child. Using money saved up from allowances and grandparent handouts, I bought new collections such as *Speak*

Softly, and Carry a Beagle as soon as they came out—that book's very title occasioning a potted history by my father of Teddy Roosevelt's approach to diplomacy. When I had cash to spend but there was no new *Peanuts* title, I'd pick up something from the back catalogue, even the '50s material, which I considered inferior because Schulz's drawing style was more straitjack-eted and crew-cutted then, and because Shermy, Violet, and (non-Peppermint) Patty were so dull compared with the char-acters who followed them.

I even bought stuff that was beyond my reading comprehen-sion, such as *Charlie Brown and Charlie Schulz*, a 1970 hardcover book by Lee Mendelson (who, with Bill Melendez, produced the animated *Peanuts* TV specials) that was essentially a histor-ical *Peanuts* monograph for grown-ups, prepared on the occa-sion of the strip's twentieth anniversary, and peppered with morose, therapy-informed quotes from Schulz about depres-sion and anxiety. (Some years later, when I became devoted to Garry Trudeau's *Doonesbury*, I made a similar mistake with my precious dollars, purchasing *Trout Fishing in the Reflecting Pool*, an unreadable collection of sub–Hunter S. Thompson satiri-cal essays about Watergate written by the journalist Nicholas von Hoffman, solely because Trudeau had provided the book's illustrations.)

My *Peanuts* books were not treated cavalierly, tossed on the floor or shelved haphazardly. No, I devoted a corner of my tiny bedroom to an arrangement evoking a display at a children's li-brary. I took a wicker picnic hamper, covered it with the downy baby blanket that I, like Linus, had carried with me everywhere as a toddler, and artfully set up the books atop the blanket at different angles, augmenting this decor with Hallmark birthday cards that I had received bearing images of the *Peanuts* characters. This installation, set up solely for my own appreciation, was OCD and a little nuts. Let's call it what it was: a shrine to Charles M. Schulz.

MY LIFE TUTORIAL via the proper nouns of *Peanuts* was an unintended consequence of Schulz's simply following his own muse; he was notoriously wary of attributing any messaging or grand philosophy to his strips. About the closest he ever came to signaling intent was when he explained why he named Woodstock "Woodstock," and, even then, he was characteristically vague and noncommittal, saying, "I thought Woodstock would be a good name for this bird and also, it will get the attention of these people that liked that kind of thing."

Schulz not only got the attention of counterculturists, who had already appropriated Snoopy's fighter-pilot image for an unauthorized "Don't Eat Yellow Snow" sew-on patch that appeared on jean jackets from Washington Square to People's Park. He also piqued the interest of this confused boy. Reading the four-panel strip that was first published in newspapers on June 22, 1970, I failed to grasp its comedic payoff. It went like this: (1) Snoopy's tousle-feathered friend flies into view, upside down; (2) Snoopy's first thought balloon reads, "I finally found out what that stupid bird's name is . . ."; (3) Snoopy's second thought balloon reads, "You'll never believe it . . ."; (4) Snoopy's third and final thought balloon, floating above the little bird, now seated atop the doghouse with a beatific grin on his face, reads, "Woodstock!"

Wait, in what way is that a punchline? It's not a particularly funny name. I knew that there had to be a topical explanation; even as a child, I understood Schulz not to trade in the sort of Dada, so-unfunny-it's-funny humor in which *Nancy*'s Ernie Bushmiller specialized. It was my brother, Ted, four years my senior, who provided me with the necessary thumbnail overview: hippies, mud, VW vans, Country Joe and the Fish, Jimi in fringed buckskin playing "The Star-Spangled Banner."

As an adult, in my capacity as a journalist and author, I have interviewed Sly Stone, Robbie Robertson, Graham Nash, and David Crosby, all of whom actually played at Woodstock. But my first inkling of that festival's very existence came from "that stupid bird." This observation is not offered in some corny, "Wow, life takes ya full circle, don't it?" spirit. Rather, it's a tribute to the path of inquiry that Schulz set me on.

It's been noted before that *Peanuts*, in its stealthy guise as a wholesome comic strip putatively about and for kids, shined a light on some big, controversial ideas that had theretofore been little discussed in the American mainstream, such as the validity of women's athletics and the value of talk therapy. In similar fashion, the strip, which reached about a hundred million readers daily at its apex, cultivated legions of dedicated followers who made Schulz's obsessions and interests their own. Well, okay, maybe not *legions*—but if you were the type of fan who kept a shrine to Charles Schulz in your bedroom, you took what was in the man's head seriously.

SOMETHING HAD CHANGED by the late '70s and early '80s. I was older, and I had caught up with Schulz in terms of pop-culture fluency. His references to Olivia Newton-John, Elton John, and John McEnroe elicited nodding recognition rather than fascinated puzzlement. Schulz was older, too, and sometimes, his topical material made me cringe: Peppermint Patty's experimentation with Bo Derek–style beaded cornrows, for example, and Snoopy's "world famous disco dancer" persona. Nearing sixty, Schulz seemed to be grasping for topicality rather than letting his weird, wintry Minnesotan mind do its thing. I actually shuddered on October 19, 1978—the day that a jiggling, white-suited Snoopy thought-ballooned the words "BOOGIE DOWN!" It pained me, in the same way that coming to grips with parental fallibility did.

Time and perspective have since healed that psychic wound. Really, would it have been any better if Schulz's taste had been cooler, or if one of his kids had clued him in to the Clash, and suddenly there'd have been a *Peanuts* arc in which Snoopy appeared in camo fatigues and a fauxhawk, thinking, "Here's Joe Strummer, getting ready to bring down the house with some righteous dub rock"?

The reality is, I was lucky to have been born during Schulz's peak creative period, and simply to have been alive while he was a working cartoonist. He was the best at what he did, his achievement in comics forever untoppable. As for the curriculum he inadvertently created—call it The History of the Twentieth Century, Four Panels at a Time—it's just another way in which Schulz surpassed everyone in his field. Wishing for anything more out of him would be as futile as wishing that McCovey had hit the ball three feet higher.

"GOOD GRIEF"

WHEN I WAS GROWING UP IN THE 1960S, "PEANUTS" WAS A VERY BIG DEAL, SUCH A BIG DEAL THAT INSTEAD OF RUNNING "PEANUTS" IN THE DAILY FUNNY PAGE, THE LOS ANGELES TIMES, MY HOMETOWN PAPER, GAVE IT A PLACE OF HONOR IN THE FRONT PAGE SECTION.

BECAUSE I GOT TO SEE THE "PEANUTS" KIDS EVERYDAY, IT WAS LIKE THEY WERE MY FRIENDS. I WAS JUST AS CURIOUS AS TO WHAT THEY WERE GOING TO DO ONE DAY TO THE NEXT AS I WAS ABOUT THE REAL KIDS WHO LIVED ON MY BLOCK. I HAD DISTINCT FEELINGS FOR EACH CHARACTER IN "PEANUTS."

WHY, YOU MAY WONDER, DID I LOVE LINUS?

BECAUSE "PEANUTS" WAS IN THE FRONT PAGE SECTION, THE "ADULT" PART OF THE NEWSPAPER, I WOULD ALMOST ALWAYS HAVE TO WAIT UNTIL THE AFTERNOON, WHEN MY PARENTS WERE DONE WITH THAT DAY'S PAPER, TO GET TO READ "PEANUTS".

I WAS FIVE YEARS OLD AND COULD BARELY READ WHEN I STARTED TO FOLLOW "PEANUTS", BUT AS THE YEARS WENT BY AND I BECAME A BETTER READER, THERE WAS AN UNFORESEEN NEGATIVE CONSEQUENCE TO "PEANUTS" BEING IN THE FRONT PAGE SECTION.

IT'S POSSIBLE THAT IF I DIDN'T READ "PEANUTS" I WOULD NOT HAVE FOUND OUT ABOUT THE EIGHT NURSES WHO WERE KILLED BY AN INTRUDER IN THE MIDDLE OF THE NIGHT. BUT I DID KNOW AND KNOWING ABOUT THAT HORRIBLE CRIME HAD A CATASTROPHIC EFFECT ON MY NINE-YEAR-OLD PSYCHE.

THERE ARE TERRIBLE MEN OUT THERE DOING TERRIBLE THINGS TO NURSES!

NURSES! WHO ARE SO NICE AND GIVE YOU LOLLIPOPS, AND HELP YOU AND COMFORT YOU WHEN YOU'RE SICK...

...AND IF TERRIBLE MEN CAN DO TERRIBLE THINGS TO NURSES, THEY CAN DO TERRIBLE THINGS TO ANYONE, INCLUDING...

...ME!

I THINK MOST KIDS BELIEVE THEIR PARENTS WILL PROTECT THEM FROM BAD THINGS, BUT TRY AS I MIGHT, I WAS NOT REALLY SURE THAT MY PARENTS WOULD COME THROUGH IN SITUATIONS LIKE THAT.

IT WOULD HAVE BEEN REASSURING IF MY SISTER, EVELYN, SHARED MY FEARS AND ANXIETY, BUT THE NURSES' MURDER DIDN'T BOTHER HER. SHE JUST WENT ON ENJOYING HER NORMAL SUMMER ACTIVITIES, SWIMMING, PLAYING WITH FRIENDS, FINDING WAYS TO UNDERMINE MY CONFIDENCE AND SELF-WORTH WHENEVER POSSIBLE. ACTUALLY, NO OTHER KIDS SEEMED PERTURBED BY THE GRISLY CRIME. THE ONLY CHILD I COULD IMAGINE UNDERSTANDING AND SYMPATHIZING WITH MY DARK OBSESSION WAS LINUS.

I TRIED TO FOLLOW MY SISTER'S LEAD AND JUST FORGET WHAT WAS GOING ON IN THE ADULT WORLD AND PLAY LIKE A NORMAL KID, BUT THEN, TWO WEEKS AFTER THE NURSES' MURDER, A SNIPER IN A TOWER AT THE UNIVERSITY OF TEXAS SHOT AND KILLED SIXTEEN PEOPLE AND WOUNDED THIRTY-TWO OTHERS. AFTER THAT, NOT ONLY WAS I TERRIFIED OF TERRIBLE MEN DOING TERRIBLE THINGS TO ME AT NIGHT, I ALSO HAD TO WORRY ABOUT SNIPERS LURKING ON OUR NEIGHBORS' ROOFTOPS.

DURING THAT SUMMER, I OFTEN TOOK REFUGE IN THE WORLD
OF "PEANUTS," READING THE STRIP IN THE DAILY PAPER,
AND MY "PEANUTS" BOOKS. THE "PEANUTS" WORLD WAS FAR
FROM PERFECT. THE KIDS WERE RARELY HAPPY, OFTEN
CRUEL, AND NEVER SEEMED TO HAVE MUCH FUN, BUT AT
LEAST, THERE WEREN'T ANY PSYCHO KILLERS HAUNTING
THEIR LIVES.

ME IN THE "REAL WORLD," COMING HOME FROM A PLAYDATE, LOOKING FOR SNIPERS ON OUR NEIGHBORS' ROOF.

ME IN THE "REAL WORLD," LOOKING FOR SNIPERS ON OUR ROOF.

ACTUALLY, THERE WERE NO ADULTS AT ALL IN "PEANUTS". IT WAS A PURELY MAKE-BELIEVE KIDS' WORLD, AND IN 1966, AS A FRIGHTENED NINE-YEAR-OLD WHO COULD NOT FIND ANY REASSURANCE OF SAFETY FROM THE ADULTS AROUND ME, THE "PEANUTS" WORLD WAS WHERE I LONGED TO BE.

MY FAVORITE FANTASY WHEN I WAS TRYING TO SLEEP AT NIGHT THAT SUMMER OF THE DEAD NURSES AND THE SNIPER IN TEXAS, WAS TO IMAGINE MYSELF SITTING WITH LINUS IN A PUMPKIN PATCH WAITING FOR THE GREAT PUMPKIN TO RISE UP TO THE SKY.

I LOVED MANY THINGS ABOUT LINUS, BUT HIS UNSHAKABLE BELIEF IN THE GREAT PUMPKIN WAS ONE OF THE THINGS I LOVED BEST.

AND IN MY IMAGINATION, I WOULD PRETEND TO BELIEVE IN THE GREAT PUMPKIN TOO. (ALTHOUGH I REALLY DIDN'T.)

I WOULD PRETEND THAT I DIDN'T CARE ABOUT MISSING TRICK-OR-TREATING. (ALTHOUGH IN REALITY I WOULD NEVER NOT GO TRICK-OR-TREATING.)

Duck Boy

Maxine Hong Kingston

I wanted to adopt Britt Masy. He was not preliterate—he was fifteen—but he could not read, and he never did learn how to read during the two years he had to come to my classes. We would both grin and grin at each other so happily because he read two pages of a first-grade reader, and the next day he would have forgotten it all. To adopt him or marry him would have been the only way I could have changed him a little, and even then it would have been too late—unless I could have adopted him when he was born. He had no mother, and his father, an alcoholic, had given him away. His foster parents took in a different child every few years for the $75 a month from the state. They must have done it for the money. Who else would take on Britt as a daily responsibility? Short. Skinny. Pimply. Glasses. Scared, darting, jumping eyes when he did not understand something or when the others teased him or hit him. But he was scared only when they pounced from hiding, or jumped on him from the back. After the surprise and pain, always sweet words and sweet smiles, not idiotic smiles. When I made an incomprehensible assignment to the class (it was a regular public-school class, not Special Ed or E. H., whatever that stands for), I watched him staring around at the corners of floor and ceiling, startled and panicked, a bird, a wild mouse, then the amazing smile if he understood.

Britt hungered after a reality that leaped into him now and then. It seemed to come like a hard light that flashed too quickly to examine. Like one hammer blow. Like a curtain yanked aside for a moment. The reality would be some emergency from a special television news report, a war picture of bodies in an old *Life* magazine, that picture of the Vietnamese guerrilla with the blindfold and gag, a disfigurement in the *National Enquirer*. Newspapers and news magazines with "actual photos" impressed him; they were "real." I watched him see. He would first glimpse the picture accidentally, then quickly turn the page or slap the magazine shut. Fear shot through his eyes. He looked around at the rest of us to see whether anyone else had *seen*. He would turn away, but return later to touch the picture, to trace it through a piece of typing paper, to copy it in margins and on the blackboard. Sometimes I would sit by him and try to explain until the fear let up and the good smile came. The next few days the two of us would play grown-up-discussing-current-events, and he would smile and smile at his normalcy.

One day the whole school was snickering and guffawing at a new joke. Everywhere kids drew graffiti of *Peanuts*'s Lucy, her stomach sticking out huge and pregnant. "Good grief, Charlie Brown," she said. Britt copied the picture in his seven notebooks, which had no particular order as to content or front and

back or top and bottom. Other students had six or seven notebooks, too, one for each class. He carried his seven notebooks
in a black clarinet case. Sometimes he came to school early or
stayed late and played his clarinet for this one or that one of his
teachers. He played while we graded papers. He drew the simple Lucy figure over and over again in his notebooks and on the
blackboards, coloring in the dress and the hair, tracing the lines
with his index finger (sometimes with his middle finger; ninth
graders make a great fuss over their middle fingers)—and still
could not understand. Britt began to whine, "What is it? What
is she? Why is it funny? Why is it funny? Tell me. Why don't you
tell me?" I told him. And told him, and told him, and he did not
understand. He followed me everywhere, all over the campus.
He came out of hallways and doorways to ask me, "Why is it
funny? Please tell me why it's funny. Please. Tell me. Tell me."
The panicked eyes. The pleading.

"Lucy is pregnant, Britt. She's going to have a baby. See?
That's why she is so fat, because there's a baby in there. And
Charlie Brown is the father. She says, 'Good grief, Charlie
Brown.' That's funny because in the comics, she says that all
the time for all kinds of situations. Now here is a situation they
never show in the comics. She says the same old thing even in
this unusual situation, which happens quite often, really, in real
life, but not in comics. Now do you understand why it's funny?"

Nodding his head, but still the eyes dazed with confusion.
"I guess so."

"Listen, Britt. I'll try to explain it better later. O.K.? I have
a class now. I have to go. I just cannot be late. So I'll see you
later. O.K.? You go to your class, too. You're late already. Go
on." A fresh jerk of fear in the eyes; I have told him to go away.

For many weeks, he drew the picture on book jackets, on folders. I watched his fingertips trace Lucy's contours on his desk top. He stopped asking me about the cartoon.

He started to tell me his dreams. He drew pictures of the dreams. He dreamed about his clarinet. In his dreams, his clarinet has gotten fat and puffy in the center. He drew his clarinet, fat and puffed up. That is all that happens in the dreams, the clarinet growing.

I asked him why he didn't just play his clarinet to me for the next couple of mornings while I thought about the dream. Once he started playing, he did not care whether I was grading papers or listening. He did not notice bells going off. To him I must have faded away and reappeared like people in dreams; we are all part of his dream, upon which particularly horrible news items impinge strongest. How can I, one of the dreamed, explain things to my dreamer? Surely, the dreamed cannot make more sense than the dreamer.

I took the picture of the fat clarinet from him, and next to it, I drew Lucy. From the clarinet's mouth I drew notes and other clarinets, not puffed up. Above Lucy, I drew other children, not puffed up, playing and smiling. I drew children and notes mingling in a dance. They dance in a circle until they turn into fat Lucy and fat clarinet. The girl children become Lucy. The boy children are the clarinets. I drew circles and arrows connecting everybody.

Britt nodded, smiling and laughing. "Girls and clarinets love each other, don't they?" he said. "That's what it means."

In stories, even in psychiatric case histories, that would be the denouement, and Britt would be cured. Britt got worse. What is one good dream that turns out useful when you have to dream every night, and no one answers but your own phantoms? I had not taught him to speak like the rest of us. He had taught me to speak like him. (Boys are *not* clarinets. Girls are *not* Lucy.) He continued to tell me his dreams, but I came up with no more inspired interpretations. I was only bored, as you are bored with listening to normal people's dreams.

Then he stopped dreaming. He had stepped into another new world. He spoke like this.

"The two ducks came to visit me last night. They talked together, and I laughed. They do not pay attention to human beings."

"Three nights in a row, close."

"I know a boy whose ears ring so loud even other people can hear them. I heard them."

"One of the ducks did not come last night. I tried to talk to the one who came. He walked back and forth across my room, and pretended he didn't see me."

I could no longer follow him. I asked him silly questions to satisfy my curiosity, not to help him.

"What color are the ducks?"

"They are white."

"Do they ever answer you?"

"No, they talk to each other. They pretend they aren't watching me all the time."

"What do they talk about, Britt?"

"They tell jokes and make me laugh."

"How big are they?"

"They are four or five feet tall, with orange bills and orange feet."

He usually seemed happy now. When somebody hurt him

or if I said something difficult, his head still jerked up with surprise, confusion, bewilderment, a scurrying-about look of dis-
may on his face. But then almost immediately came the smile.
Now he was not so often afraid of the people around him.

At first, he was concerned that the ducks and the voices
were not normal. By the end of the year, he was only unhappy
when one or the other of the ducks did not come to visit him.
He was worried that it would not return the next night or the
next, that it had decided to abandon him. After a while he gave
up trying to make them talk to him, and was satisfied to laugh
at their jokes and to know they secretly cared, only pretending
indifference, another one of their jokes.

He was an innocent, too dumb not to forgive, unable to
remember grievances clearly.

I abandoned him, too.

There were so many like him.

Happiness Is Fleeting

Hilary Fitzgerald Campbell

There are so many topics and themes and recurring jokes in the wonderful world of *Peanuts*; if it were allowed I would just sit here and write a list of all my favorite cartoons.

But since I don't have a podcast called *My Favorite Peanuts* (yet), and since we all have short attention spans, I'm going to write about my two favorite topics, which I believe are intrinsically connected: *disappointment* and *dancing*.

Among the thousands of life lessons found throughout *Peanuts*, I believe there is one that stands out among the rest: **At the end of the day, you can either be disappointed, or**

you can be dancing, but you cannot be disappointed while you're dancing. So take your pick.

To begin to explain this, I have to go back and start at the beginning of me and *Peanuts*. The beginning is often a good place to start.

I was born into a family that was already *very* into Schulz. I'm sure there are many of these types of families. You're probably from one, or maybe you will start one, or maybe you wish you were from one. In which case, feel free to join mine! Each of my parents is one of seven children, I am the youngest of four. There are so many cousins, we wouldn't notice or question your presence at the family reunion.

My maternal grandfather, Dr. Daniel Vaughan, was golfing buddies with Charles Schulz, Sparky to his friends. In 1964 Grandpa Dan cofounded a pro-am charity tournament in San Jose and Sparky did custom drawings for it for the following twenty or so years. I grew up inside a home filled with Schulz sketches addressed to my mother and original cartoons that referenced an ophthalmologist in San Jose, that of course being my grandfather. I already, and quite literally, had someone to look up to.

But that someone, at first, was not Sparky. It was Snoopy. Here we have not only an adorable cartoon dog, but one that *dances*. I loved dogs and dancing, so I believe that is what they call "kismet."

Grandpa Dan gave me my first Snoopy doll when I was probably about six or seven. It was one of those authentic Snoopys. Not those plush things you see at every drugstore across the world these days. *This* Snoopy was made in San Francisco in 1968 (now that I think about it, it's incredibly impressive

Grandpa Dan hung on to this thing until 1997). I have slept with it in my arms nearly every night since. As a twenty-seven-year-old, I've even boarded planes clutching it. It elicits a certain *concerned* look from the flight attendants and, like Charlie Brown, I'm almost always looking for sympathy.

Snoopy was essentially a god. His style, his moves. I wanted to dance just like him. His hands in the air, his feet, everywhere! He always embraced the music, and usually alone. Who needs a partner when you've got two feet? Between Snoopy and my mother, I had two dancing role models to set me up for complete success, at least on the dance floor.

Second to dancing, the thing I loved the most was drawing. When I began to draw, I was extremely concerned with my ability to draw Snoopy and Charlie Brown *just like Schulz did*. No tracing, I needed to be able to do it myself. Get all the strokes and shapes just right. Schulz, without knowing it, taught me how to draw. I think a lot of his expressions (and, well, his whole outlook on life) still exist in my work today.

In an effort to keep me entertained, my parents bought me many *Peanuts* books for me to copy. The more I copied, the more I read, and the more I read, the more my connection grew. This was more than cool drawings of a beagle around our home. I still loved the dancing bits, but this stuff was hitting my little soul. Hard.

By age ten, I was in the height of my "copying Snoopy" phase. I believed myself to be a young artist. Fully equipped with self-confidence *and* self-doubt, with contradicting thoughts like "I'm incredibly unique and important" and "No one really wants me here, maybe I should go home and watch a movie instead." And then, one day in fourth grade, something happened. Sammy Wallace told me that I was, in fact, not a real artist because I was copying someone else's work. Plus, I used an eraser.

His sister Carly did not use an eraser, and she was definitely a real artist. I was horrified. I was embarrassed. I was Charlie Brown.

All my fears were confirmed. Clearly, everyone at school thought I was a joke, the laughingstock of all the other fourth-grade artists. No one liked me; in fact, *everyone hated me*.

That was the moment *Peanuts* started to change for me. I like to think all *Peanuts* readers have some sort of pivotal memory in their life when the cartoon took on new relevance. Almost *too* much relevance. I wanted so badly to be liked by everyone, just like Charlie Brown, and somehow nothing was working out for either of us. It never would. And yet . . . there was still this hope inside of me, that maybe things would change. Maybe one day, I'd be as cool as my big brother, maybe I'd be the best dancer at the party, even know how to tell a good joke without messing up the punchline! That push and pull of hope and despair, expectation and disappointment, in a nutshell, is life. And life is a *Peanuts* cartoon.

This revelation wasn't exactly funny to me at first, but I did feel very understood by the gang. What started off as an innocent love affair with a group of kids and their beagle soon became a heavy-duty, serious relationship that would shape my understanding of myself and the world around me. These weren't jokes, but tales of love, loss, and the human condition! *Peanuts* taught me that despite the little engine of hope inside you convincing you otherwise, you know timing will always be a little off with you and the Little Red-Haired Girl, Christmas will never be quite as amazing as you expected, and you'll never be satisfied with what's in your bowl. So you better take what you can get because, happiness is . . . fleeting.

Or as Linus would put it, "Good things last eight seconds. Bad things last three weeks."

There are so many ways in a *Peanuts* cartoon that you can be disappointed. You can be disappointed at home, in love, at school, on vacation, over holiday, during baseball, golf, or any sport under or out of the sun. You can be disappointed in a kite, a book, a play, your classmates, your parents, your friends, and even your dog.

Most importantly for each of these li'l folks, if all else fails, you can be disappointed in yourself. Who else is there to blame, Charlie Brown, when you're the one setting the high expectations?

Every day they have a list of great expectations of how their day will go, and by age five they are learning that life is mostly not going to go as planned. Lucy will "probably never get married" and as much as Peppermint Patty studies she will somehow always know less than before. I think Schulz could have written a great self-help book entitled *How to Be Disappointed*. In fact, if he were coming up today, literary agents would probably be forcing him to do so.

Let's examine some of my favorite examples of disappointment in *Peanuts* . . .

CHARLIE BROWN IS the *king* of disappointment. He's been disappointed in everything and everyone. His dog has forgotten his name, his kite can't keep away from the trees, and no matter how much they practice, his baseball team will never win a game.

If the world is not disappointing Charlie Brown, he's disappointing them. Why can't he just take his therapist's advice and "snap out of it" already?

More than anything, Charlie Brown is disappointed in love. Will he ever be loved by the Little Red-Haired Girl or will he have to settle for a peanut butter sandwich? Luckily, Charlie Brown has an amazing ability to turn the disappointment in his relationship (or lack thereof) into complete dissatisfaction with himself. One of the best examples of this is when Charlie Brown is so mad at himself for not talking to the Little Red-Haired Girl, telling himself as he walks away, "I hate myself for not having enough nerve to talk to her!" and then, after a moment, "Well, that isn't exactly true . . . I hate myself for a lot of other reasons, too. . . ."

That's what I love about *Peanuts*. The disappointment is the joke. When you learn that, you learn to laugh at yourself and that is so important for survival.

It's not just Charlie Brown who has been let down, time and time again. Lucy is also frequently disappointed. If it isn't with one of her patients, it's always with her brother. She cannot get him to ditch that blanket. If only she could've had a better brother, one with more personality. In one strip, Linus confronts Lucy about this, asking, "Why should **you** care if I have any opinions or personality or character?" Lucy responds, "Because if **you** don't have any character, it's a reflection on **me**!"

Like Charlie Brown and the Little Red-Haired Girl, Lucy's love life with Schroeder continues to fall short. Try as she might, she may never convince him to pay more attention to her than to the piano.

Sally, though innocent, is no stranger to disappointment. Her latest field trip is nothing to write home about, literally, and "What's so much fun about a balloon" anyway? According to Sally, nothing. What a letdown.

Along with her brother and Lucy and pretty much the whole cast, love is a disappointment for Sally. Linus, her sweet babboo, still hasn't asked her out yet. Even when she's dropped so many hints! And who can forget when she practices all week for her role in the Christmas play, only to get onstage and recite "HOCKEY STICK!" instead of "hark!"

Sally is not the only one to be let down by the buildup of the holiday. Lucy waits for what seems like forever for Christmas to arrive, counting down the months, the days, the hours, the minutes . . . only to leave her completely unsatisfied . . . sigh. Will we ever be happy?

Linus has *great* resilience for his disappointment in the Great Pumpkin. My favorite example: He starts off writing a letter to express just how disappointed he is that the Great

Pumpkin did not show up yet again, noting, "If I sound bitter, it's because I am." But before he can finish the letter and save some dignity, hope finds its way back in. After writing off the Great Pumpkin for good, Linus adds, "P.S. See you next year."

That is the thing about disappointment; it cannot exist without expectation. Try as they might, these kids are never going to get rid of expectation. One day, sitting at the brick wall, Linus shares his worries about his worries, lamenting, "I guess it's wrong always to be worrying about tomorrow. / Maybe we should think only about today." Charlie Brown responds, "No, that's giving up . . . / I'm still hoping that yesterday will get better."

Hope lives on, and so does disappointment.

Schroeder's friends will never understand Beethoven. No one will want to listen to Woodstock's long-winded stories. Peppermint Patty will never be appreciated as the great caddy she knows she is, and her gal Friday, Marcie, will probably never stop being disappointed in, well, Peppermint Patty. "Always an embarrassment, sir."

So it would appear that, according to Schulz, just about anything can and will let you down.

As dark as all of this was for a preteen to come to terms with, there was one thing that stood out in the comic, one sigh of relief from the existential crises of childhood and beyond. While everyone's life is going horribly downhill (Sally signed up for conversational French, not *controversial* French, as she thought), there is this dog. And there was a lot of frustration with this dog because he is too happy and *always dancing*.

Lucy, honestly, can't stand it. On more than one occasion she's yelled at a dancing Snoopy, "With all the trouble in this world, you have no right to be so happy!" It drives Charlie Brown nuts as well. "What makes you think you're happy?"

By default, dancing becomes one of the only pure moments of bliss: the rare time when you cannot worry or take yourself too seriously, you simply cannot be upset! Lucy could shout, **"Floods, fire and famine! / Doom, defeat and despair!"** but dancing saves you from all life's downers. "Nothing seems to disturb him!"

Dancing can never be a disappointment. It is the savior of sadness.

It is no surprise that the one who dances the most is a dog. As Lucy says, "It's easy for him to be so happy . . . he doesn't have any worries!" The deep irony is the idea that Snoopy is a ball of pure happiness, unaffected by consciousness. That is wildly untrue. Snoopy has so many disappointments of his own. He wishes he were anything but a dog. Why couldn't he be an alligator or a snake! Or better yet, a World War I fighter pilot?

I particularly love the contrast between Snoopy's hopes and dreams, which are way out of the realm of possibility, and those of someone like Lucy, who wants to be a psychiatrist. She could very well become one but Snoopy will always be a dog.

"Yesterday I was a dog . . . today I'm a dog . . . / tomorrow I'll probably still be a dog . . . / *sigh* / There's so little hope for advancement!"

Even though his aspirations may be futile, they embody the crises of consciousness we all know too well. There is no satisfaction! Plus, whenever Snoopy does try to live out his fantasies, he usually comes to the conclusion that he isn't suited for the role. Can't be a hunter because of his "weed-claustrophobia." Can't be a giraffe because it's "too hard on the neck."

As much as he loves to golf and get some quality time in on the typewriter, all these activities often leave him a little discouraged. He may never be satisfied with life or food—"Needs salt!"—but dancing is one guarantee of a good time. With dancing, Snoopy can be himself! He can let it all go! Sure, he still hasn't gotten his invite to play in the Masters, but it must be in the mail. Anyway, none of this worldly stuff matters while you're doing the Charleston!

Though the whole gang likes to act as if they are very annoyed by all of Snoopy's dancing, the fact of the matter is they are quite jealous. They wish they didn't have to worry about being alive. Or do they?

One day, as Snoopy dances around, Charlie Brown comments, "I sure wish I could be that happy all the time." Lucy replies, "Not me . . . / it's too hard to feel sorry for yourself when you're happy."

Lucy's response here might be the most definitive cartoon in defense of my argument. Sure, they *could* be happy, but they are choosing not to be, because it's much more entertaining to live the emotional roller coaster of hope and despair. But you *do* always have the option to dance.

Every once in a while, they give in to Snoopy's ways and when they do, they love it. In one strip Schroeder presses a frustrated Lucy, "What in the world do you have to worry about?" Lucy thinks a moment, realizes what the answer is (nothing), then joins Snoopy with a huge smile on her face. And why wouldn't she love it? Dancing is great! If only they'd let themselves do it more often . . .

"To dance is to live! / For me, dancing is an emotional

outlet . . . / I feel sorry for people who can't dance . . . / If you can't dance you should at least be able to do a happy hop!"

Snoopy's words, not mine.

Lucy is usually the one who succumbs to Snoopy's carefree calypso, "If you can't lick em, join 'em!" Though she tries very hard to resist most of the time. One of my favorite dancing cartoons that has really stuck with me has Lucy screaming at Snoopy, "Just because you're happy today, doesn't mean you'll be happy tomorrow!"

Isn't that the whole reason Snoopy chooses to dance? Who knows what small disaster is on the horizon. Your novel could be rejected, someone might call you "fuzzy face," or even worse, you could find out there's a new "No Dogs Allowed" sign at the beach.

What is life but a series of small disasters with a little dancing in between!

They say don't sweat the small stuff. But for the *Peanuts* gang, small stuff is all they've got and they are *sweating*. When each day is another question of whether to be disappointed or to dance, the answer is simply which kind of sweat you're looking for.

Of course there has to be a balance. As much as we'd like to, we can't always be dancing. And I never meant to suggest there is any problem with being disappointed. It's good for you. I don't know who I'd be if I wasn't always just a *little* let down. I would probably be a very boring person. *Peanuts* would be a very boring cartoon. They say comedy is tragedy plus time. The great comedy (and tragedy) in *Peanuts* is that every day there is newfound hope, as Linus would put it, that they will grow up to be "outrageously happy!" despite all the evidence that points to the contrary. As if total satisfaction were something to be desired. If we were all outrageously happy, I have no idea what we'd talk about. And yet, the *idea* of happiness . . . sure sounds nice.

Maybe it's because I read so much *Peanuts* as a kid or maybe it's just who I am, but I find the balancing act between the fountain of hope and the forecast of disappointment to be the essence of life. It seems I wake up every morning cheerfully wondering . . .

Big or small, I know something will. Charlie Brown knows something will. Linus knows something will. We all know something will. But it's fun to believe otherwise. It's fun to believe Lucy won't pull the football out from under you, even when you know better.

As an adult my hero has shifted from Snoopy to the creator of Snoopy. Through his work, Schulz taught me that in the middle of the mess of day-to-day life, the one thing I (and the *Peanuts* gang) can rely on for a truly good time is to dance. Like Lucy, it's just a matter of whether or not I want to be pulled out of my pity party.

We've all got a little Snoopy, Charlie Brown, and ultimately Schulz in us. Sometimes our similarities scare me. When I saw the new *Peanuts* movie a couple years back, I recognized myself so much in Charlie Brown that I came home in tears. My mother had to put her twenty-five-year-old daughter to bed, crying . . .

And . . . that very well may be true, but, the next day, we had a glass of wine and ended up dancing all night to the Beach Boys and that was great, so I think that's what Snoopy would call "par for the course."

The Gospel
According to Linus (II)

David L. Ulin

Here's where it begins for me: a four-panel strip, Lucy and Linus, simplest narrative in the universe. As the sequence starts, we see Lucy skipping rope and, like an older sister, giving Linus a hard time. "**You** a doctor! **Ha**! That's a big laugh!" she mocks. "You could never be a doctor! You know why?" Before he can respond, she turns away, as if to say she knows him better than he knows himself. "Because you don't love mankind, that's why!" she answers, seeking (as usual) the final word. Linus, however, defies her, standing alone in the last frame, shouting his rejoinder out into the distance: "**I** love mankind . . . it's **people** I can't stand!!"

When I say *begins for me*, I mean it figuratively; that strip ran on November 12, 1959, nearly two years before I was born. What I'm describing, rather, is a sensibility, a way of looking at, or engaging with, the world. I still remember the moment I stumbled across that set of images, entirely by accident—which is as it should be. It was the middle of June 1968, and I was in the finished basement of a cousin's house in suburban Michigan. I still remember encountering the punchline with the flash of recognition someone else might call epiphany. Me, I don't believe in epiphanies, or perhaps it is more accurate to say that they seem too convenient, that life (my life, at any rate) rarely unfurls itself in such a way. Nonetheless, I can tell you that even at the age of six—I would turn seven later in the summer—I knew I shared some of Linus's . . . misanthropy is not quite the right word here, but distance, self-containment, solitude, that this was how I understood who I was.

What were we doing in Michigan? My family—my parents, my two-year-old brother, and myself—were driving from Southern California, where for the last year my father had been on a fellowship, to Connecticut, where we would spend the summer at my grandparents' house. The cousin in question was not mine, not really, nor my mother's, but my *grandmother's*, which left us twice removed. He and his wife had older children, one a son in college, whom I admired for his long hair and his politics. (We were a political family, had left California a few weeks before we'd meant to, after one of my father's colleagues told my mother he did not regret the death of Bobby Kennedy, who had just been gunned down in Los Angeles, in a kitchen of the Ambassador Hotel.) The Michigan house was modern, with sliding wooden doors that, I chose to imagine, worked like those on the starship *Enterprise*. I was a huge *Star Trek* fan; my father and I would sit on the couch in the living room and watch it together every week. In Michigan, I spent a good amount of time sliding those doors open and shut as if they were automatic while making a whooshing sound between pursed lips. The college-age son, he observed this; he also observed that I enjoyed reading. On the second or third day of our visit, while the adults were upstairs doing who-knows-what, he found me in the basement and introduced me to what I would later come to think of as his secret stash. "Do you like Charlie Brown?" he asked, and when I told him yes, he gestured at a shelf of mass-market paperbacks, twenty or so of them in a variety of primary colors, collections of *Peanuts* comics going back close to twenty years. I was familiar with the television specials, loved the theme song by Vince Guaraldi, the lilting piano riff I could hum from memory. (I am humming it now as I write this: *da da da da da dada da da.*) But these books—they were a revelation, because I had never seen the strip. My parents didn't read the funnies, believed them to be a form of lowbrow entertainment; at least, this was how my mother put it a decade later when she announced she was throwing out my comic books. In Southern California, they did not subscribe to the local *Times*, which featured comics pages, but to that other, grayer *Times* out of New York.

Over the next three or four days, until we left Michigan for Columbus, Ohio, where my mother's brother was serving a two-year stint as a doctor at Lockbourne Air Force Base, I sat in that basement and tore through every one of those books. If they didn't include all the *Peanuts* strips then in existence, they must have come pretty close. What I remember most, though, is that punchline: "**I** love mankind . . . it's **people** I can't stand!!" So much so that when I looked it up online to make sure I was quoting it correctly, it was exactly, down to the punctuation, as I recalled.

This interests me because I would not describe myself as a

Peanuts obsessive, nor as anything more than a casual fan. Yes, I had a Snoopy throw pillow on my bed in grade school (as a teenager, I used to exhale bong hits into it, so my room wouldn't reek of weed), but hey, it was the early 1970s, and so did everyone. Yes, I knew the characters: Lucy, Charlie Brown, and Linus; Schroeder, Violet, and Woodstock. In college, after I met the woman I would later marry (she was a redhead), I would jokingly call her, on occasion, "the Little Red-Haired Girl." Such signifiers, however, are now so common that they function as a kind of cultural wallpaper. We take them for granted, we do not see them; their power to surprise or even stir us has been, on the most basic terms, stripped away. "He was the king and he showed us how to do it," *Bloom County* creator Berkeley Breathed said to me of Charles M. Schulz (one of his primary inspirations) during a 2003 interview. "Why didn't he stop and leave us with those memories, rather than, in the last ten years of his life, drawing Woodstock falling off the doghouse over and over?" At the same time, does it really matter? Breathed regarded Schulz as a figure on the level of Elvis, not the burnt-out one in the white jumpsuit, but the hungry one who made those Sun recordings, which literally—and in every way that counts—reframed the world. "Don't worry about it," Schulz's widow Jean told Breathed. "You have to understand that Sparky lived to do this. He would have died if he had stopped." And in fact, that's just what happened. He died on February 12, 2000, less than two months after announcing his retirement, and the day before the publication of the last new *Peanuts* strip.

Still, Linus. For me, he offered something of a gateway—less a weird kid than one who encouraged me to be . . . myself. I liked that he stood apart, clinging to his security blanket even when Snoopy tried to grab it away. I liked his faith, and his lack of faith: that tension between mankind and people again. "I was the victim of a false doctrine," he declares after being disappointed by the Great Pumpkin, although the following year, he is (how could he not be?) in the pumpkin patch once more. "Why worry about the future when the present is more than most of us can handle!" he reflects, articulating a belief system that allows him to occupy a middle territory between despair and hope. He is the boy philosopher, wise beyond his years. "Here's something to think about," he avers in a May 1981 strip. "Life is like a ten-speed bicycle . . . / Most of us have gears that we never use!" Potential, in other words, the insistence that we are always growing, or could be—ironic since his physical persona, his face and hair and body, never changed. Perhaps this is why my favorite image of him is not from Schulz, but from a *Mad* magazine satire in which the *Peanuts* crew is portrayed in their teens. Linus has become a beatnik, scruffy beard but still clutching that blanket, as if all the ages, childhood through adolescence, had come together in one body, which is, of course, the way it has to be. Think of me as a high schooler, breathing smoke into that Snoopy pillow. Do we ever change? I don't think so, no, not really. Linus rendered this notion three-dimensional to me.

In that sense, Linus was my earliest countercultural hero, the first to indicate a certain set of possibilities. And not just him, but *Peanuts* in general, although he was (and remains) the avatar of this idea. "To the countercultural mind," Jonathan Franzen writes, "the strip's square panels were the only square thing about it. A begoggled beagle piloting a doghouse and getting shot down by the Red Baron had the same antic valence as

Yossarian paddling a dinghy to Sweden. Wouldn't the country be better off listening to Linus van Pelt than to Robert McNamara? This was the era of flower children, not flower adults." Partly, this is a function of the moment: Ron McKernan, the Grateful Dead's notably unkempt harmonica and organ player, took his stage name from the character of Pig-Pen. At the same time, the strip represented a safe place in a chaotic world. Schulz's Pig-Pen is filthy, yes, but McKernan was a severe alcoholic who was only twenty-seven when he died of a gastrointestinal hemorrhage. In reality, potential, possibility, don't always pan out; they can take us places we don't want to go. Art can do that also, but it doesn't have to—or better, when it does, it does so for a reason, even (or especially) when there are no epiphanies. As I've suggested, *Peanuts* led me to *Mad*, which led me to *Wacky Packs* and *Monty Python*, which revealed to me the conditionality of . . . everything. Adult life looked ridiculous because it *was* ridiculous: "All those egos," to borrow a line from J. D. Salinger, "running around feeling terribly *char*itable and *warm*."

The dynamic is one in which *Peanuts* regularly trafficked; think of Lucy, who is all ego—or, more fundamentally, all id. But somehow the strip managed to be gentle also, to clear a space, within its fractured moment (and maybe ours, as well), for everyone. That may explain my offhand relation to the strip—I was looking for something more provocative, with rougher textures—even as I came to know it well. Comics, Art Spiegelman insists, move us in just such a fashion: with their familiarity, which is enhanced by our repeated interactions over days and years. "Comics aren't made to be read," he told me once, "they're made to be reread. If you only read them once, they weren't worth bothering with." On the one hand,

Spiegelman is referring to accessibility; comics are the original disposable art. And yet, this doesn't mean that they are low-brow, but the opposite. What they offer is a shared vernacular. What they offer is a language we all understand. The four-panel arc is as natural to us now as the rhythm of a Bible verse must have been to an earlier generation: anticipation, setup, and release. This is why the parodies are so effective, because we are all in on the joke. Take "Good ol' Gregor Brown," in which R. Sikoryak conflates Schulz with Kafka in a brilliant act of visual ventriloquism. Nine four-panel strips retell the story of *The Metamorphosis*, with Charlie Brown as Gregor and Linus as the office manager. Nowhere does an adult appear; you can almost imagine Gregor's parents, not unlike the teachers in a *Peanuts* television special, making *wah-wah-wah* sounds as they fret beyond the edges of the frame. This, too, was part of Schulz's achievement, to recognize that childhood was an existential landscape, in which, say, the struggle to hold on to a security blanket or believe in the Great Pumpkin is the struggle to keep hope alive: as important and defining as anything in the adult world.

In the end, what makes this meaningful is decency, which is also what Linus is about. It is, after all, people he dismisses in favor of humanity, and not the other way around. The same, I would submit here, was also true of that long-ago college student, my grandmother's cousin's son. He saw a six-year-old—bored, a little lonely—and reached out with a whisper of consolation, a glimpse of something bigger, something else. He didn't have to do it; I don't know that I would have, nor that I would have noticed, even, much about that little boy at all. Decency again, or empathy, a sense that we are all in it together, joined in the collective known as humankind. The last time he and I saw one another, a decade ago at my parents' fiftieth anniversary celebration, I recalled his kindness, as I do whenever our paths cross. I have never said a word about it, though; I'm not sure he would remember, and it doesn't matter anyway. What is resonant to one of us is often (usually?) forgotten by another; it is the subjectivity upon which identity depends. Who's to say what his experience was in that basement? Who's to say what he thought, or what he imagined he was doing, or what, if anything, about it was important to him?

No, what lingers is the comic. What lingers is the voice. What lingers is Linus, alone but also with his sister, as I was alone with, well, everyone. "I love mankind . . . it's **people** I can't stand!!" The distinction he is making is a subtle one, but it is also unmistakable. It represents the voice of the iconoclast, the individual, eager, desperate even, to be a part of it (whatever it is) at the same time as he wants to stand apart. Do I need to say that I still feel like this, half a century after discovering those words? Indeed, I feel the sentiment as strongly now—perhaps more than that—as I ever have. We live in a world Schulz couldn't have imagined, with its hyperlinks and networks, social media and connectivity. We live in a world where a sense of shared humanity seems the most impossible of conceits. It is a world that the *Peanuts* kids wouldn't recognize, although if Linus has anything to tell us, it is that mankind, humanity, what exists at the heart of us, remains the same. What does it mean to speak for yourself? What does it mean to feel that pull? I began to ask and (yes) to comprehend these questions on the afternoon, in that basement in suburban Michigan, I first encountered Linus's fervent charge.

Pilgrimage

Seth

I f anyone made me want to be a cartoonist, it was Charles
Schulz. I was reading *Peanuts* before it even occurred to me
that someone must be drawing it. I distinctly remember the moment this thought appeared in my young child's mind. I looked
down into the bottom right-hand corner of the panel I was reading and noticed, for the first time, that magical name: *Schulz*.

I have a deep abiding love for the *Peanuts* characters. They
stand out as perfectly real to me in the same way that Emma Bo-
vary, Holden Caulfield, Gregor Samsa, and Charlotte the spider
do. I was a socially awkward child, and the daily plight of Charlie Brown said something to me. I understood in a profoundly
personal way the guaranteed failure that made up his world. It
was my world too. Some of the very first comic strips I drew
were primitive imitations of Schulz's work. I recall, sometime
during grade school, publishing my own mimeographed book-
let of these embarrassing, crudely rendered drawings.

I never stopped reading the strip but as I grew older I started to take it for granted. My adolescent tastes turned to the more direct power fantasies of comic books like *Spider-Man* or *The Fantastic Four*. Only in my early twenties, when I started to see the strip through adult eyes, did it come back to life. Rereading all those old paperback collections—stretching back thirty years at that point—I began to recognize the sophisticated wit and poignant social commentary that were the foundation of Schulz's writing. But above all I saw the strip as a poem to unrequited love. Lucy for Schroeder, Sally for Linus, Charlie Brown for the Little Red-Haired Girl. An ode to failure and loneliness. The very best of the individual strips read like polished haikus. Those *Peanuts* characters, so familiar to all of us, wander through a bleak suburban landscape like miniature existentialists. Most people turn up their noses at cartooning— it's lowbrow stuff. And I'd be the first to admit that most of it is worthless . . . but Schulz, he was a *great* artist. The real thing.

In 2003 I found myself traveling to the mecca of *Peanuts*: Santa Rosa, California. That's where Charles Schulz had lived and had his studio since the late 1960s. It looked likely that I would be the designer for a series of books collecting the entire fifty years of *Peanuts* comic strips. A dream assignment: I can't help but return to the image of myself as a lonely child, sitting on my bed, reading those Charlie Brown paperbacks. Now I'd be playing a major role in shepherding Schulz's life's work. It was not a task I took lightly. I had put a lot of thought and effort into coming up with a design for these books, which I hoped would do justice to the quiet masterpiece that is *Peanuts*. I was going to Santa Rosa to meet his widow, Jeannie, to seek her approval.

With Tania, my wife of less than a year, I flew to San Francisco and checked into a hotel. The next morning we found ourselves crammed into the rented sports car of publisher Gary Groth. Gary is the man behind Fantagraphics Books of Seattle, the leading publisher of underground comics in the United States. He had built a reputation as a supporter of innovative cartooning in the 1980s and '90s. His company had also branched out by reprinting classic comic strips like *Pogo* and *Little Orphan Annie*. For years he had tried to secure the rights from Schulz to reprint the complete *Peanuts*, but Schulz had always procrastinated about the project. Clearly he had thought of the strip as a living thing. It's possible he'd felt that publishing an archive of his work would be more of a tombstone to *Peanuts* than a monument. Now Schulz's widow was determined to erect that monument and get these books published. Gary knew of my enthusiasm for the strip and brought me on board.

Gary Groth is a highly erudite fellow with a deeply cynical turn of mind. He's not the kind of guy to give you a pep talk before a meeting. Thankfully, though, between the effort of trying to keep up with him conversationally and fearing for my life because of his aggressive driving, I didn't have much time to fret on the trip to Santa Rosa. However, when we finally came into town I felt the reality of our meeting coming into focus. I don't know what I expected from Santa Rosa—but as I gazed out the window of the sports car it appeared to be one long touristy strip mall. I imagined that when Schulz had moved here from snow-blown Minneapolis the place had probably seemed like some sort of sun-bleached promised land. Certainly it was like a warm spring afternoon that day. There had been a foot of snow in Guelph, Ontario, when we had departed, and bitterly cold too. Still, Santa Rosa seemed depressingly like a highway rest stop. As we drove along I spotted statues and signs of Snoopy and Charlie Brown respectfully placed in every public space. Schulz was this town's bread and butter.

In no time we pulled up to the address I had known for years—Number One Snoopy Place, Schulz's studio. I got out of the car and slid my portfolio out of the trunk. Inside were the presentation designs I had labored over in preparation for this meeting. Even though I had given up smoking years ago, I took a cigarette and puffed away on it to calm my nerves. I had been warned that Jeannie Schulz says what she thinks. If she didn't like the designs I was sure to hear about it. This project was important to me, but I'm an artist myself. With enough arrogance to feel that I knew what was the right look for these books. If she rejected my ideas I had no intention of simply becoming a pair of hired hands. It was necessary that I insist on my vision. Her reaction would determine whether I would be involved.

The studio building itself was unthreatening. A one-story brick-and-wood structure probably tossed up in the early '70s, more suited to a podiatry office than an artist's studio. Schulz, though, was the most unpretentious of artists. He probably would have winced over the term. He saw himself as a cartoonist, a craftsman. I always admired the fact that no matter how rich he became—and God knows, he was rich—he never hired assistants to take over the drawing. For him, the joy was in the doing.

Inside, we were greeted by Paige, the creative director, and after a brief wait we were led to the conference room where Jeannie and her lawyer were working on the details of some other complicated project.

I was well aware that this conference room had actually been Charles Schulz's studio. His drawing table and most of his instruments had been moved out after his death to the *Peanuts* museum down the street, but I could see that much of the room had remained unchanged. Several of his bookshelves were still there, still stocked with his books. I quickly scanned them as I made my way toward the conference table. Mostly standard reference works and what appeared to be a hefty assortment of books on the Second World War. Not surprising for a man of his generation. I also noted a record box sitting there with a hand-drawn picture of Schroeder carefully painted on its side. On the walls were some terribly bland realist paintings of wildlife. What had he seen in these? I wondered.

Jeannie Schulz was a small woman—slim, tight-skinned, but youthful. In her sixties, I guessed. I was somewhat tongue-tied as I shook her hand. I realize that this woman had nothing to do with the work I admired so much. Yet somehow, now that he was gone, being his wife had made her possess a strange kind of resonance in my mind. Much like the aura around those connected to a holy man after he passes on. A ridiculous comparison, I know—but this visit was something of a pilgrimage.

I retreated into the background while she and Gary hashed out the matter-of-fact details of contracts and rights. Finally the time came to present my designs. As I opened up my parcel of drawings I recited a short speech that I had rehearsed in my mind repeatedly for the last week.

Now I am no public speaker, but I think I managed, even with my nervousness, to impart to her my deep appreciation for her husband's work. I explained how I had kept my designs simple and austere, the colors dark and moody. How it was important that these books present the strips as the sensitive work that they are. I wanted to steer away from the bright colors and pop-culture sensibility that had tied the strip to children's entertainment. Twenty-five years of TV specials and mountains of merchandising had pulled the image of *Peanuts* away from the place it once had in our culture. In the '50s and '60s it had been considered sophisticated fare—with a cutting-edge mix of cynicism, melancholy, and psychoanalytical jargon. During this little talk I watched her closely. I could read in her eyes her honest belief that her husband, Sparky, was a genius.

I should digress here and explain that everyone called Charles Schulz "Sparky." Even I call him that, although in there I didn't—I called him Mr. Schulz.

Jeannie had simply sat back and taken in what I was showing her. She didn't ask for any changes. She didn't say that much one way or the other but I felt the atmosphere in the meeting literally warm after I'd finished. I suspect seeing the designs for the books right in front of her had moved the project from an idea to a reality. The plans took a remarkably optimistic swing from this point on. While the discussions continued, I slipped back from the conference table. I could see where Sparky's drawing board had sat. There on the wall were the marks from where his chair had leaned back year after year. I walked over and quietly stood facing that wall. In the man's shoes, so to speak. I looked out his window—the window he must have stared out every working day of his last thirty years.

The meeting ended. Paige escorted us over to the museum. She was very enthusiastic and told me that things had gone well. I was a bit shell-shocked but felt good about it. We crossed a parking lot, then made our way through a vacant lot and across a baseball diamond. A lawn mower noisily drove by and the air was full of the smell of fresh-cut grass. How perfect, I thought, to be walking through Charles Schulz's baseball diamond. I thought of mentioning this aloud—but it seemed too trite a comment.

The museum was lovely but I was more interested in getting to the ice arena across the street. Schulz had built it in 1969 and it was his pride and joy. Next to his comic strip, it was probably the center of his life. This wasn't a billionaire's private vanity project—this was a fully functioning community arena, open to all. Sparky's daily routine had been to sit by the window of its coffee shop, The Warm Puppy, eating a warm English muffin with grape jelly. (The name is taken from Schulz's wildly popular gift book of the 1960s, *Happiness Is a Warm Puppy*.) I have cartoonist friends who made the trip here while he was alive, knowing they could find him at that front table and have a chance to talk to him.

My wife and I chose a table near the back, beside large glass windows that overlooked the ice. Behind us were stained-glass designs of various Snoopys figure skating. The whole coffee shop had an odd mountain-chalet kind of design to it. Equal parts crummy and charming. This was the moment I had long contemplated. I had walked on his baseball diamond, I had stood in the spot where he drew, and now I was sitting in his coffee shop. This was the place where I figured I would somehow make my connection to the man. Gary came in and joined us. We all started to chat. This wasn't right. I don't mean any disrespect to Tania or Gary, but I knew I should be alone here. I excused myself and went out into the arena. I passed through the double doors and felt the rush of cold air as I entered.

Perhaps I had missed out on something by never meeting him. I don't think so. Sometimes, when you like a thing enough it's better not to meet the people behind it. They all get mixed up together, the people and the work, and that's the sort of situation that can ruin something so delicate and meaningful. When it came down to it I was glad I'd never met him. Still, he was dead. It left an empty feeling in the world.

I walked up to the railing and leaned over. On the ice a group of children were practicing figure skating. One boy was repeatedly falling down in a deliberate manner, then doing an awkward spin in a style that reminded me of break dancing. Obviously, he had invented this move and was very proud of it. Showing it off over and over again. It was kind of amusing. The cold air had that frosty and musty smell that only an arena has. It's a Canadian smell and it was odd to be experiencing it here in sunny California. It's also a childhood smell. A certain melancholy descended on me: a pleasant sadness not unlike that feeling when Charlie Brown says "Good Grief." I knew Sparky had looked at this ice a thousand times and here I was, doing the same thing in the same place. As I looked out over the dimly lit ice I faced the simple facts: this place was just a mundane place like anywhere else in the world. Whatever I was looking for here—this was as close as I was going to get to it.

Contributors

JILL BIALOSKY is the author, most recently, of the memoir *Poetry Will Save Your Life*. She has published four collections of poetry, most recently *The Players*; three novels, most recently *The Prize*; and the memoir *History of a Suicide: My Sister's Unfinished Life*. With Helen Schulman, she coedited the anthology *Wanting a Child*. An Executive Editor and Vice President at W. W. Norton & Company, she was honored by the Poetry Society of America in 2014 for her distinguished contribution to poetry.

LISA BIRNBACH wrote and edited *The Official Preppy Handbook* in 1980. Since then she has published more than twenty books and has written for television, stage, and film. She has also been a network television correspondent and radio host, and was deputy editor of *Spy* magazine and a contributing editor to *Parade* and *New York*. The first Broadway show she took her three children to see was the 1999 revival of *You're a Good Man, Charlie Brown*. She hosts the podcast *Five Things with Lisa Birnbach*.

SARAH BOXER is the creator of two cartoon novels, *In the Floyd Archives*, based on Freud's case histories, and its sequel, *Mother May I?* She is also the editor of the anthology *Ultimate Blogs*, a contributing writer for *The Atlantic*, and a critic who has written for *The New York Review of Books*, the *Los Angeles Review of Books*, *The Comics Journal*, and *Artforum*. For many years she was on the staff of *The New York Times*, serving variously as an editor of the Book Review, a photography critic, a Web critic, and an Arts & Ideas reporter covering psychoanalysis, philosophy, photography, art, animals, and comics.

JENNIFER FINNEY BOYLAN is the inaugural Anna Quindlen Writer-in-Residence at Barnard College of Columbia University. She is also contributing opinion writer for *The New York Times*, where her column appears on alternate Wednesdays. She is the author of fifteen books, most recently the novel *Long Black Veil*. Her memoir *She's Not There: A Life in Two Genders* (2003) was the first best-selling work by a transgender American.

IVAN BRUNETTI is a teacher, illustrator, editor, and cartoonist. He is an Associate Professor of Design at Columbia College Chicago, where he edits the annual(-ish) student anthology *Linework*. He is the author of *Cartooning: Philosophy and Practice* and *Aesthetics: A Memoir*, as well as the editor of both volumes of *An Anthology of Graphic Fiction, Cartoons, and True Stories*. His most recent books are *Wordplay*, *3x4*, and *Comics: Easy as ABC*. His drawings occasionally appear in *The New Yorker*, among other publications.

HILARY FITZGERALD CAMPBELL is a Brooklyn-based cartoonist, writer, and documentary filmmaker. Her cartoons have appeared in *The New Yorker* and *The New York Times*, among other publications. Campbell has illustrated books such as *Are You My Uber?* and *Feminist Fight Club*; her first book of cartoons, *Breaking Up Is Hard to Do, But You Could've Done Better*, was published in 2016. Her films *Small Talk* and *This Is Not the End* premiered at festivals across the United States before each becoming a Vimeo Staff Pick. *Mashable* recently named her one of the top female artists on Instagram.

RICH COHEN is the author, most recently, of *The Last Pirate of New York*, as well as other books, including *Tough Jews* and *The Fish That Ate the Whales*.

GERALD EARLY is the Merle Kling Professor of Modern Letters and Chair of the Department of African and African American Studies at Washington University in St. Louis. He is the author of *The Culture of Bruising: Essays on Prizefighting, Literature, and Modern American Culture*, which won the 1994 National Book Critics Circle Award for Criticism. His latest book is the edited volume *The Cambridge Companion to Boxing*.

UMBERTO ECO (1932–2016) was an Italian semiotician, philosopher, cultural critic, and the author of novels including *The Name of the Rose* and *Foucault's Pendulum*. His essay on *Peanuts* was first published as the introduction to the book *Arriva Charlie Brown!* in 1963.

JONATHAN FRANZEN is the author of five novels, including *Purity*, *Freedom*, and *The Corrections*, and five works of nonfiction and translation, including, most recently, his essay collection *The End of the End of the Earth*.

IRA GLASS is the host of the public radio show *This American Life*.

ADAM GOPNIK is the author of several books, including *Paris to the Moon*, *The King in the Window*, *Through the Children's Gate*, and *The Table Comes First: Family, France, and the Meaning of Food*. A three-time winner of the National Magazine Award, he has been writing for *The New Yorker* since 1986.

DAVID HAJDU is a staff critic for *The Nation* and a professor at Columbia University's Graduate School of Journalism. His books include *Heroes and Villains: Essays on Music, Movies, Comics and Culture* and *The Ten-Cent Plague: The Great Comic Book Scare and How It Changed America*. He is working on a book of graphic nonfiction set in the vaudeville era. For his final ninth-grade English class report he submitted an analysis of theological themes in *Peanuts*.

BRUCE HANDY is the author of *Wild Things: The Joy of Reading Children's Literature as an Adult*. A journalist, essayist, critic, and cartoonist manqué, he has spent most of his career writing and editing for magazines, including *Spy*, *Time*, *Vanity Fair*, and *Esquire*, where he is currently features director. He has also contributed humor pieces to *The New Yorker* and wrote for one season for *Saturday Night Live*. His first book for children, *The Happiness of a Dog with a Ball in Its Mouth*, will be published in 2020.

DAVID KAMP is an author, journalist, humorist, lyricist, and longtime *Vanity Fair* contributor, and has also worked for *Spy* and for *GQ* as an editor. He is the author of *The United States of Arugula*, a chronicle of American foodways.

MAXINE HONG KINGSTON is the author of *The Woman Warrior: Memoirs of a Girlhood Among Ghosts*; *China Men*; *Hawai'i One Summer*; *Tripmaster Monkey: His Fake Book*; *To Be the Poet*; *The Fifth Book of Peace*; and *I Love a Broad Margin to My Life*. She has edited the anthologies *The Literature of California: Native American Beginnings to 1945* and *Veterans of War, Veterans of Peace*. She is the recipient of, among many other awards, the National Humanities Medal and the National Medal of Arts.

CHUCK KLOSTERMAN is a writer and journalist who has written for *Spin*, *The New York Times Magazine*, *GQ*, *Esquire*, *The Guardian*, *Billboard*, and *The Washington Post*. He is the author of eleven books, including *But What If We're Wrong?* and *Killing Yourself to Live*.

PETER D. KRAMER is the author of seven books, including *Ordinarily Well*, *Against Depression*, *Should You Leave?*, the novel *Spectacular Happiness*, and *Listening to Prozac*. He hosted the nationally syndicated public radio program *The Infinite Mind*, and his essays, op-eds, and book reviews have appeared in *The New*

York Times, *The Wall Street Journal*, *The Washington Post*, *Slate*, *The Times Literary Supplement*, and elsewhere. He is Emeritus Professor of Psychiatry and Human Behavior at Brown University. He is at work on a novel built around a psychotherapist's encounter with an erratic, egotistical political leader.

JONATHAN LETHEM is the author of *Girl in Landscape*, *Chronic City*, and eleven other novels. His fifth, *Motherless Brooklyn*, won the National Book Critics' Circle Award. His essays and stories have been collected in six volumes, and his writing has been translated into more than thirty languages.

RICK MOODY is the author of six novels, three collections of stories, and three works of nonfiction, most recently the memoir *The Long Accomplishment*. He writes about music regularly at *The Rumpus* and teaches writing at Brown University.

ANN PATCHETT is the author of eight novels, most recently *The Dutch House*, and three books of nonfiction. Her numerous honors include the PEN/Faulkner for Fiction and the Tennessee Governor's Award for the Arts. Her work has been translated into more than thirty languages. She is the co-owner of Parnassus Books in Nashville, Tennessee, where she lives with her husband Karl and their dog Sparky.

KEVIN POWELL is a writer, activist, and public speaker. He is the author or editor of thirteen books, including his most recent essay collection, *My Mother. Barack Obama. Donald Trump. And the Last Stand of the Angry White Man*. He is working on a biography of Tupac Shakur.

JOE QUEENAN is the author of nine books, including *Red Lobster, White Trash and the Blue Lagoon*, and *If You're Talking to Me, Your Career Must Be in Trouble*. His memoir *Closing Time* was a 2009 *New York Times* Notable Book. He writes the "Moving Targets" column for *The Wall Street Journal* and regularly hosts radio features for the BBC. His stories have appeared in many publications, including *The New York Times*, *The Guardian*, *GQ*, *Esquire*, *The New Republic*, *Playboy*, *Golf Digest*, *Vogue*, and *New York*.

NICOLE RUDICK is a New York–based writer and editor whose writing has appeared in books including *What Nerve! Alternative Figures in American Art, 1960 to the Present* and *Return of the Repressed: Destroy All Monsters 1973–1977* (PictureBox), and in *The New York Review of Books*, *The New Yorker*, and *Artforum*.

GEORGE SAUNDERS is the author of eight books, including the novel *Lincoln in the Bardo*, winner of the Man Booker Prize, and the story collections *Pastoralia* and *Tenth of December*. In 2006 he was awarded a MacArthur Fellowship. In 2013 he was awarded the PEN/Malamud Award for Excellence in Short Fiction and was named one of *Time*'s 100 most influential people in the world. He teaches in the creative writing program at Syracuse University.

ELISA SCHAPPELL is the author of two books of fiction, *Use Me*, runner-up for the PEN Hemingway Award and a *New York Times* Notable Book, and *Blueprints for Building Better Girls*. With Jenny Offill, she coedited the anthologies *The Friend Who Got Away* and *Money Changes Everything*. She is a contributing editor at *Vanity Fair*, former senior editor of *The Paris Review*, and a founding editor and editor-at-large of *Tin House*. She teaches in the MFA Fiction Writing Program at Columbia University and the low-residency MFA program at Queens University in Charlotte, North Carolina.

SETH is the cartoonist behind the long-running comic-book series *Palookaville*. His books include *Wimbledon Green*, *George Sprott*, and *It's a Good Life If You Don't Weaken*, and most recently *Clyde Fans*, issued in a deluxe edition after twenty years of serialization. He is the designer for *The Complete Peanuts*, *The Portable Dorothy Parker*, *The Collected Doug Wright*, and *The New World: Comics from Mauretania*. The subject of the documentary *Seth's Dominion*, Seth was awarded the Harbourfront Prize in 2011.

JANICE SHAPIRO is the author of *Bummer and Other Stories*. She has taught courses on screenwriting at Columbia University and on the graphic memoir at Politics and Prose in Washington, D.C. Her stories and comics have been published in *The Rumpus*, *Catapult*, *The North American Review*, *52 Stories*, *The Santa Monica Review*, *Everyday Genius*, *Real Pants*, and other places. Her contribution to this volume is a chapter in her graphic memoir *Crushable—My Life In Crushes From Ricky Nelson to Viggo Mortensen*.

MONA SIMPSON is the author of the novels *Anywhere but Here*, *The Lost Father*, *A Regular Guy*, *Off Keck Road*, *My Hollywood*, and *Casebook*. Her work has been awarded a Whiting Writers Award, a Guggenheim Fellowship, a grant from the National Endowment for the Arts, a Lila Wallace–Reader's Digest award, a *Chicago Tribune* Heartland Prize, and a Literature Award from the American Academy of Arts and Letters.

LESLIE STEIN is the creator of the three-volume series *Eye of the Majestic Creature* and the diary comic *Bright-Eyed at Midnight*. Her autobiographical comics have appeared in *The New Yorker*, *Vice*, and the Best American Comics series. Her most recent book, *Present*, won the Los Angeles Book Prize for Graphic Novel of the Year in 2018.

CLIFFORD THOMPSON is a writer and poet whose book *Love for Sale and Other Essays* received a Whiting Writers Award for nonfiction in 2013. He is the author of the memoir *Twin of Blackness*, the novel *Signifying Nothing*, and the forthcoming *What It Is: Race, Family, and One Thinking Black Man's Blues*. His writings on books, film, jazz, and American identity have appeared in publications including *The Best American Essays 2018*, *The Washington Post*, *The Wall Street Journal*, *The Times Literary Supplement*, *The Threepenny Review*, *Commonweal*, *Cineaste*, and the *Los Angeles Review of Books*. He has taught creative nonfiction writing at the Bennington Writing Seminars, New York University, Columbia University, Queens College, and Sarah Lawrence College.

DAVID L. ULIN is the author or editor of ten books, including *Sidewalking: Coming to Terms with Los Angeles*, shortlisted for the PEN/Diamonstein-Spielvogel Award for the Art of the Essay; Library of America's *Writing Los Angeles: A Literary Anthology*, which won a California Book Award; and *The Lost Art of Reading: Books and Resistance in a Troubled Time*. He is the recipient of a Guggenheim Fellowship, a Tom and Mary Gallagher Fellowship from Black Mountain Institute at the University of Nevada, Las Vegas, and a Lannan Foundation Residency Fellowship.

Formerly the book editor of and a book critic for the *Los Angeles Times*, he teaches at the University of Southern California.

CHRIS WARE is the author of *Jimmy Corrigan: The Smartest Kid on Earth*, *Building Stories*, and *Rusty Brown*. A regular contributor of comic strips and more than two dozen covers to *The New Yorker*, his work has been exhibited at the Museum of Contemporary Art Los Angeles, the Museum of Contemporary Art Chicago, and the Whitney Museum of American Art. He was featured on the PBS program *Art21: Art in the Twenty-First Century* in 2016. An eponymous monograph was published by Rizzoli in 2017.

Quarterly Concern 13 (2004). Copyright © 2004 by Ira Glass. Reprinted by permission of the author.

Maxine Hong Kingston, "Duck Boy." *The New York Times*, June 12, 1977. Copyright © 1977 by Maxine Hong Kingston. Reprinted by permission of the author.

Joe Queenan, "Why I Love *Peanuts*." *The Guardian*, October 20, 2010. Copyright © 2010 by Joe Queenan. Reprinted by permission of the author.

George Saunders, "Strip Mind." *The New York Times*, January 7, 2001. Copyright © 2007 by George Saunders. Reprinted by permission of the author.

Janice Shapiro, "Good Grief." Previously published in *The Rumpus*, January 10, 2017: therumpus.net/2017/01/spotlight -good-grief-by-janice-shapiro/.

Clifford Thompson, "On Unhappiness, Friendship, and Charlie Brown." Previously published in a different form in *The Reading Room* 6 (2006).

Sources and Acknowledgments

The following essays and one comic have previously been published and are reprinted here from the following sources:

Sarah Boxer, "The Exemplary Narcissism of Snoopy." *The Atlantic*, November 2015. Copyright © 2015 by Sarah Boxer. Reprinted with permission.

Umberto Eco, "On *Krazy Kat* and *Peanuts*," trans. William Weaver. *New York Review of Books*, June 13, 1985. Copyright © 1985 by Umberto Eco. Reprinted by permission of the estate of the author. The translation is an excerpt from Eco's introduction to *Arriva Charlie Brown!* (Milan: Cartonato Milano Libri, 1963).

Jonathan Franzen, "Two Ponies." From Jonathan Franzen, *The Discomfort Zone* (New York: Farrar, Straus & Giroux, 2006). Copyright © 2006 by Jonathan Franzen. Reprinted by permission of Writers House LLC acting as agent for the author. The essay had previously been published under the title "The Comfort Zone" in *The New Yorker*, November 29, 2004.

Ira Glass, "Charlie Brown, Spider-Man, Me, and You." Adapted from an earlier version of the essay published in *McSweeney's*